New Interpretations in
Naval History

U.S. GOVERNMENT
OFFICIAL EDITION NOTICE

Use of ISBN Prefix

This is the Official U.S. Government edition of this publication and is herein identified to certify its authenticity. ISBN 978-1-884733-91-8 is for this U.S. Government Printing Office Official Edition only. The Superintendent of Documents of the U.S. Government Printing Office requests that any reprinted edition clearly be labeled as a copy of the authentic work with a new ISBN.

Legal Status and Use of Seals and Logos

The logo of the U.S. Naval War College (NWC), Newport, Rhode Island, authenticates *New Interpretations in Naval History: Selected Papers from the Sixteenth Naval History Symposium Held at the United States Naval Academy 10–11 September 2009,* edited by Craig C. Felker and Marcus O. Jones, as an official publication of the College. It is prohibited to use NWC's logo on any republication of this book without the express, written permission of the Editor, Naval War College Press, or the editor's designee.

ISBN 978-1-884733-91-8

For Sale by the Superintendent of Documents, U.S. Government Printing Office
Internet: bookstore.gpo.gov Phone: toll free (866) 512-1800; DC area (202) 512-1800
Fax: (202) 512-2104 Mail: Stop IDCC, Washington, DC 20402-00001

ISBN: 978-1-884733-91-8

NAVAL WAR COLLEGE HISTORICAL MONOGRAPH SERIES NO. 20

The historical monographs in this series are book-length studies of the history of naval warfare, edited historical documents, conference proceedings, and bibliographies that are based wholly or in part on source materials in the Historical Collection of the Naval War College.

The editors of the Naval War College Press express their special gratitude to all the members of the Naval War College Foundation, whose generous financial support for research projects, conferences, and printing has made possible the publication of this historical monograph.

New Interpretations in Naval History:
Selected Papers from the Sixteenth
Naval History Symposium Held at the
United States Naval Academy
10–11 September 2009

Edited by Craig C. Felker and
Marcus O. Jones

NAVAL WAR COLLEGE PRESS
NEWPORT, RHODE ISLAND
2012

The contents of this volume represent the views of the authors. Their opinions are not necessarily endorsed by the Naval War College or by any other agency, organization, or command of the U.S. government.

Printed in the United States of America

Historical Monograph Series

NAVAL WAR COLLEGE PRESS
Code 32
Naval War College
686 Cushing Road
Newport, R.I. 02841-1207

The Library of Congress Cataloging-in-Publication Data

United States Naval Academy History Symposium (16th : 2009)
 New interpretations in naval history : selected papers from the sixteenth Naval History Symposium held at the United States Naval Academy, 10-11 September 2009 / edited by Craig C. Felker and Marcus O. Jones. — 1st ed.
   p. cm.
 Includes bibliographical references and index.
 ISBN 978-1-884733-91-8 (pbk.)
 1. Naval art and science—History—Congresses. 2. Naval history—Congresses.
I. Felker, Craig C., 1959- II. Jones, Marcus O. III. Title. IV. Title: Selected papers from the sixteenth Naval History Symposium held at the United States Naval Academy, 10-11 September 2009.
 V27. U55 2009b
 359.009—dc23
                                                            2012000736

TABLE OF CONTENTS

Foreword, by *John B. Hattendorf* ix

Preface xi

Program of Events of the 2009 Naval History Symposium xvii

I. Colonial American Resistance to British Naval Impressment in the
   Revolutionary Era 1
   Christopher P. Magra

II. Medium Powers and Ironclad Construction: The Spanish Case, 1861–1868 11
    by *Carlos Alfaro Zaforteza*

III. Water Wings: The Early Years of Navy and Marine Corps Aviation 23
     Laurence Mitchell Burke II

IV. Riverine Operations of the Danube Flotilla in the Austro-German
    Romanian Campaign of 1916 35
    Michael B. Barrett

V. "There's Nothing a Marine Can't Do": Publicity and the
   Marine Corps, 1911–1917 49
   Heather Pace Marshall

VI. Arms and the Man: Some Approaches to the Study of
    British Naval Communities Afloat, 1900–1950 61
    Bruce Taylor

VII. *Ostfriesland,* the General Board of the Navy, and the Washington Naval Treaty:
     A Relook at a Historic Sinking 73
     John T. Kuehn

VIII. "This Temporary Strategical Withdrawal": The Eastern Fleet's
      Wartime African Sojourn 87
      Andrew Stewart

IX. Escort Oilers: The Untold Story of the Battle of the Atlantic 99

   Kenneth P. Hansen

 X. See Fido Run: A Tale of the First Anti-U-boat Acoustic Torpedo 115

   Kathleen Broome Williams

XI. Hiding in Plain Sight: The U.S. Navy and Dispersed Operations under

   EMCON, 1956–1972 127

   Robert G. Angevine

XII. Turbulence and Terrorism: The Story of Headquarters Support Activity Saigon,

   1964–1966 143

   John Darrell Sherwood

   About the Authors 161

   Titles in the Series 165

FOREWORD

The U.S. Naval Academy's Naval History Symposium, held regularly in Annapolis, Maryland, since 1971, continues to be one of the most important events for the scholarly exchange of ideas on naval history. It serves this purpose not only in the United States for American naval history but in the world at large for global naval history. It is certainly the largest regular meeting of naval historians. The Naval Academy, with its historic grounds, large and active history department, fine museum, rich historical collections, and numerous naval memorials, is an ideal place to bring together such a large group of highly informed experts, including naval professionals and civilian academics, to exchange research information and ideas on a scholarly level.

A dozen published volumes of selected papers have captured the essence and growth of the Naval Academy's symposium over the decades. Like this volume, most have carried the now well established title of *New Interpretations in Naval History.* Typically, each volume in the series has been a selection from the many papers presented at each symposium and has ranged widely across all periods of naval history and the histories of many navies. Not limited to any particular theme, other than presenting new interpretations of whatever subjects researchers are working on, each symposium and its resulting volume present very useful samplings of current thinking, new themes, and new approaches in naval history. Collectively, the series has been a great stimulus to advancing and encouraging naval history and continues to chart the state of naval history as a field of research and inquiry.

This particular volume, from the Sixteenth Symposium, adds further to the fine tradition established by its predecessors. The full range of the more than seventy papers presented at the symposium can be seen in the program of events, while the volume itself presents twelve excellent papers selected by the editors—papers ranging from the mid-eighteenth century to the late twentieth century, with topics that vary from aspects of American, British, and Spanish naval history to strategic, technological, and social history.

In publishing this volume, the Naval War College, as a graduate-level educational and research institution, and the Naval Academy, at the undergraduate level, join together with the mutual interest of helping to promote a better understanding of navies and naval history.

JOHN B. HATTENDORF, D.PHIL.
Ernest J. King Professor of Maritime History
Chairman, Maritime History Department

PREFACE

In *The Influence of Sea Power upon History,* Alfred Thayer Mahan criticized historians who had overlooked the "profound determining influence of maritime strength" on the events that shaped the history of Western Europe in the seventeenth and eighteenth centuries. Competition for control of overseas trade, the naval captain argued, had been a historical catalyst for a "clash of interests," "angry feelings," and war. We may debate the relevance of Mahan's theories over the ensuing 120 years. But his belief in the link between history and man's use of the sea seems no less important to the contemporary world of globalized economies, transnational threats, and techno-centric navies than it was in Mahan's day.

Four decades ago the History Department of the U.S. Naval Academy sponsored its first naval history symposium. Over the years the symposium gained a reputation as the hallmark conference dedicated to naval and maritime history, drawing scholars from around the world. In 2001, the attacks on the World Trade Center and Pentagon preempted the Fourteenth Symposium and left the future of the conference in doubt. Four years later the History Department sought approval from Academy leadership to resume the conference on its biennial schedule. With the Academy's enthusiastic support, the Fifteenth Naval History Symposium was held in September 2007.

The Sixteenth Symposium was held on 10–11 September 2009. Despite the global recession, over two hundred participants from seventeen countries gathered in Annapolis to share insights on an incredibly diverse range of topics. Over the two days, eighty-four historians presented their scholarship, debated questions, and renewed old acquaintances in an atmosphere that was as dynamic as it was collegial.

To those who could not attend the symposium, the enclosed essays offer but a brief glimpse of the diversity and energy of the naval and maritime history community. The slate of scholars includes some of the leaders of the field but also young authors who are the future of this community. Like the prior editions, this book is international in scope. Also, in keeping with the 2007 proceedings, the essays were not tied to a central theme. Consequently, they stand out for their superb scholarship. But just as importantly, they represent the quality of the symposium and the vitality of naval and maritime history studies. The only failure of this book is that it could not include all the exceptional essays. Fortunately, many of those have been nominated to Dr. Gary Weir of *The International Journal of Maritime History* and Dr. Richard Gimblett of *The Northern Mariner*. Each of these gentlemen has our appreciation for their assistance to the symposium and commitment to the scholarly community.

This book and many of the symposium functions were funded through the generosity of the McMullen Sea Power Fund, managed by the Naval Academy Foundation. The McMullen Fund permitted us to keep registration fees to a minimum and still maintain the quality expected of an international conference. This support also allowed the symposium to offset travel expenses for many graduate students and foreign scholars, as well as to offer research grants for future conference presentations. The symposium committee and the Academy's History Department are deeply grateful to the McMullen family and to the Naval Academy Foundation for their support of the conference.

Preparing for and executing a naval history symposium can be best described in the U.S. Navy's lexicon as an "all-hands evolution." The conference would not have been possible without the unqualified support of the Naval Academy's leadership. The Superintendent of the Naval Academy, Vice Adm. Jeffrey Fowler, approved the continuation of the symposium and the use of Naval Academy facilities and services. His introductory remarks at the plenary session conveyed the institution's unwavering support for naval and maritime history. Dr. William Miller, academic dean and provost, strongly endorsed our request for the 2009 symposium and was instrumental in securing support from the Naval Academy Foundation. Although newly arrived as the director of the Division of Humanities and Social Sciences, Col. John Kennedy, USMC, kept the faith that a group of academics could coordinate and execute the conference without stepping on too many toes. The final link in the leadership chain, though by no means the least important, was the chair of the History Department. Dr. David Peeler brought the symposium back to life and provided superb guidance to the 2009 symposium committee. Dr. Richard Abels, who relieved Professor Peeler as chair in 2008, rallied departmental support for the myriad administrative and logistical requirements essential to the symposium's success.

While the Naval Academy reflects many attributes of civilian undergraduate universities, the added responsibility of our faculty members to develop midshipmen into Navy and Marine Corps officers places incomparable demands on their time. Yet the professors and military faculty of the History Department, many of whom are not naval historians, gave their valuable time and wholehearted support to the symposium. They served on the registration desks, set up classrooms, participated in the various social functions, and attended many of the seminars. Their efforts, mostly behind the scenes, are testaments to their professionalism and dedication to history. They are colleagues in the finest sense of the word.

Coordinating major aspects of the symposium was the responsibility of the Symposium Executive Committee. Associate Professor Marcus Jones proved a superb deputy. He kept the planning process focused and ensured that the symposium was executed flawlessly. When the publication process and my impending deployment to Afghanistan appeared to put this book in extremis, he willingly carried the process to completion. Lt. John Cauthen oversaw the registration of over two hundred participants and still found the time to present an excellent paper that is being considered for publication. Associate Professor Lori Bogle identified the leading publishers in naval and maritime history and coordinated their participation in the conference. Their displays not only offered the latest scholarship to conference participants but also served to enhance the symposium's professional reputation. Symposium participants were some of the first patrons to enjoy the newly renovated Naval Academy Museum, during the Thursday evening reception, courtesy of its director, Dr. Scott Harmon. Lt. Col. Brian Ross developed and implemented a transportation plan that moved participants with an efficiency that could be achieved only by a combat-experienced Marine, while Maj. Mark Deets led colleagues in the tiring but essential task of transforming classrooms into seminar rooms and then back again for Monday classes. Finally, Mrs. Connie Grigor, whose "day job" is taking care of the department's administrative requirements, was called into service to process extremely important stipend packages for our visiting scholars. Her patience with the symposium director's administrative clumsiness is much appreciated.

Special recognition also goes out to departments within the Naval Academy that provided services that made this conference a first-class affair. The Special Events Department oversees hundreds of events a year and yet took a genuine interest in the symposium. The Superintendent's protocol office proved extremely helpful when for a brief time the symposium was on the radar screens of some very senior officers. Mr. Greg Zingler oversees the day-to-day operations of Alumni and Mahan Halls. His deputy, Jim McManamay, has the unique talent of solving dicey logistical problems quickly and painlessly. Without the use of those exquisite facilities, the symposium simply could not have been pulled off. Diane Greene's artistic talents produced eye-catching posters and programs for two successive symposia. Finally, a special thank-you goes to the Naval Academy security office. One can only imagine the problems associated with moving two hundred people off the Yard in the middle of a formal parade, but the Defense Department police and U.S. Navy security force personnel went beyond the call to ensure that our guests got on buses and on their way with little inconvenience.

Our sincere appreciation also goes out to organizations outside the Naval Academy that have proved themselves deeply invested in the success of the symposium. Adm. Bruce DeMars of the Naval Historical Foundation (NHF) graciously accepted our invitation to speak at the symposium luncheon and offered engaging insights on challenges facing the preservation side of naval history. Dr. Andrew Gordon, who held the Class of 1957 Chair in American Naval History, offered an impassioned speech at the symposium banquet on the fate of the cruiser USS *Olympia*. Dave Winkler, Director of Programs and Development for the NHF, advertised the symposium through the foundation's newsletter, *Pull Together*. The robust participation of faculty from the Naval War College lent much prestige to the conference. Similarly, the Naval History and Heritage Command is recognized for its sustained and much appreciated presence at the symposium. Rear Adm. Jay DeLoach was an active participant in panel sessions, chaired a panel on Abraham Lincoln and his admirals, and entertained our foreign guests at the Washington Navy Yard. The historians on his staff offered panels on some of the most engaging and lively topics of the conference. Particular recognition goes to Dr. Sarandis Papadopoulos, whose enthusiasm for the symposium and professional networking skills are unparalleled. He reached out to the most distinguished scholars in the field to serve as chairs, commentators, and moderators on many of the panels. Randy is truly one of the leaders in the naval and maritime history community, and he was instrumental in the Sixteenth Symposium's success.

The publication process can be daunting, even with essays of such superb caliber. Add the vagaries of the Navy's contracting system, and it becomes an almost insurmountable task. But the Naval War College Press arrived in the nick of time, and the enthusiastic response of its managing editor, Pelham Boyer, to this manuscript is greatly appreciated. One can say that this book illustrates the potential of a Navy University system.

Finally, special recognition goes out to all who attended and participated in the Sixteenth Naval History Symposium. They can all feel justifiably proud of their contribution to the success of this conference and its future as the flagship event for naval and maritime history. The scholarship was diverse, substantive, and insightful. The social events provided opportunities to share ideas in an informal setting. Our attendance was global, the food was exceptional, and the buses ran on time— for the most part.

In 2011 the Naval History Symposium enters its fifth decade of service to the scholarly community of naval and maritime historians. Under the direction of Professor Marcus Jones and his deputy, Cdr. John Freymann, we can all look forward to coming together in the future in Annapolis to exchange ideas, debate great questions, and further the study of naval and maritime history. Mahan, I think, would be pleased.

CRAIG C. FELKER, *Captain, U.S. Navy*
Director, Sixteenth Naval History Symposium

PROGRAM OF EVENTS OF THE 2009 NAVAL HISTORY SYMPOSIUM

Thursday, 10 September

ONE HUNDRED YEARS OF U.S. NAVY AIR POWER

Hill Goodspeed, U.S. Naval Aviation Museum, "Advancements in Navy Aircraft Design, 1922–1945"

Tim Jackson, U.S. Naval War College, "The Two-Ocean Navy Act of 1940: The Impact on American Preparedness for World War II"

Douglas V. Smith, U.S. Naval War College, "Adm. Joseph Mason 'Bull' Reeves (USNA Class of 1884), the Father of Navy Carrier Aviation"

Robert "Barney" Rubel, U.S. Naval War College, "The Transition to Swept-Wing Jets"

Kevin Delamer, U.S. Naval War College, "History of Navy Helicopter Aviation"

Chair: Thomas Cutler, U.S. Naval Institute

Moderator: Stanley D. M. Carpenter, U.S. Naval War College

ROUNDTABLE ON U.S. NAVY DOCUMENTARY EDITIONS

Michael Crawford, Naval History and Heritage Command

Rear Adm. Joseph Callo, USNR (Ret.), New York, New York

George C. Daughan, Portland, Maine

James L. Nelson, Harpswell, Maine

Chair: Rear Adm Jay DeLoach, USN (Ret.), Naval History and Heritage Command

*CHANGES AND CONTINUITY IN THE U.S. MARINE CORPS IN
THE 20TH CENTURY*

Heather Pace Marshall, Duke University, "'There's Nothing a Marine Can't Do': Publicizing the Marine Corps from Above and Below"

Colin M. Colbourn, University of Southern Mississippi, "Pride and Progressivism: John A. Lejeune and the New U.S. Marine Corps, 1914–1929"

David J. Ulbrich, Ohio University, "Transitions in the Second World War: Thomas Holcomb and the Making of a Modern Marine Corps"

Earl J. Catagnus, Temple University, "Intellectual Warrior: General Alfred Gray's Transformational Commandancy, 1987–1991"

Chair: Gregory J. W. Urwin, Temple University

Moderator: Charles D. Melson, U.S. Marine Corps History Division

LUNCHEON—BO COPPEDGE ROOM, ALUMNI HALL

Speaker: Adm. Bruce DeMars, USN (Ret.), Chairman, Naval Historical Foundation

THE RISE AND FALL OF NAVAL REPUTATIONS

Roger Dingman, University of Southern California, "Commodore Matthew C. Perry: Devil or Dove?"

Barry Gough, Wilfred Laurier University, "Admiral Sir David Beatty's Ghost: Historians and the Hero of Jutland"

Asada Sadao, Doshisha University, "Admiral Kato Tomosaburo: Angel of Peace Restored"

Chair: Ronald Spector, USNA Class of 1957 Chair in Naval Heritage, U.S. Naval Academy

Moderators: Jon T. Sumida, University of Maryland, and Ronald Spector

THE SEARCH FOR CAPTAIN JOHN PAUL JONES'S BONHOMME RICHARD

Robert S. Neyland, Naval History and Heritage Command, and Peter Reaveley, Independent Scholar, "The Naval Engagement between *Bonhomme Richard* and HMS *Serapis:* Battle Won and Ship Lost"

Peter Guth, U.S. Naval Academy, "Track the Sinking Ship: GIS and Ocean Modeling in the Search for the *Bonhomme Richard*"

George Schwarz, Naval History and Heritage Command; Melissa Ryan, Ocean Technology Foundation; and Alexis Catsambis, Naval History and Heritage Command, "Searching for *Bonhomme Richard*"

Chair: Joseph Kirschbaum, U.S. Government Accountability Office

PUSHING THE ENVELOPE ON THE HIGH SEAS: U.S. NAVAL TECHNO-LOGICAL DEVELOPMENT FROM THE CIVIL WAR TO WORLD WAR II

Claude Berube, U.S. Naval Academy, "American Thunder Child: Barron, Ellet, Ammen and U.S. Ram Ships in the 19th Century"

K. C. Epstein, The Ohio State University, "Early American Development of the Whitehead Torpedo: Technology, Industry, and Tactics"

Laurence Mitchell Burke II, Carnegie Mellon University, "Water Wings: The Early Years of Navy and Marine Corps Aviation"

Jonathan Reed Winkler, Wright State University, "The Navy and Strategic Communications in the Era of World War Two"
Chair: Hal M. Friedman, Henry Ford Community College
Moderator: Sarandis Papadopoulos, Naval History and Heritage Command

TOPICS IN EASTERN EUROPEAN NAVAL HISTORY

Michael Barrett, The Citadel, "The Danube Flotilla in the 1916 Romanian Campaign"
Marcus O. Jones, U.S. Naval Academy, "The Type XXI and Innovation in the German Navy during the Second World War"
Chair: Col. Thomas Julian, USAF (Ret.)

SAILING SHIPS AND NAVAL CONSTRUCTION IN SPAIN AND LATIN AMERICA

Feliciano Gámez Duarte, Universidad de Cádiz, "Beyond Kolkhis: The Busy Life of the Spanish Frigate *Veloz Pasajera*, 1807–1830"
Carla Rahn Philips, University of Minnesota, "Theory and Practice in Spanish Ship Construction in Early Modern Times"
Francisco Fernandez-Gonzalez, Universidad Politécnica de Madrid, "Spanish Shipbuilding Regulations *(Ordenanzas)* in the 17th Century"
Ivan Valdez-Bubnov, Universidad de México, "Antonio de Gaztaneta and the Seville-Cadiz Political Conflict (1700–1725)"
Chair: Lawrence Clayton, University of Alabama
Moderator: Jorge Ortiz-Sotelo, Shifrin Chair in Military History, U.S. Naval Academy

ROUNDTABLE ON ORAL HISTORY

Jan Herman, U.S. Navy Medical Department
Evelyn Cherpak, U.S. Naval War College
Representative of Navy Combat Documentation Detachment 206
Robert Taglianetti, U.S. Marine Corps History Division, Oral History Branch
Chair: Regina Akers, Naval History and Heritage Command

RESISTANCE BY THE COMMON SAILOR

Christopher P. Magra, California State University at Northridge, "Colonial American Resistance to British Naval Impressment in the Revolutionary Era"
Keith Mercer, Saint Mary's University, Halifax, Nova Scotia, "Press Gangs and Naval-Civilian Discord in Atlantic Canada, 1775–1815"
Thomas Malcomson, George Brown College, "Resistance and Punishment in the British Navy on the North American and West Indies Station, 1812–1815"

Chair: John Hattendorf, U.S. Naval War College
Moderator: Rich Gimblett, Staff Historian for the Canadian Navy

THE U.S. NAVY IN VIETNAM: ON THE COAST AND ON THE SHORE
Edward J. Marolda, former Chief Historian, Naval History and Heritage Command, "The Sand Sailors of Vietnam"
Mark Moyar, U.S. Marine Corps University, "Maritime Infiltration during the Vietnam War"
John Sherwood, Naval History and Heritage Command, "Turbulence and Terrorism: The Story of Headquarters Support Activity Saigon, 1964–1966"
Chair: John Prados, National Security Archive
Moderator: Jay Veith, Independent Scholar

Friday, 11 September

SCIENCE AND THE WAR AT SEA, ASW TECHNOLOGY
David Zimmerman, The University of Victoria, "The Chilowsky and Langevin Patent Dispute and the Origins of Asdic"
Gary Weir, National Geospatial-Intelligence Agency, "Allyn Collins Vine and the Birth of Undersea Warfare, 1940–1946"
Kathleen Broome Williams, Cogswell Polytechnical College, "See Fido Run: The Tale of an Anti-U-boat Acoustic Torpedo"
Chair: Michael Whitby, Directorate of History and Heritage, Department of National Defence, Canada
Moderator: Malcolm Llewellyn-Jones, Naval Historical Branch, Naval Staff, U.K. Ministry of Defence

STEAM SHIPS AND NAVAL CONSTRUCTION IN SPAIN AND
LATIN AMERICA
Carlos Alfaro Zaforteza, King's College London, "The Ironclad, the Spanish Naval Dockyards and the Challenge of New Technology, 1861–1868"
Carlos Tromben, Centro de Estudios Estratégicos de la Armada de Chile, "Replica of the Chilean Steam Corvette *Esmeralda* c. 1870"
Jorge Ortiz-Sotelo, Shifrin Chair in Military History, U.S. Naval Academy, "The Peruvian Corvette *Union* (1865–1881)"
Larrie D. Ferreiro, Defense Acquisition University, "Shipbuilders to the World: Evolution and Revolution in Spanish and Chilean Shipbuilding from the Cold War to the 21st Century"
Chair: Francisco Fernandez-Gonzalez, Universidad Politecnica de Madrid
Moderator: John Harbron, Canadian Institute of Strategic Studies

PRESIDENT ABRAHAM LINCOLN AND THE U.S. NAVY

Craig L. Symonds, U.S. Naval Academy, "Lincoln and Combined Operations"

Robert J. Schneller, Jr., Naval History and Heritage Command, "Lincoln: 'I Must See Dahl[gren]'"

Andrew C. A. Jampoler, Independent Scholar, "The U.S. Navy and John Harrison Surratt, Jr., 'The Last Lincoln Conspirator'"

Chair: Rear Adm. Jay DeLoach, USN (Ret.), Naval History and Heritage Command

Moderator: William Dudley, former Director of Naval History

TOPICS IN GLOBAL MARITIME HISTORY

Sabrina Guerra, Universidad San Francisco de Quito, "Guayaquil, 'Lady of the Pacific': Its Maritime Trade and the Impact of the Independence Process"

Manohar Banger, Maharashtra Maritime Board, "Ancient Shipbuilding in India: A Historical Review"

Erin Greenwald, The Historic New Orleans Collection, "On the French Atlantic Circuit: Company Ships, Cargoes, and Crews between Lorient and Louisiana, 1720–1731"

Chair: Capt. Christopher Page, RN, Royal Navy Naval Historical Branch

JFK, VIETNAM, AND COUNTERINSURGENCY

Christopher K. Ives, Independent Scholar, "Between Doctrine and Ethos: The U.S. Marine Corps and Army, Counterinsurgency, and the Vietnam War"

Leo J. Daugherty, U.S. Army Accessions Command, "Partners in Counterinsurgency: Lieutenant General Victor H. Krulak, USMC, and President John F. Kennedy, 1961–1966"

Rhonda L. Smith-Daugherty, Alice Lloyd College, "An Alliance with Progress: Kennedy, Diem, and a Distant Jungle"

Chair: Nicholas Evan Sarantakes, U.S. Naval War College

Moderator: Andrew J. Birtle, The Center for Military History

"DOES ANYONE KNOW WHERE WE ARE? DOES ANYBODY CARE?" THE BRITISH EASTERN FLEET AND ITS BASES IN WORLD WAR II

Ashley Jackson, King's College London, "Ceylon, the Indian Ocean, and the Second World War"

Augustine Meaher, University of Melbourne, "'The Inability of Effective Action without Singapore': The Ups and Downs of the Singapore Naval Base"

Andrew Stewart, King's College London, "East Africa, the British Commonwealth and the Second World War"

Chair: Adam Kane, U.S. Naval Institute

NAVAL EDUCATION AND KNOWLEDGE TRANSFER

Keith Neilson, Royal Military College of Canada, "Mental Maps, Institutional Values and the Effects of Bolshevism on British Perceptions of Russia as a Naval Power, 1917"

Greg Kennedy, King's College London, "Anglo-Japanese Naval Relations and Technology Transfer in the 1930s"

Harry Dickinson, King's College London, "Not Much Wisdom, Not Much War: Sir Astley Cooper Key and the Royal Naval College Greenwich 1873–1876"

Chair: Eugene Rasor, Emery and Henry College

THE UNITED STATES NAVY ON THE PERIPHERY

Claire Phelan, University of Mary Hardin-Baylor, "'The Inconvenience, Extravagance, and Perplexities of New Orleans!' U.S. Naval Officers on the Periphery"

C. Herbert Gilliland, U.S. Naval Academy, "The U.S. African Squadron: Exhortations to Operational Success"

Diana L. Ahmad, Missouri University of Science and Technology, "Two Captains, Two Regimes: Benjamin Franklin Tilley and Richard Phillips Leary: America's Pacific Island Commanders, 1899–1901"

Dennis J. Ringle, Henry Ford Community College, "Black-Hull Sailor with Commodore Perry in Japan"

Chair: Suzanne Geissler Bowles, William Paterson University

ISSUES OF NAVAL TRANSFORMATION, COMMAND, AND CONTROL

Jorit Wintjes, University of Würzburg, "The Biggest of All? The Battle of Ecnomus and Naval Command and Control in Ancient World"

Bob Angevine, George Washington University, "Hiding in Plain Sight: The U.S. Navy and Dispersed Operations under EMCON, 1956–1972"

Steven Ippolito, Monroe College, and Benjamin Armstrong, USS *Wasp*, "The Transformation of Mongol Military Formations in the 13th Century"

Thomas B. Grassey, U.S. Naval Academy, "Halsey's Two Mistakes and Leyte Gulf"

Chair: Alexandre Sheldon-Duplaix, French Service Historique

TOPICS IN ROYAL NAVY HISTORY

John A. Cauthen, U.S. Naval Academy, "Spithead Mutiny, 1797"

John Beeler, University of Alabama, "The Royal Navy, Education, and Officer Competence: Challenges of the Mid-nineteenth Century"

Cori Convertito-Farrar, University of Exeter, "Tattooing in the Victorian Navy: An Investigation into the Motivations"

Bruce Taylor, Los Angeles, California, "Arms and the Man: Some Approaches to the Study of Naval Communities Afloat"

Chair: Christopher McKee, Grinnell College

BUREAUCRACY AND THE U.S. NAVY

Edward L. De Rosa, Rutgers University, "A Fleet Grows in Brooklyn: The New York Naval Shipyard and the Building of the U.S. Navy"

Michael L. Weisel, Duke University, "Joseph Wharton: A Quaker Vulcan—The Political Economy of Big Steel and the U.S. Navy, 1885–1895"

John T. Kuehn, U.S. Army Command and General Staff College, "The *Ostfriesland*, the Washington Naval Treaty, and the General Board of the Navy: A Relook at a Historic Sinking"

Dennis Conrad, Naval History and Heritage Command, "Were They Really So Unprepared? Josephus Daniels and the U.S. Navy's Entry into World War I"

Chair: Marcus O. Jones, U.S. Naval Academy

WORLD WAR II

Donald Chisholm, U.S. Naval War College, "Naval Support to Anti-Japanese Guerilla Operations in the Philippines, 1942–1945"

Kenneth P. Hansen, Center for Foreign Policy Studies, Dalhousie University, "Escort Oilers: The Untold Story of the Battle of the Atlantic"

Kathleen M. Ryan, Miami University, "Nice Girls, Camp Followers, and the Construction of World War II Femininity"

Nicholas Evan Sarantakes, U.S. Naval War College, "The British Pacific Fleet Visits Japan"

Chair: Jeffrey G. Barlow, Naval History and Heritage Command

NAVAL HISTORY SYMPOSIUM BANQUET

Remarks: Dr. Andrew Gordon, USNA Class of 1957 Chair in Naval Heritage

I Colonial American Resistance to British Naval Impressment in the Revolutionary Era

CHRISTOPHER P. MAGRA

In the summer of 1768, between 6:00 and 7:00 PM on 10 June, American colonists in Boston, Massachusetts, rioted against British authority. Three to four hundred seafarers gathered at Boston's waterfront as a British naval officer painted the king's broad arrow on the mainmast of John Hancock's sloop *Liberty* and began to unmoor the vessel in order to tow it toward the security of a nearby warship. Customs officials had accused Hancock of illegally stowing contraband on *Liberty*. The seafarers gathered near the water's edge and hurled insults at the naval officer and at the seamen and customs officials assisting him. The officer cut the mooring cables. The customs agents jumped ship and attempted to escape the scene. The mob of sailors chased them through the streets of Boston. Crowds of colonists joined the sailors pursuing the customs agents, and the mob swelled to an estimated two thousand. The customs agents somehow made good their escapes. The mob vented its frustration by breaking the windows of the agents' homes. Then the mob dragged one of the warship's boats from the waterfront to Boston's Liberty Tree. Bostonians conducted a mock vice admiralty court and condemned the navy's property. The mob then carried the boat to the Common and set it ablaze. Such riotous behavior posed enough of a threat to induce British naval officers and customs collectors to flee to a nearby fortified position, Castle William.[1]

Most historians see this riot simply as colonists' resistance to the seizure of John Hancock's sloop. The 1768 riot is also commonly interpreted within the wider context of colonial resentment toward the British government's post–Seven Years' War crackdown on colonial smuggling. In an effort to pay off its massive war debts, the British government had decided to force colonists to pay various tariffs. Hancock's *Liberty* reportedly carried Madeira wine and other goods on which the Boston merchant had not paid impost duties. Thus, the seizure of *Liberty* can be seen as one battle in a larger British campaign to snuff out colonial clandestine commerce, in response to which colonists rioted against what they perceived to be an infringement on their free trade.[2] What is often overlooked is the fact that the British warship and the officer responsible for seizing Hancock's *Liberty* had been conducting impressment raids in the weeks leading up to the riot.[3]

This neglect is symptomatic of the lack of scholarly attention given to the maritime dimensions of the American Revolution. The sea is commonly seen as a vast empty space in between lands, where history unfolds.[4] As a result, peoples' interaction with the sea and the historical repercussions associated with this interaction are not taken seriously. Even among maritime historians, only a handful of scholars have ever examined the role that British naval impressment played in the origins of the American Revolution and the birth of the United States of America.

In general, there have been two schools of academic thought on the role British naval impressment played in the origins of the American Revolution. There are historians like Jesse Lemisch, Marcus Rediker, and Gary Nash, who present a "bottom up" interpretation of naval impressment as a chronic imposition on the rights of American workers.[5] For the most part, these historians tend to focus on the plight of the American workingman. In contrast, such historians as N. A. M. Rodger and Denver Brunsman present a "top down" portrait of naval impressment.[6] They argue that impressment was rare and that while it regrettably robbed workers of the ability to choose their careers themselves, it nonetheless afforded the lower sort a career path, discipline, food, and shelter. Historians in this latter camp align more with British naval administrators than with the pressed men, and they do not see impressment as playing an important role in the rift between colonies and mother country. To date, Lemisch has provided the only book-length investigation of the connections between British naval impressment and the origins of the American Revolution, and his study focuses on New York City.[7] For the most part, historians interested in the connections between British naval impressment and the breakdown of Anglo-American relations have restricted their studies to the War of 1812.[8]

My research provides new evidence that reinforces the bottom-up interpretation of the connections that existed between British naval impressment and colonial resistance to British authority. Colonial business owners and workers clearly likened impressment to tyranny and corrupt government, and they viewed coerced military service as a form of slavery. My research also expands on Lemisch's study of New York City. Impressment raids occurred throughout the British North American mainland colonies, and they generated fierce resentment and resistance among a cross section of colonists. Widespread colonial resentment and resistance to British naval impressment contributed to colonists' willingness to resist British authority during the late-eighteenth-century imperial crisis.

Naval impressment can be defined as a system of coercion that puts people into military service on warships for various, normally extensive, periods of time. First, the British monarch would authorize use of the system. The Board of Admiralty, a governing body of seven men (usually four admirals and three members of Parliament) that administered the British navy, then printed and distributed press warrants to commissioned officers along with sets of orders. Like arrest warrants, press warrants were legal documents that empowered naval officers to use force to take men to warships; these warrants were good for only a specified amount of time. Press warrants stipulated that "Seamen, Seafaring Men and Persons whose occupations and callings are to work in Vessels and Boats upon Rivers" were to be pressed.[9] The Board of Admiralty typically sent these warrants to the captains of warships, who in turn gave them to lieutenants to execute.[10] Lieutenants and loyal, physically tough seamen then took tenders into ports or used tenders to board vessels at sea.[11] The lieutenants and their loyal seamen were collectively known as "press-gangs." Pressed men were placed on the tenders and taken back to the warships. Volunteers were given the king's shilling and allowed shore leave and freedom of movement about the ship. Those who refused to volunteer for military service were kept in chains below deck and were denied shore leave. This was impressment.

There was a complex set of reasons for the deployment of this coercive system. Most obviously, British authorities authorized naval impressment to man the navy.[12] The size and number of vessels involved with the British navy expanded over the second half of the eighteenth century, increasing 26 percent in terms of total displacement.[13] Because seafarers typically chose work on merchant vessels, for their higher wages, the British government authorized press-gangs to force subjects into military service in order to meet the manpower demands of a larger navy. There were other reasons for naval impressment, however. Impressment functioned as a form of social control; press warrants were issued specifically to suppress riots in port cities, and admirals, receiving written requests from masters, authorized press-gangs to seize troublesome sailors on merchant vessels.[14] Impressment was used to man shorthanded merchant vessels.[15] It was used to man shorthanded army transport vessels.[16] This coercive system was used forcibly to procure pilots for navigational assistance.[17] There is even evidence that admirals operating overseas authorized press-gangs out of personal animosity.[18] The navy also pressed men into service for sundry short-term labor in shipyards.[19] It was for a variety of reasons, then, that the British navy pressed men around the Atlantic World.

British naval press-gangs operated in and around North American colonial ports prior to the Revolution. There were reported incidents of impressment in coastal communities ranging from northern seaports like Falmouth, Maine, to Norfolk, Virginia, in the south prior to April 1775, when the "shot heard around the world" rang out at Lexington, Massachusetts.[20] For example, Captain Corner of HMS *Romney* had pressed men on at least three separate occasions prior to the riot in the summer of 1768.[21] Despite the riot that followed, Captain Corner and his crew continued to press men in Boston. Several months after the mob action, a press-gang boarded a London vessel entering Boston's harbor and took sixteen of its crew.[22] The navy then had the prudence to relocate Captain Corner to Philadelphia; however, Corner pressed three seamen off a vessel bound from Newcastle, England, to Philadelphia in July 1769.[23]

The British navy also pressed colonial fishermen directly off fishing vessels while they were working on the Atlantic Ocean. Skipper Jonathan Millet and company of the schooner *Hawke,* out of Salem, Massachusetts, were "a-Fishing in the Straits of Belle Isle near Bradore [Labrador]" in July 1766, when, according to Millet's deposition, Captain Hamilton, "the Master of his Majesties' [*sic*] Sloop *Merlin* with a Number of Armed Men in several Boats came on board my Schooner, and demanded my Business there." The surprised yet pugnacious Yankee skipper "told him I was on a cod fishing Voyage from New England." The British naval officer treated Millet "as an Enemy.... He damned me and gave a Blow with his Fist on my Face. I told him it was hard Usage. He again damned me & then ordered a Number of armed Men to seize me which they did. One of them at the same time shoving a Loaded Pistol against my Breast." Captain Hamilton informed the colonial fishing crew they "were a Pack of Damned Rascals several times." According to Millet, "He then seized my Vessel & Fish and put a Sentry on board." The captain of HMS *Merlin* "kept [i.e., pressed] one of my Men, viz. Francis Con, & threatened that if he ever Catched any New England Men Fishing there again that he would seize their Vessels & Fish and keep all the Men, beside inflicting severe Corporal Punishment on every man he took."[24]

This case of impressment had little to do with manning.[25] The British navy was enforcing the tenets of the 1763 peace treaty, which included keeping British fishermen out of fishing waters reserved for the French, and the Strait of Belle Isle was one of the regions the treaty made strictly off-limits to British fishermen.[26] Indeed, when Millet demanded to know why *Hawke,* its crew, and its catch were being seized, Captain Hamilton informed the skipper that he "had broke the Law."[27] The navy was also responding to the commercial lobby of fish merchants in England, which had been pressuring the British government to keep colonists out of the rich fishing waters around Newfoundland. Fish merchants in England wanted these waters as their private preserve.[28] Despite the fact that manning was not the primary motivation behind this case of impressment, it was still impressment. Fishermen were forcibly appropriated for military service in the navy.

Such British naval impressment generated much resentment among North American colonists. In fact, colonists in this part of the British Empire were particularly resentful of naval impressment, because it violated a law passed in 1708 that made it illegal for the British navy to press men in American ports.[29] The law, known as the "Sixth of Anne," was on the minds of leading Bostonians when in 1768 a town meeting resolved to send "instructions" to representatives in the Massachusetts legislature, which included such future revolutionaries and founding fathers as Samuel Adams, John Hancock, and James Otis. The instructions required

> that nothing be left undone that may conduce to our relief; and in particular we recommend it to your consideration and discretion, in the first place, to endeavor that impresses of all kinds may if possible be prevented. There is an act of Parliament in being, which has never

been repealed, for the encouragement of the trade to America; we mean, by the 6th Anne, chap. 37, sect. 9.[30]

For business owners in Boston, "any impresses of any mariner, from any vessel whatever, appears to be in direct violation of an act of Parliament," and therefore press-gangs posed a direct threat to colonial legal rights.[31] That is why during the 1768 riot Bostonians held emergency town meetings and wrote protest letters demanding the dismissal of the offending naval officers from the British navy. They then sent these letters to their representatives in the Massachusetts legislature. They also sent letters to the governor of Massachusetts and to their lobbyist in Parliament.[32]

The town meetings and protest letters responding to impressment were part of a larger American demand that the British government respect colonists' constitutional rights.[33] The Sixth of Anne inspired more than meetings and letters. It heightened colonists' awareness of their legal rights, and it elevated their willingness to defend those rights. At Charleston, South Carolina, in 1743, Capt. Charles Hardy observed that the "Spirit of Prosecuting on that Statute [6 Anne, c. 37] reigns here more than ever."[34] Hardy nervously noted that colonists were taking naval officers to court for violating this law. Two years later in Boston a mob verbally accosted naval officers who had been pressing colonial seamen. One of these officers, Capt. John Rouse of HMS *Shirley,* later acknowledged that he "dared not" set foot on shore in the colonial port city after this mobbing, "for fear of being prosecuted on the [6 Anne, c. 37], or murdered by the mob for pressing."[35] Colonists resented the fact that the navy ignored the Sixth of Anne. They perceived it as a violation of their legal rights, and it made them especially sensitive to any additional infringements.

North American colonists further perceived naval impressment to be a threat to their political rights as British subjects. By the eighteenth century, England was a constitutionally limited monarchy.[36] A Bill of Rights limited the Crown's prerogative powers. The liberty of British subjects was supposed to be sacrosanct, and colonists believed they were entitled to the same rights and liberties as people living in Great Britain. Indeed, Adm. Peter Warren, the naval officer in charge of, among other things, impressment in North America in 1745, warned the Admiralty that American colonists maintained "the highest notions of the rights and liberties of Englishmen."[37] Distance from the mother country perhaps made colonists more sensitive about these matters, but so did naval impressment, which constantly grated on colonial sensibilities and rubbed raw colonial nerves.

When colonial maritime laborers resisted a British press-gang that had boarded their vessel at sea in 1768, they killed a naval officer in defense of their liberty. James McGlocklin, the cook on board *Pitt Packet,* testified in the murder trial of the colonial seamen that his fellow crew members had responded to the British naval officer's command that he be allowed to come up on the deck of their ship that "they were Freemen born free, and would not go aboard a Man of War."[38] James Siley, a

British marine who accompanied the lieutenant onto the colonial brig, and John Roney, the brig's master, both testified they heard them "say they wanted nothing but their Liberty."[39] Peter Bowen and William Peacock, the British warship's midshipmen, both testified that the Americans "said they were resolved to die, sooner than be pressed on Board a Man of War."[40] Patrick Henry was not the only American to maintain a "liberty or death" ethos. More colonists were willing to square off against British authority to defend their rights on the eve of the Revolution.

North American colonists also resented the violation of custom inherent in certain cases of impressment. Fishermen, along with masters, mates, carpenters, and cabin boys, were traditionally exempt from naval impressment. In London in 1739, for example, it was reported that there was "no Certainty of any Protections being granted" by the Admiralty Board against impressment "except [for] Coasters and fishing Vessels."[41] Whenever the navy pressed fishermen from fishing vessels, then, it was a violation of what E. P. Thompson has referred to as the "moral economy" of English working peoples.[42] Whereas infringements on this moral economy stimulated the rise of class consciousness and riots against a revolution in England (that is, the Industrial Revolution), they fueled revolutionary energies in America.

North American colonists further resented the fact that British naval impressment disrupted transatlantic shipping to and from the colonies. Bostonian businessmen believed press-gangs "ruined" the "trade and business of this and the other towns," and this economic ruination "raised such a spirit of resentment in the people."[43] Insufficient crews delayed merchant vessels, which cut into profit margins, discouraged trade, and threatened unemployment and higher prices. British colonists in Nova Scotia expressed similar concerns in a petition they laid before their royal governor in 1775. The Nova Scotians believed "it our duty to lay before your Excellency the Discouragement [that] the trading part of the People meet with in their Commerce with Great Britain, the West India Islands, and also the Coasting Trade, by having their Seamen and other persons employed by them in that Business impressed and put on Board Ships of War, which unless speedily prevented must utterly ruin the small Trade of this province."[44] While the Nova Scotians restricted their protests to legal channels, most likely due to the presence of a naval base in Halifax, other North American colonists took to extralegal and illegal forms of protest against what they perceived to be a direct threat to their legal and economic rights and freedoms.

Naval impressment fueled militant and forceful colonial resistance to British authority in colonial America, resistance that was part of the violence associated with the wider revolutionary movement.[45] In addition to the *Pitt Packet* murder case, the 1768 riot in Boston mentioned earlier, and the more famous Knowles riot there in 1747 (in which sailors seized control over the port city for several weeks), colonists in Norfolk, Virginia, forcibly resisted naval impressment in 1767.[46] The sloop *Hornet* came into Norfolk on 5 September, and Capt. Jeremiah Morgan landed with "several of his officers and about 30 seamen." After imbibing "a little Dutch courage" at the local tavern, Morgan and his press-gang, armed with "large clubs," attempted to force American colonists into military service. The town watch raised an alarm, however, and "at least 100" members of the colonial community turned out to fight off Captain Morgan and his crew. The British press-gang retreated to *Hornet*, but not before town members seized some of the British sailors, arrested them, and placed them in jail for the weekend.[47]

This resentment and resistance culminated in outright demands for separation from the British Empire, as evidenced in the Declaration of Independence. Thomas Jefferson, its principal author, listed impressment as one of the foremost reasons colonists considered the British government to have abused its authority, and in a corrupt fashion. Jefferson wrote that King George III "has constrained our fellow Citizens." These citizens had been "taken Captive on the high Seas." They were forced to serve in the British military, and they were made "to bear Arms against their Country, to become the executioners of their friends and Brethren, or to fall themselves by their Hands."[48] Americans were justified in their rebellion and the formation of an independent nation because of this abuse of power.

In conclusion, peoples' interaction with the sea contributed to the late-eighteenth-century imperial crisis that brought about the birth of the United States of America. The British government and its navy forced colonial subjects to perform military service at sea. Colonial maritime laborers were forcibly taken from their ships and from their port communities. American colonists resented and resisted coerced military service at sea, and this resentment and resistance directly informed the American decision to break with the British Empire. This setback for the British Empire and the rise of the United States cannot be fully understood if we end history at shorelines.

NOTES   1 Dirk Hoerder, *Crowd Action in Revolutionary Massachusetts, 1765–1780* (New York: Academic, 1977), pp. 164–84.

2 Merrill Jensen, *The Founding of a Nation: A History of the American Revolution, 1763–1776* (New York: Oxford Univ. Press, 1968), p. 347; O. M. Dickerson, "John Hancock: Notorious Smuggler or Near Victim of British Revenue Racketeers?" *Mississippi Valley Historical Review* 32, no. 4 (March 1946), pp. 517–40; William M. Fowler, Jr., *The Baron of Beacon Hill: A Biography of John Hancock* (Boston: Houghton Mifflin, 1980), pp. 82–100; and John W. Tyler, *Smugglers & Patriots: Boston Merchants and the Advent of the American Revolution* (Boston: Northeastern Univ. Press, 1986), pp. 5, 13, 16, 114, 266.

3 Hoerder's account is an exception to this general scholarly neglect. Hoerder, *Crowd Action in Revolutionary Massachusetts, 1765–1780.*

4 For a thorough discussion of this historical interpretation in general and for arguments against it, see John R. Gillis, *Islands of the Mind* (New York: Palgrave Macmillan, 2004); Bernhard Klein and Gesa Mackenthun, eds., *Sea Changes: Historicizing the Ocean* (New York: Routledge, 2003); and Martin W. Lewis and Kären E. Wigen, *The Myth of Continents: A Critique of Metageography* (Berkeley: Univ. of California Press, 1997). Also, see W. Jeffrey Bolster, "Putting the Ocean in Atlantic History: Maritime Communities and Marine Ecology in the Northwest Atlantic, 1500–1800," *American Historical Review* 113, no. 1 (February 2008), pp. 19–47; and Marcus Rediker, "Toward a People's History of the Sea," in *Maritime Empires: British Imperial Maritime Trade in the Nineteenth Century,* ed. David Killingray, Margarette Lincoln, and Nigel Rigby (Rochester, N.Y.: Boydell, in association with the National Maritime Museum, 2004), pp. 195–206.

5 Jesse Lemisch, *Jack Tar vs. John Bull: The Role of New York's Seamen in Precipitating the Revolution* (New York: Garland, 1997); Marcus Rediker, *Between the Devil and the Deep Blue Sea* (Cambridge, U.K.: Cambridge Univ. Press, 1987); and Gary B. Nash, *The Urban Crucible: Social Change, Political Consciousness, and the Origins of the American Revolution* (Cambridge, Mass.: Harvard Univ. Press, 1979). Also, see Peter Linebaugh and Marcus Rediker, *The Many-Headed Hydra: Sailors, Slaves, Commoners, and the Hidden History of the Revolutionary Atlantic* (Boston: Beacon, 2000). For a bottom-up examination of British naval impressment in ports in England, see Nicholas Rogers, *Press Gang: Naval Impressment and Its Opponents in Georgian Britain* (London: Continuum, 2007).

6 Denver Brunsman, "The Evil Necessity: British Naval Impressment in the Eighteenth-Century Atlantic World" (PhD diss., Princeton Univ., 2004); and N. A. M. Rodger, *The Wooden World: An Anatomy of the Georgian Navy* (London: Collins, 1986).

7 Book chapters and articles include Matthew Raffety, "A Sea of Rebellion: Maritime Workers in the Age of the American Revolution," in *American Revolution: People and Perspectives,* ed. Andrew K. Frank and Peter C. Mancall (New York: ABC-CLIO, 2007), pp. 189–206; William Pencak, "Thomas Hutchinson's Fight against Naval Impressment," *New England Historical and Genealogical Register* 132 (January 1978), pp. 25–36; Neil R. Stout, *The Royal Navy in America, 1760–1775: A Study of Enforcement of British Colonial Policy in the Era of the American Revolution* (Annapolis, Md.: Naval Institute Press, 1973); Neil R. Stout, "Manning the Royal Navy in North America, 1763–1775," *American Neptune* 23 (April 1963), pp. 174–85; Roland G. Usher, Jr., "Royal Navy Impressment during the American Revolution," *Mississippi Valley Historical Review* 37, no. 4 (March 1951), pp. 673–88; Richard Pares, "The Manning of the Navy in the West Indies, 1702–63," in *Transactions of the Royal Historical Society,* 4th series (n.p.: 1937), vol. 20, pp. 31–60; and Dora Mae Clark, "The Impressment of Seamen in the American Colonies," in *Essays in Colonial History Presented to Charles McLean Andrews by His Students* (New Haven, Conn.: Yale Univ. Press, 1931), pp. 198–224.

8 See, for example, Reginald Horsman, *The Causes of the War of 1812* (Philadelphia: Univ. of Pennsylvania Press, 1962).

9 "Lords Commissioners, Admiralty, To All Captains," [London?], 7 November 1775, in *Naval Documents of the American Revolution,* ed. William Bell Clark (Washington, D.C.: U.S. Government Printing Office, 1964) [hereafter NDAR], vol. 3, p. 349. The actual press warrant read: "I do hereby depute ———belonging to His Majesty's——under my Command, to impress Seamen, Seafaring Men, & Persons whose occupations & callings are to work in Vessels & Boats upon Rivers according to the tenor of this Warrant. In testimony whereof I have hereunto set my Hand & Seal this Day of——."

10 "Last Night, about eight o'Clock, Vice Admiral Pye came down and hoisted his Flag on Board the *Barfleur.* He ordered all the Ships in Commission to take on Board six Months Provisions, to complete their full Complement of Men, and get ready for Sea with all possible Expedition; in Consequence of which Orders, Lieutenants from every Ship went immediately to London to open Houses of Rendezvous. . . . Press Warrants are expected down [from the Admiralty Board] this Day." *Virginia Gazette,* 24 June 1773.

11 Tenders were so ubiquitously used in naval impressment raids that the vessels came to be defined in terms of this impressment. William Falconer, for example, defined a tender as a "small vessel employed in the King's service, on various occasions; as, to receive volunteers and impressed men, and convey them to a distant place; to attend on ships of war or squadrons; and to carry intelligence or orders from one place to another, &c." William Falconer, *Dictionary of the Marine,* 1780 ed. (London: Printed to T. Cadell, in the Strand, 1780), p. 1345.

12 "The King having been pleased by his Order in Council of the 16th of June 1775 to order my Lords Comm[isione]rs of the Adm[iral]ty to issue out such Warrants as they should find requisite for pressing so many Seamen, Seafaring Men & Persons whose occupations & callings are to work in Vessels & Boats upon Rivers in His Majesties Dominions in North America as should from time to time be necessary for Manning His Maj[es]t[ie]s Ships & Vessels employed in those parts." Philip Stephens to Vice Adm. Samuel Graves, Admiralty Office, 24 June 1775, NDAR, vol. 1, p. 493. "The Ships with me at Boston are beginning to be sickly, they have lately lost several men by deaths, and as desertions happen, notwithstanding the utmost care is taken to prevent it, I have ordered the *Scarborough* at Piscataqua, and the *Lively* at Marblehead, to raise men for the Squadron, and have directed Captain [Thomas] Bishop of the *Lively* to press thirty Seamen, if that Number of Volunteers cannot be procured. Necessity obliges me, contrary to my inclination, to use this method to man the King's Ships, and as it shall be done with all possible moderation, though at a place extremely violent in supporting and carrying into execution the Resolutions and Directions of the Continental Congress respecting the Non-importation Agreement, I trust their Lordships will not disapprove thereof." Vice Adm. Samuel Graves to Philip Stephens, Secretary of the British Admiralty, *Preston*, Boston, 20 February 1775, NDAR, vol. 1, p. 98.

13 Niklas Frykman, "Seamen on Late Eighteenth-Century European Warships," *International Review of Social History* (April 2009), p. 1.

14 See *Virginia Gazette*, 31 December 1772; and Vice Adm. Graves to Gen. Thomas Gage, Boston, 11 June 1775, NDAR, vol. 1, p. 656.

15 A merchant-ship captain, Thomas Caulson, was breaking the American Continental Association's ban on trade by attempting to land certain manufactured goods at Falmouth, Maine, and the British navy was helping him do it. The navy was even pressing men to supply Caulson with a crew for the return trip to Bristol. "[Thomas] Caulson no sooner arrived, but the next day had the [HMS] *Canso* Man-of-War up to Town, and his old Bristol Sloop alongside of his new Ship, taking out the goods. But it seems he cannot get any of our people to help him; and I do not think he will be able to get his Ship loaded and rigged unless he gets the Man-of-War's men to do it. And I hear that Capt. [Henry] Mowat has been pressing men; some he releases, and some retains; and it is suggested by some, that his design is to supply Captain Caulson with men from his own Ship." NDAR, vol. 1, pp. 179–80; Peter Force, *American Archives* (Washington, D.C.: M. St. Clair Clarke and Peter Force, 1838) [hereafter AA], series 4, vol. 2, p. 318.

16 "I beg leave to Remark the great want of Seamen experienced this Summer, for the navigating of Transports, for manning armed Vessels, and Boats on particular Services, and on many other occasions, which induces me to urge the Necessity of sending out Seamen to complete the Transports to their proper Number. . . . It is also to be wished that the Kings Ships had their War Establishment [i.e., complement], as they would then be able to spare Men for extra Services and not have the same Reason for Pressing out the Vessels from Europe, and other Parts coming with Supplies for the Navy and Army, a Practice which may greatly affect us in future, unless your Lordship shall be pleased to direct that Protections be given to Vessels sailing from Britain, and Exemptions to others who may bring such Supplies." Maj. Gen. William Howe to Lord Dartmouth, Boston, 27 November 1775, NDAR, vol. 2, p. 1155.

17 "I have also their Lordships' commands to send you herewith two Press Warrants empowering you to impress Seamen in North America, and to signify their further direction to you, in case the Pilots abovementioned ('to engage, upon your arrival at those Provinces ["Carolinas, Georgia, & East Florida"], as many Pilots as you can who may be acquainted with any part of the Coasts thereof') should not be willing to engage in His Majesty's Service, to impress them by virtue of those Warrants, and to keep them on board the Sloop you command until you receive directions from Sir Peter Parker, or the Commander in Chief of His Majesty's Ships in North America, for their further disposal." Philip Stephens to Captain Robert Cooper, RN, of HM Sloop *Hawke*, Spithead, Admiralty Office, 21 November 1775, NDAR, vol. 3, p. 381.

18 "The Admiral [Graves] issued press-warrants at Marblehead on account of the detention of some wax-candles imported for his own use, and which were seized by the Committee of Inspection." "A Private Letter from a Gentleman at Boston, Dated Feb. 19, 1775," *Morning Chronicle and London Advertiser*, 8 April 1775, cited in NDAR, vol. 1, pp. 93–94.

19 Admiral Graves "sent four Press Gangs, under the Command of Captain [John] Linzee [Lindsey] to secure all the Shipwrights, Caulkers and Seamen they could lay hold of, and three hundred men were thus impressed, among whom were found many sailors who were taken for the Ships, and the Artificers, after some days confinement, consented to work and were released." "Narrative of Vice Adm. Samuel Graves," *Preston*, Boston, 18 June 1775, NDAR, vol. 1, p. 714.

20 For impressment at Norfolk, Virginia, see "News from Norfolk, dated September 5, 1767," *Virginia Gazette*, 1 October 1767. For Philadelphia, Pennsylvania, see "News from Philadelphia, dated July 10, 1769," *Virginia Gazette*, 27 July 1769. For impressment in Boston, Massachusetts, see "News from Boston dated June 16, 1768," *Virginia Gazette*, 14 July 1768; "News from Boston, dated November 17, 1768," *Virginia Gazette*, 12 January 1769; and "Diary of Lieutenant John Barker," entry dated Boston, 8 February 1775, NDAR, vol. 1, pp. 81–82. For Marblehead, Massachusetts, see NDAR, vol. 1, pp. 93–94, 98. For Portsmouth, New Hampshire, see NDAR, vol. 1, pp. 69, 126, 224, 329, 362. For Falmouth, Maine, see NDAR, vol. 1, pp. 179–80; and AA, S4, vol. 2, p. 318.

21 "There were some occurrences respecting the officers of the *Romney* preceding this affair [i.e., the seizure of Hancock's sloop] which raised the resentment of the populace. On the Sunday evening

before, a press gang went on board a vessel just arrived from Glasgow, and which came to anchor off the long wharf [in Boston]. . . . A few days after a young man, that had served an apprenticeship in this town, was impressed out of an inward bound ship. . . . The day following a man was taken out of an Eastern vessel [possibly a cod fishing vessel; a banker] by an armed schooner, that was bound to Halifax [Nova Scotia]." "News from Boston dated June 16, 1768."

22 "News from Boston, dated November 17, 1768."

23 "News from Philadelphia, dated July 10, 1769."

24 Jonathan Millet, deposition, 13 September 1766, Misc. Bound Manuscripts, 1766–1769, MHS. The Strait of Belle Isle divides the north coast of Newfoundland from the southern tip of Labrador. Salem fish merchant Jonathan Orne owned *Hawke.*

25 Naval impressment is commonly associated with manning concerns. See, for example, Stout, "Manning the Royal Navy in North America, 1763–1775"; and Pares, "The Manning of the Navy in the West Indies, 1702–63." The following paragraph lists additional concerns that prompted impressment over and above the factors discussed at the beginning of the essay. The fact that manning was not the primary reason for impressment does not make it something other than impressment.

26 Article 5 of the 1763 Paris Peace Treaty stipulated that "the subjects of France shall have the liberty of fishing and drying on a part of the coasts of the island of Newfoundland, such as is specified in the XIIIth Article of the Treaty of Utrecht [i.e., from Bonavista to Point Riche]." Clive Parry, ed., *The Consolidated Treaty Series* (New York: Oceana, 1969), vol. 42, p. 325. For article 13 of the 1713 Utrecht Peace Treaty, see ibid., vol. 27, p. 486.

27 When the British naval officer informed Millet that by international law the colonial fishermen were operating in illegal waters, the maritime laborer replied, "If I had it was through Ignorance"; Millet, deposition. Lines drawn in peace treaties were not easy to see on the ocean. For more on this point, see Joshua M. Smith, *Borderland Smuggling: Patriots, Loyalists, and Illicit Trade in the Northeast, 1783–1820* (Gainesville: Univ. Press of Florida, 2006).

28 Christopher P. Magra, *The Fisherman's Cause: Atlantic Commerce and Maritime Dimensions of the American Revolution* (Cambridge, U.K.: Cambridge Univ. Press, 2009), pp. 127–58.

29 6 Anne, c. 37, Great Britain, *Statutes at Large from the Tenth Year of King William the Third to the End of the Reign of Queen Anne . . . ,* vol. 4 (London: 1769), p. 336. The Sixth of Anne formally stated: "That no mariner, or other person, who shall serve on board, or be retained to serve on board, any privateer, or trading ship or vessel that shall be employed in any part of America, nor any mariner, or other person, being on shore in any part thereof, shall be liable to be impressed or taken away by any officer or officers of or belonging to any of her Majesty's ships of war, empowered by the Lord High Admiral, or any other person whatsoever, unless such mariner shall have before deserted from such ship of war belonging to her Majesty, at any time

after the 14th day of February 1707, upon pain that any officer or officers so impressing or taking away, or causing to be impressed or taken away, any mariner or other person, contrary to the tenor and true meaning of this act, shall forfeit to the master, or owner or owners of any such ship or vessel, £20 for every man he or they shall so impress or take, to be recovered with full costs of suit, in any court within any part of her Majesty's dominions."

30 "News from Boston dated June 20, 1768," *Virginia Gazette,* 14 July 1768.

31 Ibid.

32 Ibid.

33 For more on these constitutional rights, see Bernard Bailyn, *The Ideological Origins of the American Revolution,* 2nd ed. (Cambridge, Mass.: Harvard Univ. Press, 1992).

34 Cited in Douglas Edward Leach, *Roots of Conflict: British Armed Forces and Colonial Americans, 1677–1763* (Chapel Hill: Univ. of North Carolina Press, 1989), pp. 148–49.

35 Ibid., pp. 152–53.

36 J. C. D. Clark, *English Society 1660–1832,* 2nd ed. (Cambridge, U.K.: Cambridge Univ. Press, 2000).

37 Peter Warren to the Duke of Newcastle, 18 June 1745, in *The Royal Navy and North America: The Warren Papers, 1736–1752,* ed. Julian Gwyn (London: Navy Records Society, 1973), p. 126.

38 L. Kinvin Wroth and Hiller B. Zobel, eds., *Legal Papers of John Adams* (Cambridge, Mass.: Harvard Univ. Press, 1965), vol. 2, p. 320.

39 Ibid., pp. 309, 319.

40 Ibid., pp. 294, 300.

41 "News from London, dated July 11, 1739," *Virginia Gazette,* 12 October 1739. Also, see Vice Adm. Samuel Graves to Capt. William C. Burnaby, RN [captain of HM Sloop *Merlin*], 5 July 1775, NDAR, vol. 1, p. 820.

42 E. P. Thompson, *Customs in Common* (New York: New Press, 1992), pp. 185–351.

43 Ibid.

44 NDAR, vol. 2, p. 877.

45 For more on this violence, see Wayne E. Lee, *Crowds and Soldiers in Revolutionary North Carolina: The Culture of Violence in Riot and War* (Gainesville: Univ. Press of Florida, 2001).

46 For more on the Knowles riot, see William Pencak and John Lax, "The Knowles Riot and the Crisis of the 1740s in Massachusetts," *Perspectives in American History* 10 (1976), pp. 163–214. This is the definitive study of the riot. For a treatment more recent but less detailed, see Denver A. Brunsman, "The Knowles Atlantic Impressment Riots of the 1740s," *Early American Studies* 5, no. 2 (Fall 2007), pp. 324–66.

47 "News from Norfolk, dated September 5, 1767."

48 "The Charters of Freedom," *The National Archives,* www.archives.gov/exhibits/charters/declaration.html.

II *Medium Powers and Ironclad Construction*
The Spanish Case, 1861–1868

CARLOS ALFARO ZAFORTEZA

In April 1866, the newly commissioned armored frigate *Tetuán* struck a rock as it sailed out of Ferrol Dockyard. As the damage appeared not too serious, it continued its trip to Cadiz. Upon arrival, however, it was decided that the ship should undergo repairs to mend its false keel, to clean the heavy fouling, and to fix the effects of three years of galvanic action between the copper sheathing and armor plate. But then a second problem arose, as none of the available docks was large enough to accommodate what was at the time the largest ship built in Spain. Owing to lack of funds, the new docks were not yet finished. The frigate was forced to sail to Toulon, where it waited, since all the docks at the French port were occupied by French warships. Finally, after having its hull cleaned and repaired, the crew conducted proper trials and took reliable speed measurements.[1] But the delays had significant consequences. *Tetuán*'s original mission was to join the squadron in the Pacific. But by the time it was finally ready for sea, the attack on the Callao forts had taken place and the Spanish fleet had sailed away.

The 1860s witnessed a surge in warship construction across Europe and the Americas. The introduction of armor, rifled guns, and iron construction revolutionized naval architecture. Undeterred by the huge costs involved, both great and small powers launched building programs to acquire the new ships. Several secondary navies strove not only to replace their wooden ships but also to increase their naval strength. These included the fleets of Italy, Austria, and Spain, none of which had had a squadron of capital ships before. By the end of the decade, the Spanish navy comprised seven seagoing ironclads and a dozen wooden frigates. Except for three of the former, all were built at naval dockyards, for which the necessary infrastructure and technology had to be acquired. This paper addresses the challenges involved in building the ironclads.[2] To this end, the need for such ships and the political decisions to authorize them will be briefly sketched. Then the technological, economic, and industrial challenges will be explored. Through comparisons with other countries, the general conclusion is drawn that the use of indigenous naval construction made the cost of sea power much higher for aspiring naval powers than for the great powers. Economic and technical difficulties plagued the domestic construction of the Spanish ironclads.

The Need for Ironclads

By the end of the 1850s, Spain's major external security concerns were the Balearic Islands and Cuba. Anglo-French rivalry after the Crimean War and the question of Italian unification raised the prospect of a general European war. The Spanish feared that Britain or France might seize Minorca as a base to strangle the other's imperial routes. Spanish concerns, though, were not isolated to the Mediterranean. Cuba was seen as an objective of U.S. expansionism as well. The attempts of Presidents Franklin Pierce and James Buchanan, although futile in retrospect, only increased tensions. The matter for the Spanish government was not whether but when the United States would strike. Indeed, by 1860 the two countries were already fighting by proxy in the Mexican Civil War. Both government and public opinion saw a naval force as a necessary element to preserve Spanish neutrality in Europe and defend Cuba against the United States. This meant first-class vessels capable of intercepting an invasion force or of escorting a relief expedition.

The most adequate model for these duties was the *Gloire*-type armored frigate. The key decisions were made in 1860, 1862, and 1866. The first decision was the completion of an initial seagoing ironclad and subsequent evaluation of its potential. The second reflected the fears of an impending war with the United States. By 1866 the Spanish government was sensing an imminent threat. But it was also suffering the consequences of delays in the completion of the ships, since all ironclads should by then have been completed. In May 1860, the Junta Directiva de la Armada (navy executive board) had included two armored frigates in the naval expansion program. This was considered sufficient as long as only European navies built ironclads. The main force was to be made up of nine fifty-gun frigates, at an estimated cost of seventeen million reales apiece;[3] that compared with thirty-five million for an armored frigate. A proven technology, frigates were considered the optimum solution.[4] But, hedging their bets, the Spanish authorized the construction of two armored ships at the Ferrol (Tetuán) shipyard, and another (*Numancia*, subsequently canceled) at a foreign shipyard.

These views changed as soon as the Navy Ministry learned the details of the battle of Hampton Roads and of the U.S. Navy's monitor-building program. The junta met on 13 April to make sense of events. Its members came to the conclusion that the Americans were indeed a potential threat to the empire and that Cuba could be defended only with armored ships. Regardless of the Civil War's outcome, they believed that at the war's end the Americans would resume their southward expansion. Suddenly, wooden ships seemed obsolete. After considering its options, the junta determined to

- Convert the fifty-gun frigates *Zaragoza* and *Arapiles* into armored ships.

- Build another armored frigate *(Príncipe Alfonso)* at La Carraca dockyard, using the timbers earmarked for the fifty-gun *Navas de Tolosa* and the eight-hundred-horsepower engines building in France for a canceled ship.[5]
- Award the contracts for the building of two armored frigates abroad *(Vitoria* and *Sagunto),* whose tenders had been under consideration for some time.
- Order armor plates from the French firm Petin et Gaudet for the following ships: *Zaragoza, Tetuán,* the ship to be built at La Carraca *(Príncipe Alfonso),* and a "floating battery."
- Apply a set of 360-horsepower engines built at Ferrol to an "armored battery," presumably the "floating battery" mentioned above; this ship was subsequently canceled.
- Build a further twelve "armored batteries" for harbor defense (also canceled).[6]

The first four points constituted the foundation of the subsequent building effort. But most of these measures also depended to a great extent on indigenous resources. Optimistic estimates about the completion of the ships were widespread. The Spanish ships were scheduled to be completed by the end of 1864. This radical change in the naval program was a widespread phenomenon, a product of the assessment of the new technology. In many ways the Spanish decisions were representative of those of smaller naval powers trying to determine how to fit in with their more powerful rivals. The Italians, for example, canceled the construction of four ninety-gun wooden battleships. Additionally, three wooden frigates were converted into armored ships, and several ironclads were ordered from abroad.[7]

Another event that affected ironclad construction was the war against Chile and Peru.[8] Once war was declared by Chile in September 1865, and then by Peru in January 1866, the British government embargoed armaments ordered by both belligerents. Nevertheless the Peruvian government managed to get the ironclads *Huascar* and *Independencia* completed by delaying its declaration of war. The Spanish *Vitoria* and *Arapiles,* as well as the Chilean corvettes *Chacabuco* and *O'Higgins,* remained in Britain for the duration of hostilities.

After the Spanish fleet sailed away from the Pacific in May 1866, the government was concerned over the possibility of an allied attack on Cuba or the Philippine archipelago. The defense of Cuba was assured by the presence of *Tetuán,* but by May 1867 *Numancia,* flagship of the South Atlantic Squadron, badly needed docking to have its iron hull cleaned and painted. A third ironclad was urgently needed to replace it.[9] *Zaragoza* would still take a year, *Príncipe Alfonso* longer. Meanwhile, the Peruvians were shopping around for ironclads. To lay down new hulls was out of question. Time, dockyard resources, and finance precluded it. After unsuccessful attempts to purchase ironclads in Denmark and the United States, the only solution left was to convert some wooden frigates into belt-and-battery armored corvettes.

This scheme was tested in *Resolución,* which was scheduled for a large refit. Still, by 1868 the de facto cessation of the hostilities, the effects of the 1866 financial crisis, and the return of political strife led to a virtual standstill in the dockyards. The 1868 revolution effectively ended the cycle of the first ironclads. *Príncipe Alfonso* was completed only in 1877, after the country had gone through another period of political turmoil. Foreign and colonial policy requirements were powerful enough to create the political will to fund a domestic building capability. However, the Spanish exchequer proved unequal to the task.

Coping with Technological Change

To choose the right technology in a period of rapid technological development was a complex decision. The first step was the adoption of the ironclad as the capital ship, which was made only after the battle of Hampton Roads. Even the most advanced navies opted for solutions difficult to explain, such as the British mammoth ironclads derived from *Warrior* or the American concentration on the monitor type. Secondary powers could not afford such costly experiments. They could adopt only proven technology, even at the risk of being conservative.

The restored corps of Spanish naval constructors played a vital role in this task. Many of its members had studied naval architecture at the Lorient school, then had placements in the Brest Dockyard, completing their training with spells in the naval mission to Britain. As a result, they had a good knowledge of the progress in both countries, complemented by occasional visits to the United States and other countries. They were responsible for the design and construction of the ships studied in this paper. Naval intelligence was also crucial; naval missions in Britain and France played essential roles in tracking new developments.

But it proved extremely difficult to keep up with the pace of technological change in naval warfare. By 1866 the fully armored *Gloire,* with its twelve-centimeter armor and sixteen-centimeter rifled guns, had been superseded by the belt-and-battery *Océan,* with twenty-centimeter armor and twenty-four-centimeter rifled guns. Yet the Spanish ironclads—*Tetuán* commissioned and *Numancia* in the Pacific—had conformed to the basic design of *Gloire,* with thin armor, vulnerable to rifled guns. Moreover, their armament consisted of twenty-centimeter smoothbore guns, already obsolete and ineffective against armor, as was confirmed by the experience of the attack on the Callao forts in May 1866 in Peru and the battle of Lissa on 20 July that same year in the Adriatic. Keeping up with these developments required substantial modifications in the design of *Príncipe Alfonso,* including

- Replacement of the original eight-hundred-horsepower engines by a thousand-horsepower set
- Building of a central battery and an upper-deck armored redoubt and increase of the thickness of the waterline belt to sixteen centimeters

- Replacement of the original armament of thirty twenty-centimeter smoothbore guns with thirteen heavier, more powerful guns protected by the central battery and redoubt
- Rebuilding of the unarmored ends of the battery deck in iron, to protect them from catching fire.[10]

The changes reflected the struggle between gun and armor, and they introduced a higher proportion of iron in the ships' structure. They also reflected the difficulty of having at least one state-of-the-art ship under construction. Austria and Italy experienced the same problems. After the 1866 war both nations sought to cut expenses. Consequently, though the Austrian navy resumed ironclad construction in 1867, it did so at a more leisurely pace. Italian ships lingered on the stocks for years, just like the Spanish *Príncipe Alfonso,* which was finally completed only in 1877. No Italian ironclads were laid down between 1865 and 1873.

Economic Constraints

Ferrol Dockyard built the thousand-horsepower engine of *Príncipe Alfonso,* the largest to date. The casting of the block was straightforward, but the forging of large parts was beset by problems. The crankshaft turned out to be defective, because the forging hammer was not powerful enough. The solution was to order a new crankshaft from John Penn & Sons of London, which doubled the estimated cost.[11] Nevertheless, importing a crankshaft was cheaper than ordering a larger forging hammer and paying the high wages of British instructors.

The predicament at the Ferrol yard reflected the problems of naval modernization for a smaller naval power. Essentially there were two ways of acquiring advanced naval armaments. The easier was to order the ships abroad, which offered the attraction of moderate cost and quick delivery. However, it also entailed the use of foreign currency and long-term dependence on foreign suppliers, as well as on their governments' policies. Alternatively, facilities, plant, and know-how could be acquired to produce the ships locally. This usually meant huge investments in time and money, which included refurbishing the dockyards or building them anew, to procure a relatively small number of ships, of uncertain quality in the initial output. For reasons of prestige and industrial development, aspiring sea powers attempted the second method. But once in operation, the shipyard had to be kept busy with new construction to remain economically viable. The size of the Italian, Austrian, and Spanish fleets simply did not allow this. With the exception of Austria, neither could they thrive on civilian or foreign contracts.

At the top end of the economies of scale, Britain enjoyed the lowest cost of sea power. The "workshop of the world" could deliver high-technology products at the most competitive prices. A strong exchequer and a parliament willing to spend virtually any amount of money on the Royal Navy completed this almost ideal scenario. Unfortunately, few of these benefits were available to small and medium powers. Spain, for example, could not count on its underdeveloped maritime industries. Their contribution to the naval expansion of the 1860s was three small, wooden gunboats and six small-crew engines. True, the country enjoyed three substantial naval dockyards, a legacy of its eighteenth-century navy. However, they needed extensive, costly refurbishment to cope with the much larger modern, steam-propelled ships.

Russia also suffered a low degree of industrialization, but it enjoyed the financial strength of a great power. Its 1863 ironclad program included the construction of a brand-new dockyard in Saint Petersburg for the special purpose of building iron-armored ships. The magnitude of the project was enough to attract British capital, plant, and technical expertise.[12] Such an undertaking, though, was not feasible for Spain. The investment in plant and the overheads increased unit costs unacceptably, while the weak finances of the Spanish government made working for it unattractive to foreign technical advisers.

Furthermore, four factors restricted the funds available for ironclad construction within the Spanish naval budget: high unit cost, the need to adapt dockyard facilities, the building of other ship types, and current naval activity. The cost of a *Gloire*-type ship, for example, was roughly double that of a large frigate. By the time the navy decided that smaller, cheaper, coastal-defense vessels were more appropriate for certain duties, cost overruns had consumed all the funds allocated for ironclad construction.

Similarly, new dry docks had to be built to accommodate the new ships. The British and French navies were faced with the same problem. But due to their large numbers of ships, their ships/docks ratios were higher and thus represented smaller proportions of their naval budgets. In Spain, the Navy Ministry scheduled the building of four docks in Ferrol, one in La Carraca, and two in Cartagena.[13] This meant an investment of around 120 million reales—equivalent to the cost of four armored frigates. The project was only partially completed and was much delayed by cost overruns and budgetary problems.

Between 1858 and 1866 the three peninsular dockyards built nine wooden frigates, a type considered essential for overseas service. Yet their construction consumed a large proportion of available funds. Despite Spain's desire to keep pace with the great naval powers by building ironclads, the far-flung interests of the Spanish state required a more balanced naval force. Extensive operations conducted in support of the government's active foreign policy during the 1860s impinged on the naval budget and dockyard resources. These operations included the war with Morocco (1859–60), interventions in Mexico (1861–62) and Santo Domingo (1861–65), an 1863 crisis with United States over Cuban territorial waters, the establishment of the Pacific Station (1862), and the subsequent war with

Chile and Peru (1865–68). The logistical and refit work involved meant heavy, unforeseen expenses, which competed with new construction in a dwindling naval budget.

Simultaneous financing of a large building program and operational demands could not be achieved through the ordinary annual budget. At the time the Spanish treasury benefited from the Disentailment Law of 1855. This piece of legislation was central to the economic policies of Spanish Liberal governments, as it put up for sale a large mass of common land. This source of extra income was directed primarily to public works and the armed forces. By an act of 1 April 1859, the navy received a supplementary credit of 450 million reales for dockyard plant and facilities and ship construction. A supplementary credit of 250 million was provided two years later.[14] As previously mentioned, the program was subsequently modified by, on one hand, the increased importance of the ironclad and, on the other, budget reductions and cost overruns.

By 1864 the budget deficit caused by heavy spending—not only foreign interventions but also railway subsidies—as well as a rising public debt placed a heavy burden on the treasury. Simultaneously, income began to dwindle through a severe downturn of an economy already weakened by the cotton decline caused by the American Civil War. The effects of the 1866 financial crisis, together with the failure of the 1866 and 1867 harvests, aggravated the situation. As a result, the naval budget was subjected to severe cuts that precluded payments to foreign contractors. In June 1867, John Brown and Company in Britain claimed overdue payments totaling £28,000 for the plates of *Zaragoza* and *Príncipe Alfonso*.[15] Once *Zaragoza* was completed, work in the dockyards came to a standstill; for all practical purposes, the building program ended with the 1868 revolution, in which Queen Isabella II was deposed.

A Weak Industrial Base

Because of the lack of industrial infrastructure, construction was delayed beyond 1864 and the period of economic prosperity. The main aspects of this lack of resources were procurement difficulties and lack of private industry, building materials, and dockyard facilities. In this period the Spanish dockyards made the transition from the traditional, centuries-old supply system of working with basically raw materials to a mixture of raw materials, manufactured components, and machinery. The introduction of steam power and iron in naval construction made procurement of the new materials more complex. As an example, sometimes armor plate had to be trimmed to account for wrong templates or modifications to the hull. This was a time-consuming job, since neither adequate means nor personnel was available.[16] The navy had to specify details and cost estimates for the different components, put them out to tender, conclude contracts, make payments, and conduct quality control. The other problem was integrating foreign components into

Spanish ships. To deal with the growing proportion of foreign-produced items, the navy maintained two standing naval missions abroad, one in Britain and one in France, in constant communication with the ministry and the dockyards. The efforts of these, in which administrative personnel and naval constructors worked in close collaboration, needed close coordination. These management skills were critical factors in the procurement process; they kept delays and cost overruns within reasonable limits, but they took time to acquire.

A further disadvantage was the lack of a domestic private sector that could supplement this building effort. The ideal case of Britain has been mentioned. Though smaller, less industrialized countries like Austria or Italy benefited from fledgling private sectors. The Austrian navy relied on the maritime industries around the active port of Trieste, where the steam packet company Österreichischer Lloyd was based. These companies included the Stabilimento Tecnico Triestino shipyard, which built the hulls of all the Austrian navy's ironclads; engineering firms that built the engines and boilers; and even an armor-plate manufacturer, in Zeltweg.[17] This high degree of nationalization avoided payment in foreign currency, further investment in the Pola Dockyard, and strain on the limited capacities of the naval dockyards. The Italian navy too was assisted by the private sector, albeit to a lesser degree. While the new establishment at La Spezia was being built, it had to make do with the obsolete dockyards of Genoa and Naples. Italian ship engines were of domestic manufacture, and the Orlando Shipyard, of Livorno, built one ship.[18] Still, the Italian navy had to resort to foreign shipyards for more than half of its ironclads. By comparison, Spanish industries did not help the navy to any considerable extent.

Only in 1867 did Portilla Hermanos y White, of Seville, start the domestic production of sheet and angle iron, rivets, screws, and nuts. This undertaking was in direct response to an urgent appeal from the navy to complete the as-yet unarmored sides of *Príncipe Alfonso*.[19] As all the materials for the railway construction boom were imported, its contribution to the development of the Spanish iron industry was nil. Due to financial difficulties, the navy was able neither to pay foreign contractors nor to set up a new workshop in a dockyard. The main difficulty in producing iron components lay in recruiting the necessary skilled labor, virtually nonexistent in Spain. This inevitably meant British workers and instructors. The navy was unable to pay their high wages punctually.

Timber supply was another significant problem. Most ironclads continued to be built of wood. But in the nineteenth century the Spanish navy no longer ran its own timber-supply system, relying instead on private contractors. Just as the 1859 program was launched, this arrangement came under severe strain, for three reasons. First, the 1859–61 program meant a significantly heavier demand than previously. Also, the Anglo-French naval race following the end of the Crimean War led to a general shortage of large, seasoned timber in the European market. Finally, substantial contracts concluded with suppliers in the United States failed to materialize, because of the onset of the American Civil War and the subsequent blockade of the Southern ports. To get around the first problem, the Spanish ordered some of the projected ships from abroad, but this arrangement was thwarted by timber shortages in foreign shipyards. Additionally, poor-quality timber was responsible for the cancelation of contracts for one armored and one fifty-gun frigate with Forges et Chantiers de la Méditerranée of La Seyne, and of another fifty-gun frigate in Britain. The builder of *Arapiles* asked for permission to reduce the scantlings of its floor timbers, since he was unable to find sound timber of the required dimensions.[20] Consequently, the navy had to revise its plans. It concluded new timber contracts for the construction of additional ships. The third factor delayed the launching of *Tetuán*. Since pine deck beams from the southern United States were not forthcoming, iron deck beams were ordered from England.[21] As a result of this dearth of large timber pieces in the international market, *Zaragoza,* sister ship to the British-built *Arapiles,* had more iron worked into its hull. This led to the future increase of iron components in shipbuilding, such as deck beams, frames, and knees (which supported the deck beams at the ends, where they joined the frames).

Owing to the lack of suitable personnel, the facilities for ironworking remained very limited. The hardware needed to cut, shape, and punch sheet iron was acquired in Britain and sent to Ferrol Dockyard but was then put aside for lack of skilled labor. In 1866, in the midst of the war against Chile and Peru, quick servicing of the fleet was critical. Nevertheless, only through the collaboration of Portilla and the transatlantic steam line Antonio López y Cía. of Barcelona, which supplied two dozen engineers and boilermakers between them, could Cadiz Dockyard complete the fitting out of two wooden frigates.[22]

Even the physical configuration of the dockyards was inadequate for the construction of large ships. *Príncipe Alfonso* was scheduled to be built in Cadiz.[23] But infirm slipways and the progressive silting of the channels around the dockyard precluded the building of large ships. Moreover, once launched, the ironclad would not be able to enter any of the existing dry docks.[24] Therefore, it was decided to have the ship built at Ferrol, which was spacious, had long and firm slipways, and deep draft. Moreover, it was expected that the dry dock ordered in Britain would be ready before the ship was completed. Cartagena also needed heavy investment in slipways and docks, but the dockyard there was built on firm ground, unlike Cadiz, and the harbor was deep enough. That is why the ironclads were built at Ferrol and Cartagena.

Spain's particular, changing circumstances and its economic structure proved to be impediments to building an ironclad squadron. The window of opportunity comprised only the five years from 1859 to 1864. If the dockyard facilities had been more up-to-date and the Spanish maritime industries had been more developed, as in Austria or Italy, the project could have been feasible. Thereafter, political and budgetary stability disappeared. At the same time, an unexpected war demanded the urgent completion of the new ships. By 1868 the building activity had come to a standstill. Yet the results were acceptable, if not wholly satisfactory. The errors made were much like those of the British and French. By 1870 the Spanish navy could field six seagoing ironclads; if their armor was already too thin, they were armed with rifled guns.

The cases of Austria and Italy are comparable. This leads to the wider question of why secondary powers were willing to face the staggering costs of domestic ironclad construction. Nationalism was certainly important. Like their larger counterparts, these powers had independent national policies. It was only reasonable for them to develop a certain degree of naval self-sufficiency and the means to pursue it. This course of action often turned out to be much costlier than originally envisaged. Furthermore, it proved almost impossible to keep up with the latest developments. Despite the disadvantages, however, the Spanish navy for the most part adequately supported overseas political objectives.

NOTES 1 Ferrol Chief Constructor to commander of Ferrol Dockyard, 24 November 1865, Archivo General de Marina Álvaro de Bazán, El Viso de Marqués, Ciudad Real [hereafter AGMAB], Ferrol 3872; Chief Constructor of naval mission to France to Navy Minister, 8 June 1866, AGMAB, Buques 1176/712/VII.

2 For an overview of the Spanish ironclad program see Carlos Alfaro Zaforteza, "Cambio tecnológico y política naval en la monarquía isabelina: los primeros blindados," *Revista de Historia Naval,* no. 73 (2001), pp. 75–103.

3 Approximate exchange rate: one pound sterling equals one hundred reales.

4 *Diario de Sesiones de Cortes, Congreso,* 29 January 1861, p. 1342.

5 All horsepower figures refer to nominal values rather than effective power. Nominal power was a measure of the physical size of the engine, which was directly related to its effective power.

6 Minutes of 13 April 1862 meeting, AGMAB, Buques 1176/493.

7 Mariano Gabriele, *La prima marina d'Italia (1860–1866)* (Roma: Ufficio Storico della Marina Militare, 1999), pp. 84, 88.

8 For a survey of the war from the American viewpoint see William C. Davis, *The Last Conquistadores: The Spanish Intervention in Peru and Chile, 1863–1866* (Athens: Univ. of Georgia Press, 1950). For the Spanish view see Agustín Ramón Rodríguez González, *La Armada Española, la Campaña del Pacífico, 1862–1871, España frente a Chile y Perú* (Madrid: Agualarga, 1999).

9 Navy Minister to Captain General of the Cartagena Department, minutes, 28 May 1867, AGMAB, Buques 1176/806.

10 Chief Constructor to Director of Marine Artillery, 15 November 1866, AGMAB, Buques 1176/586.

11 Memorandum, 17 July 1870, AGMAB, Buques 1176/651.

12 Jacob W. Kipp, "Das Russische Marineministerium und die Einführung der Panzerschiffe," *Marine Rundschau* (April 1981), pp. 211–12.

13 Navy Minister to president of the Junta Consultiva, 1 June 1861, AGMAB, Ingenieros 3420.

14 *Diario de Sesiones de Cortes, Senado,* 10 March 1859, app. 31, and *Congreso,* 18 May 1864, p. 2153.

15 "Proyecto de ley, presentado por el Sr. Ministro de Hacienda, relativo a los presupuestos generales del Estado para el año económico de 1866 a 1867," *Diario de Sesiones de Cortes, Congreso,* 10 February 1866, apps. 1, 3, 53; John Brown and Co. to Brigadier Acha (officer in charge of the naval mission to Britain), 20 June 1867, AGMAB, Buques 1176/651/II.

16 Captain General Ferrol Naval Department to Navy Minister, 30 August 1865, AGMAB, Buques 1176/712/VI; Chief Constructor to Director of Personnel, 20 January 1868, AGMAB, Buques 1176/806.

17 L. Sondhaus, *The Habsburg Empire and the Sea: Austrian Naval Policy, 1797–1866* (West Lafayette, Ind.: Purdue Univ. Press, 1989), pp. 210–11; "Die Panzerplatten-Fabrikation in Oesterreich," *Oesterreichische Zeitschrift für Berg- und Hüttenwesen,* 20 August 1866, pp. 268–70.

18 Gabriele, *La prima marina d'Italia,* pp. 44–45, 155–58; "La marine militaire de l'Italie en 1867," *La Revue Maritime et Coloniale* (December 1867), pp. 789–90.

19 Memorandum on materials needed for the *Príncipe Alfonso,* with comments by Chief Bookkeeper dated 23 May 1867 and by Chief Constructor dated 31 May 1867; report on the inspection visit by naval officers and constructors to the premises of Portilla Hermanos y White, 14 May 1867; all AGMAB, Buques 1176/651.

20 That is, the dimensions of the structural members laid across the keel. Navy Minister to president of the Junta Consultiva, 28 June 1861 and 25 November 1861, AGMAB, Ingenieros 3420.

21 Navy Chief Constructor, note on memorandum dated 29 December 1861; Captain General of Ferrol Department to Navy Minister, telegrams, 14 August 1862 and 5 December 1862; all AGMAB, Buques 1176/712-I.

22 Captain General of Cadiz Department to Navy Minister, 25 January 1866, dated 1, 2, and 3 February 1866, AGMAB, Maestranza 2647.

23 Navy Minister to Captain General of Cadiz Department, 9 October 1862, minutes, AGMAB, Buques 1176/576.

24 Chief Constructor of La Carraca to Captain General of Cadiz Department, 5 November 1862, AGMAB, Buques 1176/443.

III *Water Wings*
The Early Years of Navy and Marine Corps Aviation

LAURENCE MITCHELL BURKE II

The introduction of a *novum*—a new concept or new hardware—is not, by itself, sufficient to change how a military organization wages war. The *novum* must be integrated into the military in the form of doctrine governing, training in, and support for its use.[1] In the case of the airplane, several factors influenced its integration into the military. The limited performance and mechanical unreliability of early aircraft, minimal funding, and the state of domestic aircraft manufacturing all constrained the ability of the U.S. Navy and Marine Corps to develop aviation. But I will address only one factor here: the disturbed and contested (or, at best, unclear) leadership in navy and Marine Corps aviation in the years prior to World War I.

Leadership plays an important role in organizational innovation. A recent attempt to predict military innovation was unable to do so reliably but did identify factors that indicate likelihood for change. These provide a useful framework for examining the introduction of the airplane to both the navy and Marine Corps.[2] One of these conditions is the presence of "product champions"—senior officers who advocate changes.[3] The existence of a product champion, willing and able to fight for the integration of a *novum* into his (or her) organization, is an important factor. This champion works to assemble a network of support to bring about change that he (or she) believes is necessary.[4] Unstable leadership of naval aviation up to World War I hindered the emergence of product champions, contributing to its slow development.

The navy first considered the airplane in 1898: war with Spain was looming, and this drove government interest in Samuel Langley's successful unmanned flying machines.[5] Despite a positive endorsement by a joint army-navy board of Langley's plans for a man-carrying machine, the navy's Board on Construction decided that the airplane had no place in the service. Nevertheless, naval observers participated in the 1908 trials of the Wright Military Flyer. One of these prepared an enthusiastic report for William Cowles, the chief of the Bureau of Equipment.[6] But once again, the navy took no action.

Still, there was plenty of interest in airplanes among naval officers. In 1909, Cowles asked to purchase two airplanes; the acting secretary replied that airplanes had not "progressed sufficiently to warrant their purchase at this time."[7] A year later, both Hutch I. Cone, chief of the Bureau of Steam Engineering (BuEng), and Richard Watt, chief of the Bureau of Construction and Repair (BuC&R), separately requested authority to purchase airplanes.[8]

The new secretary, George von Lengerke Meyer, passed Cone's request to the navy's General Board for comment. Its president, Adm. George Dewey, recommended that "the value of aeroplanes for use in naval warfare should be investigated without delay."[9] But the assistant secretary merely ordered BuEng and BuC&R to assign officers to coordinate with Capt. Washington Irving Chambers, who was handling aviation mail for the secretary. However, these officers were only to work *with* Chambers, not *for* him.[10] Nevertheless, Chambers, though given little authority, was to have a great influence on naval aviation and to be its first successful product champion.[11]

With his ambiguous mandate, Chambers organized the 14 November 1910 flight of Eugene Ely from the cruiser *Birmingham*.[12] On 18 January 1911, Ely landed on the battleship *Pennsylvania*. These events are typically cited as the experimental beginnings of the aircraft carrier. However, these flights were simply proof-of-concept experiments to show that aircraft could operate with ships.

A third flight, almost forgotten in naval aviation histories, took place in February 1911: Glenn Curtiss demonstrated his new "hydroaeroplane" (a floatplane) by landing in the water next to *Pennsylvania* and being hoisted aboard.[13] After a reception, Curtiss was hoisted out again and returned to his base.[14] Chambers felt that the hydroaeroplane would be most useful to the navy, needing no special modifications to ships.[15] In light of these experimental successes, Chambers pushed for funding for the navy to buy its own airplanes.[16]

The next two months demonstrated the unstable position of aviation within the navy. In mid-March, Secretary Meyer, responding to Chambers's requests for clarification of his terms of reference, ordered him to "keep informed," advise, recommend, guide, and consult on aviation matters but gave him no authority. In an effort to give Chambers some support, Admiral Dewey transferred him to the General Board on 30 March. The successful flights garnered money for naval aviation, but Congress placed the twenty-five thousand dollars under the Bureau of Navigation (BuNav). Thus Chambers transferred again, on 14 April, to BuNav, where he was given a particularly cold reception.[17]

With the money, Chambers purchased three airplanes, primarily for training pilots and secondarily for experiments to explore the airplane's potential.[18] He knew that the airplane was not ready to be integrated into naval operations. But Chambers expected to have a nucleus of trained pilots by the time a plane had been developed that could accompany the fleet to sea. Thereafter, all training of aviators would take place in the fleet, to expose more sailors to aviation than would be possible if airplanes were based ashore or in special-purpose ships.[19]

Training of the first naval aviators had started well before Congress funded the planes. Taking advantage of offers from Curtiss and the Wrights, Chambers had assigned the first naval aviators. Lt. Theodore G. "Spuds" Ellyson arrived at Curtiss's San Diego camp on 23 December 1910 and helped with the two flights to *Pennsylvania*. Lt. John Rodgers (who had seen the flights as a member of *Pennsylvania*'s crew) reported to Dayton, Ohio, for training on 17 March 1911.[20] Lt. John Towers reported for training at the Curtiss plant in Hammondsport, New York, on 27 June. These men had great influence in this early period of naval aviation, training subsequent naval aviators and establishing the syllabus for further training.[21]

Once trained, these officers converged on the navy's first aeronautical station—Greenbury Point, in Annapolis, Maryland. Rodgers and Towers, along with a small cadre of enlisted men, were at the "aviation camp" by September 1911; Ellyson arrived on 3 October.[22] There the aviators began to familiarize themselves with the navy's new planes, practice their flying, and plan experiments. They were joined in November by Ens. Victor Herbster.[23] Chambers assigned Herbster to training in the Wright airplane, highlighting two sources of tension already extant in this small community of naval aviators.[24]

The first source of tension was rooted in a patent battle between the Wrights and Curtiss. While the issue played out in court, some of that animosity filtered down to the pilots the two firms trained.[25] The separation into Wright and Curtiss "camps" (which was quite literal at times) was reinforced by the fact that the two manufacturers used entirely different designs for their flight controls.[26] Herbster's assignment to the Wright B-1 meant that Rodgers had to be his instructor.

The second source of tension stemmed from questions of seniority. Rodgers was the senior lieutenant, but Ellyson had started aviation training first. That Rodgers had charge of training Herbster did nothing to clarify the relative authority between Rodgers and Ellyson. Never officially settled, the matter caused tension within naval aviation while Rodgers and Ellyson were flying.[27] That the two were also on opposite sides of the Wright/Curtiss issue exacerbated both problems and splintered the naval aviation community.

In addition to their intracamp problems, all of the aviators were occasionally frustrated with the nonflying Chambers. For instance, the flyers wanted to make their existence known to the public and demonstrate their usefulness to the rest of the navy through participation in public aeronautical meets and setting new aviation records. Chambers, on the other hand, was terribly concerned that fatal crashes would harm the reputation of naval aviation and did all he could to emphasize safety, including preventing his aviators from officially attending aviation meets and discouraging record seeking. Nor did the flyers understand how carefully Chambers needed to tread to get what was wanted from the chiefs of the various bureaus.[28] But the least tractable issues arose from the fact that Chambers was not a flyer.

Chambers based his understanding of aviation on theory, and he managed aviation accordingly. The aviators recognized that aviation theory was still a long way from describing what happened in the real world and harbored a degree of resentment that Chambers could not (or would not) appreciate their problems.[29] For instance, Chambers wanted to develop a standard control for aircraft, but when one flyer suggested trying the now familiar stick and rudder pedals in an aircraft, Chambers resisted. He felt that steering with the feet would be awkward for a sailor and was just a "European vogue" that would pass. He also objected to the stick, believing that a wheel would be more natural to a navy man.[30] Furthermore, Chambers was ordering new planes without considering the aviators' opinions. The flyers grew so frustrated that they wrote directly to the secretary of the navy, recommending that a flying officer be involved in selecting new aircraft designs.[31] There was a strong feeling among the aviators that actual flying officers should have the final say in issues connected with flying—there were too many intangibles that nonflyers would never understand.

In the spring of 1912, more officers reported for flight training. One was 1st Lt. Alfred Austel Cunningham, the first Marine Corps aviator. Before reporting to Annapolis, Cunningham had been at the Marines' Advance Base School in Philadelphia. Officers at the Advance Base School were still working on what that force would look like.[32] Cunningham envisioned the airplane as a substitute for cavalry, and on 12 February 1912 he suggested that a small aviation unit should be added to the Advance Base Force. The Major General Commandant of the Marine Corps, William Biddle, recognized that airplanes could greatly benefit advance-base defenses and recommended that Marine officers should be trained to fly, "so that a sufficient number of expert aviators . . . may be available" to conduct reconnaissance for an advance base.[33] Chambers agreed and recommended that the Marine Corps send officers to the aviation camp for training.[34] Consequently, Biddle ordered Cunningham and 1st Lt. Bernard Smith to aviation training. Cunningham reported on 22 May 1912 and Smith on 18 September.[35] Thus a new tension was introduced to aviation, one that largely continues to this day: while the Marine aviators thought of themselves as doing Corps-specific tasks, naval aviation leadership viewed the Marines as additional resources for navy missions.[36]

In the meantime, Rodgers had left aviation, requesting and receiving orders to sea duty in August 1912.[37] Among the reasons for his doing so was that the new navy secretary, Josephus Daniels, placed great importance on time at sea for promotions. At the time, many in the navy (including the aviators), saw aviation as just another assignment, not a career.[38] As well, the perishable nature of flying skills was not yet recognized; it was thought that trained officers could fly again at any time.[39] Thus, Rodgers's return to the fleet was seen as neither unusual nor a particular setback to naval aviation. Ellyson was the second officer to leave naval aviation voluntarily, following a drift away from the "action" of the aviation camp to the politics and paperwork of Washington. In mid-March 1913, Ellyson, frustrated with Chambers's leadership and also needing sea time, requested orders to sea duty and left aviation on 29 April.[40] Ellyson and Rodgers ceased to be either product champions for the airplane or part of the network supporting other champions. Both rejoined naval aviation after the Great War, but so much had changed by then that neither ever again wielded the influence they had in those first years.[41] In contrast, John Towers remained with naval aviation throughout his career, making him a particularly influential product champion.

Unlike Rodgers and Ellyson, Cunningham's departure from active participation in naval aviation was not his own idea: his fiancée forced him to choose between flying and marrying her.[42] After his departure from flying in August 1913, however, Cunningham continued to be a product champion for aviation within the Marine Corps. He was also a member of the Chambers Board, which met in October 1913 in order to set forth specific proposals for giving the navy an "adequate aeronautical service."[43] Cunningham eventually overcame his wife's objections, returning to active flight status in 1915 and remaining on aviation duty through 1922.[44]

One more "departure" in 1913 had a significant impact on naval aviation. On 30 June, a special board forcibly retired Chambers. In the service vernacular of the time, he was "plucked," ostensibly for lack of sea time as a captain—the fate feared by Ellyson and Rodgers. Chambers had wanted to go back to sea but had delayed because the navy had not assigned a relief as head of aviation within BuNav. He also feared what could happen to naval aviation without a senior officer in charge or, worse, with one who did not care about aviation.[45] Chambers had believed that his important role, managing naval aviation, would protect him. However, the real reason behind his plucking was likely the manipulation of Adm. Bradley Fiske (Aide for Operations since January 1913), who felt that Chambers was retarding naval aviation.[46]

As mentioned earlier, Chambers took a pragmatic approach to naval aviation's development. The limitations of the machines were one reason.[47] Chambers firmly believed that improvements in propulsion took precedence over tests of bombs and bombing equipment, which the planes could not yet carry anyway.[48] In any case, Chambers felt that bombing was one of the less important uses of naval aviation. Navy planes would be much more useful in scouting and reconnaissance.[49]

Fiske, on the other hand, had grand ideas for reforming the navy, including the use of naval aviation. He envisioned waves of navy bombers repulsing landing forces and torpedo planes sinking ships.[50] Although Chambers had logical reasons for his policies, his pragmatism seemed to Fiske more like outright opposition to naval aviation.[51] Ironically, though Fiske may have wanted Chambers gone in order to put his own man in place, no one else was available. Chambers remained on active duty as the head of naval aviation within the bureau; in fact, Chambers would remain on active duty with aviation through 31 October 1919. But his significance as a product champion began to wane with his plucking.[52] As a further irony, Chambers's retirement and reinstatement occurred at a time when the nascent organization was beginning to demonstrate its usefulness to the fleet.

Through the end of 1912, naval and Marine aviators had experimented with different engines, wireless telegraphy, and submarine spotting.[53] Early in 1913, the aviation camp packed up to join the fleet's winter maneuvers at Guantanamo, Cuba. While there, the seven officers of the camp (including the two Marines) flew their five aircraft as much as possible, spotting submarines, scouting for the fleet, and, perhaps most importantly, giving rides to fleet officers. This last practice not only gave naval officers a sense of what the airplane could do but generated more requests to become aviators—one of them from Lt. Cdr. Henry Mustin. Already intrigued by flying, he qualified as an aviator while in Cuba.[54] Other passengers included two future commanders of naval aviation (Cdr. Noble E. Irwin and Lt. Cdr. Thomas Tingey Craven) and a future Marine Corps Commandant (Lt. Col. John Lejeune).[55] The commander of the Atlantic Fleet, Rear Adm. Charles Badger, was so impressed by the aviators' performance that he planned to use planes in case of orders to intervene that winter in Mexico.[56] But the anticipated orders never came, and in mid-March the aviation camp returned to Annapolis.[57]

Chambers's loss of influence, which had begun with his plucking, continued during the winter of 1913–14. Capt. Mark Bristol reported to Fiske in December for "special duties" with the Aide for Operations. Fiske told him to take charge of aviation, but these orders were problematic since Chambers was still in charge of aviation in the Bureau of Navigation.[58] In January, however, Fiske succeeded in transferring aviation (and Chambers) to his sphere of responsibility and named Bristol the head of what would, on 1 July 1914, officially be called the Office of Naval Aviation.[59] Though Fiske's outspokenness eventually led to his removal from naval aviation, his rank made somewhat easier the coordination of the various (and contentious) navy bureaus.[60]

This new regime wasted no time, issuing a flurry of orders to implement the recommendations of the Chambers Board:[61] Mustin became executive officer and acting commanding officer of the old battleship *Mississippi* on 31 December 1913. Three days later, Daniels ordered the aviation camp at Annapolis to move to Pensacola.[62] Shortly thereafter, Bristol ordered *Mississippi* to Pensacola to become the station ship of the new Naval Aeronautic Station.[63] Bristol ordered Towers to establish the Navy Flying School ashore at Pensacola but confused the issue of command by noting that Mustin, as Senior Officer Present, would decide exactly where the school would be established.[64] Mustin, a lieutenant commander, clearly outranked Towers, a lieutenant, but Towers was clearly the senior aviator, having taught Mustin to fly. Despite the potential, this ambiguity never developed into a problem. More damaging over the long term was the poor relationship that eventually developed between Mustin and Bristol.[65]

While everyone else was moving to Pensacola, Bernard Smith and the newest Marine aviator, 2nd Lt. William McIlvain, took two aircraft and ten enlisted Marines to join the first Advance Base Maneuvers in Culebra, Puerto Rico.[66] As with the aviation camp the previous year, the "Marine Section of the Flying School" participated in maneuvers but also found time for flying Marine officers over the practice area.[67] Through such efforts the aviators made favorable impressions on the commander of the advance-base forces, Col. George Barnett (made Major General Commandant of the Marine Corps on his return to the States), as well as—once again—Admiral Badger.[68]

The Marine Section returned to Pensacola in plenty of time for naval aviation's first real test, though its members would be left out of it. The Mexican Revolution was heating up, and the U.S. Navy received orders to intervene. On 21 April 1914, a landing force of navy and Marine personnel occupied the Mexican port of Veracruz. Another squadron prepared to land forces at Tampico, if necessary. Naval aviation arrived a few days later—Towers, Smith, Ensign Godfrey de Chevalier, four airplanes, and ten mechanics sailed to Tampico on USS *Birmingham.*[69] Meanwhile, Mustin and *Mississippi,* with Lt. (j.g.) Patrick Bellinger, three student aviators, and the remaining two planes, steamed to Veracruz.

Bellinger did the bulk of the flying, in aircraft reconfigured as land planes, mostly in support of the landing forces. (At Tampico, Towers's section had orders to make no flights.)[70] These flights were in the nature of advance-base work, but the only Marine aviators were in Tampico (Smith) and back at Pensacola (McIlvain). Nor were the planes placed under the control of the Marine forces ashore. An army brigade arrived on 30 April to relieve the landing parties and attempted to take over the navy's aviation section. But the planes remained under navy control, supporting the Marines (who remained ashore) as well as the army until *Mississippi* returned to Pensacola in June.[71]

The beginning of the First World War later that summer had major repercussions on naval aviation. Towers immediately requested to be sent as an observer and soon received orders to London as an assistant naval attaché.[72] Towers would spend two years in London, benefiting from his friendship with Lt. Cdr. Cyril Porte of the Royal Navy Air Service. They had met in the summer of 1914, while planning a transatlantic flight with Curtiss.[73] When the war broke out, Porte returned to England, where he was able to give Towers entrée to British naval aviation.

Meanwhile, further technical development of naval aviation effectively halted. *Mississippi* was sold to Greece. The aviators had no sooner shifted the planes and all aviation equipment to the armored cruiser *North Carolina* (the new aviation station ship) than they were ordered to Boston, where the crew off-loaded it all.[74] On 7 August 1914, the ship sailed to Europe to provide relief to Americans stranded overseas, and the aviation officers were needed to help man the ship. Mustin remained as executive officer, but Capt. Joseph Oman took command just before they sailed. McIlvain was the only flyer ordered off the ship, in order to oversee shipment of the aviation gear back to Pensacola.[75] The aviators remained on board and were effectively away from aviation until their return to the United States at the end of 1914.[76] (The ship would not return to Pensacola until September 1915.)[77] The loss was not just of personnel; Pensacola was effectively operating out of the station ship. All accounts (including pay for the men left in Pensacola) and paperwork had to go through the ship.[78] Until it returned or other arrangements were made, the development of naval aviation was effectively paralyzed.[79]

North Carolina's engagement in Europe was not all bad, however. Upon arrival in France, Mustin, Bellinger, and Smith went to Paris on an impromptu fact-finding mission.[80] They toured several airplane factories and were also able to observe some of the local French army aviation squadrons.[81] Their presence in Europe also made it easier for Bristol to have Smith and Herbster assigned as assistant naval attachés in Paris and Berlin, respectively.[82] Over the next two years the information that Towers, Smith, and Herbster gained on European aviation would be of great help.

By the end of January 1915, all the aviators who had sailed with *North Carolina* (except Smith and Herbster) had returned to Pensacola.[83] That March, Congress provided one million dollars for naval aviation, which Bristol immediately used to order desperately needed new airplanes.[84] The same bill also created the office of Chief of Naval Operations (CNO), which absorbed the role of the aides for coordinating the navy bureaus.[85] Secretary Daniels appointed William S. Benson to the position in May. Benson set about establishing his new office, and his order of 8 July placed the Office of Naval Aviation under the CNO.[86] As CNO, Benson had more authority (though not much more) than Fiske to secure the cooperation of the bureaus.[87] However, Benson was at best neutral about aviation. Without Fiske, Bristol's influence with the bureaucracy weakened.

July also brought ten new officers to Pensacola for flight training, the largest class yet. The students included Marine first lieutenants Francis T. Evans and Alfred Cunningham, who returned to aviation and prepared to requalify under new regulations.[88] With an influx of new students, new planes, and the return of *North Carolina* in the fall, naval aviation could resume experiments in bombing, spotting, improving catapults, and determining what qualities were wanted in naval aircraft.[89]

In March 1916, Bristol left Washington for command of *North Carolina* and "the Air Service in the field." Though Bristol intended to exercise his influence from afar, responsibility fell to his assistant, Lt. (j.g.) Clarence Bronson, who was at least an aviator.[90] Bronson now reported to Benson's Aide for Material, Capt. Josiah McKean, who did not want to deal with aviation.[91] In April, McKean recommended reorganization: Bristol would report to the fleet commander in chief rather than directly to the CNO. Pensacola would no longer report through Bristol but instead to the CNO's Material Section.[92] Benson approved, and the changes were made by July.[93] McKean also wanted a commander to relieve Bronson; a more senior officer could relieve McKean of some of the aviation work.[94] What he got was John Towers, now a senior lieutenant, recently returned from London. Bronson was still turning over the aviation desk when he died in a bombing test on 8 November.[95] But Towers's personal knowledge of British aircraft and doctrine, both further developed than the U.S. Navy's, helped him get past this setback.

Two crashes in 1916 convinced aviators that the old pusher hydroplanes—which was all the navy had for training—were dangerous. But Bristol continued to purchase pushers rather than the safer "tractors."[96] Mustin successfully fought Bristol on this point. The CNO grounded the pushers as unsafe and replaced them with the first really modern navy aircraft.[97] Mustin's stand against Bristol contributed to his relief as commandant of the Pensacola Air Station by Capt. Joseph Jayne in January 1917. The month before, Bristol had departed naval aviation for good when he left *North Carolina* and turned over command of the navy's Air Service to Rear Adm. Albert Gleaves, commander of the Destroyer Force, Atlantic Fleet.[98] Once again, nonflyers held senior aviation positions. This was the state of leadership that would take naval aviation into the First World War.

Naval aviation made very slow progress in the prewar years. One reason was the constant turnover of people at the top combined with repeated changes in organizational structure. Marine aviation's leadership was more stable than that of the navy. There was no formal organization even there, but in a considerably smaller organization than the navy, a formal organization was perhaps unnecessary. However, the Marines depended upon the navy for their airplanes and training. Consequently, the uncertainties in naval aviation also slowed the development of Marine Corps aviation. The 1920 creation of an official Aviation Section in Marine Corps Headquarters and of the navy's Bureau of Aeronautics the following year finally spelled the end of the organizational uncertainties described in this paper. Naval aviation continued to face problems with hardware, funding, and in finding the "proper" use of airplanes (all important factors in naval aviation's development from the very beginning), but it had finally found a fixed place in the organizational chart.

NOTES   1 This has been the theme underlying I. B. Holley's work. Put another way, the adoption of any new thing (be it tool or idea) requires its integration into the culture adopting it: Oriol Pi-Sunyer and Thomas De Gregori, "Cultural Resistance to Technological Change," *Technology and Culture* 5, no. 2 (1964), p. 249.

2 Jeffery A. Isaacson, Christopher Layne, and John Arquilla, *Predicting Military Innovation* (Santa Monica, Calif.: RAND, 1999).

3 Ibid., p. 4.

4 See also Bruno Latour, *Science in Action: How to Follow Scientists and Engineers through Society* (Cambridge, Mass.: Harvard Univ. Press, 1987).

5 Assistant Secretary of the Navy Theodore Roosevelt to John Davis Long, 25 March 1898, in Theodore Roosevelt, ed. Louis Auchincloss, *Letters and Speeches* (New York: Library of America, 2004), p. 142.

6 Board of Ordnance and Fortification, "Report of Joint Board," 29 April 1898, General Correspondence, record group [hereafter RG] 165, file no. 3896, National Archives, College Park, Md., 7998; Cdr. C. H. Davis, USN, to Secretary Long, 30 April 1898, and 1st endorsement, General Correspondence, Office of the Secretary of the Navy [hereafter SecNav GC], RG 80, National Archives Building, Washington, D.C. [hereafter NAB].

7 Bureau of Equipment [hereafter BuEquip] to SecNav, 19 August 1909, 26983-20:1, SecNav GC.

8 Cone to SecNav, 7 October 1910, Washington Irving Chambers Papers, Manuscript Division, Library of Congress, Washington, D.C. [hereafter Chambers Papers].

9 President of the General Board to SecNav, 14 October 1910, file 449 [hereafter GB-449], Subject Files of the General Board, RG 80, NAB. (Further citations of "GB-*number*" are to the appropriate files in this collection.)

10 Acting SecNav [Winthrop] to Bureau of Construction and Repair [hereafter BuC&R] and Bureau of Steam Engineering [hereafter BuEng], 13 October 1910; BuC&R [Watt] to SecNav, 21 October 1910; BuEng [Cone] to SecNav, 13 October 1910; all in Chambers Papers.

11 Other officers, such as Dewey and Cowles, were also product champions, believing that aircraft could do great things for the Navy, but they were considerably less successful.

12 Chambers to SecNav, 23 November 1910, Chambers Papers.

13 Almost forgotten, that is, probably because it does not advance the carrier paradigm.

14 Whether due to problems with the engine or an inability to overcome the hydrodynamic forces on the float, Curtiss had to taxi back to his base. This did not, however, detract from the achievement. Ellyson to SecNav, 17 February 1911, Chambers Papers.

15 "The Development of Naval Aviation" (speech to the Aeronautical Society, undated, but between 9 March and 1 July 1911), Chambers Papers.

16 Chambers to SecNav, 23 November 1910, Chambers Papers.

17 Chambers to General Board, "Memorandum re 'Aeronautics,'" 8 August 1913, GB-449; Chambers, "Brief Summary of the First Steps in the Development of Naval Aviation," 24 May 1917, p. 8, Chambers Papers; Stephen K. Stein, *From Torpedoes to Aviation: Washington Irving Chambers and Technological Innovation in the New Navy, 1876–1913* (Tuscalousa: Univ. of Alabama Press, 2007), pp. 164–65.

18 The money could not be spent until the beginning of the fiscal year, on July 1, but the day Chambers issued the requisition for the planes, 8 May, is considered the birthday of naval aviation.

19 BuNav [written by Chambers] to Rodgers, 28 November 1911, Chambers Papers; *Annual Report of the Secretary of the Navy* (Washington, D.C.: 1911), p. 59.

20 Winthrop [Acting SecNav, letter prepared by Chambers] to Glenn Curtiss, 13 December 1910, 26983-72, SecNav GC; Winthrop [prepared by Chambers] to the Wright Company, telegram, 13 March 1911, 26983-109, SecNav GC; Stein, *From Torpedoes to Aviation*, p. 163; U.S. Navy Dept., *United States Naval Aviation, 1910–1980* (Washington, D.C.: U.S. Government Printing Office, 1981), pp. 3–4; George Van Deurs, *Anchors in the Sky: Spuds Ellyson, the First Naval Aviator* (San Rafael, Calif.: Presidio, 1978), pp. 54–55.

21 Ellyson, in fact, was also responsible for much of Towers's flight training. Clark G. Reynolds, *Admiral John H. Towers: The Struggle for Naval Aviation* (Annapolis, Md.: Naval Institute Press, 1991), pp. 34–44.

22 Van Deurs, *Anchors in the Sky,* pp. 133–34.

23 U.S. Navy Dept., *United States Naval Aviation, 1910–1980,* p. 5.

24 Bureau of Navigation [hereafter BuNav; prepared by Chambers] to Rodgers, 28 November 1911, Chambers Papers.

25 This was especially true of these first aviators. Van Deurs, *Anchors in the Sky,* p. 105; Reynolds, *Admiral John H. Towers,* pp. 47–48.

26 For "camps," Towers, partial manuscript for autobiography [hereafter Towers, autobiographical ms.], p. 23, Towers Papers. The reason for the separation was probably the Curtiss camp's sharing space with Glenn Curtiss's own winter operations.

27 Van Deurs, *Anchors in the Sky,* p. 105.

28 Ibid., pp. 130–31, 148–49; Chambers, memorandum, "Concerning Participation of Government Aviators in Public Meets and Celebrations," and handwritten note, "Policy—Safe & Sane—Conservative," Chambers Papers.

29 Reynolds, *Admiral John H. Towers,* p. 52.

30 George Van Deurs, *Wings for the Fleet: A Narrative of Naval Aviation's Early Development, 1910–1916* (Annapolis, Md.: Naval Institute Press, 1966), p. 94.

31 Towers to SecNav, 17 October 1913, Chambers Papers.

32 The Marine Corps did not get formal responsibility for advance-base planning until 1910, and the Advance Base School, responsible for working out such plans, was not established until 1911. Cdr. R. H. Jackson, USN, comp., "History of Advanced Base," 15 May 1913, GB-408 [Advance Base].

33 Cunningham to Officer in Charge, Advanced Base School, 12 February 1912, Chambers Papers.

34 Chambers to Aide for Personnel, memorandum, 12 February 1912; SecNav to Major General Commandant, U.S. Marine Corps [hereafter MGC], 4 March 1912; both Chambers Papers.

35 Cunningham's arrival is celebrated as the birthday of Marine Corps aviation. Edward C. Johnson, *Marine Corps Aviation: The Early Years, 1912–1940,* ed. Graham A. Cosmas (Washington, D.C.: U.S. Government Printing Office, 1977), pp. 4–5; J. W. Kinkaid [in charge of the Experiment Station at Annapolis] to Chambers, 22 May 1912, Chambers Papers.

36 Cunningham held the former view, whereas Smith was more in tune with the latter. Johnson, *Marine Corps Aviation,* p. 4 note, 11 note.

37 Van Deurs, *Anchors in the Sky,* p. 129, and *Wings for the Fleet,* 65–66; Towers, autobiographical ms., p. 29, Towers Papers; Reynolds, *Admiral John H. Towers,* pp. 51–53.

38 Chambers, "Brief Memorandum Concerning the Advance of Aviation and Its Bearing on the Foregoing Recommendations," undated but probably early 1913, Chambers Papers.

39 Van Deurs, *Wings for the Fleet,* p. 95.

40 Van Deurs, *Anchors in the Sky,* pp. 130–51.

41 Ellyson's influence on the early years of naval aviation is clear from the voluminous correspondence in the Chambers Papers between him and Chambers from Ellyson's assignment to aviation in 1911 until his return to sea service in 1913. These letters cover a variety of topics and show that Chambers relied on Ellyson's opinions and feedback to help guide the development of naval aviation (even when he overruled Ellyson). Fewer letters survive in the Chambers Papers from Rodgers, but those that do, as well as references to Rodgers in others' correspondence, make clear that Rodgers played a similar role. Though he may not have been as friendly with Chambers as Ellyson, Rodgers was the only naval aviator trained by the Wright Co. until 1914 and thus was the expert on the Wright aircraft. In addition to the fact that both had long absences from naval aviation, both Ellyson and Rodgers died in air accidents after returning to aviation and before either could rise to high rank.

42 Cunningham to Chambers, 3 September 1913, Chambers Papers.

43 F. D. Roosevelt [Acting SecNav] to Chambers, 9 October 1913, Chambers Papers.

44 Cunningham to Bristol, 3 December 1914, General Correspondence of the Office of Naval Aeronautics, 1914–1917, RG 72, 1740-14, NAB [hereafter ONA]; Johnson, p. 8; Van Deurs, *Wings for the Fleet,* p. 128. Marine Corps policy was to rotate aviators back to regular duty after five years, resulting in Cunningham's second and final departure from aviation. He requested a return to aviation in 1928 but was told he was too old to fly. Johnson, *Marine Corps Aviation,* p. 30.

45 Chambers, "Brief Summary of the First Steps in the Development of Naval Aeronautics."

46 Stein, pp. 184–88.

47 Chambers to SecNav, 28 June 1912, GB-449.

48 Many letters from Chambers to hopeful inventors emphasize his desire to make airplanes safe before dealing with aerial ordnance. For example: Chambers to BuNav, "Subject: John W. Currell Re his aerial torpedo," May [?] 1912, Chambers Papers.

49 Chambers, "Memorandum on Naval Aviation," attached to Chambers to SecNav, 28 June 1912, GB-449.

50 Fiske to President, General Board, 7 April 1911, GB-449; Bradley A. Fiske, *From Midshipman to Rear-Admiral* (New York: Century, 1919), pp. 503–506.

51 Fiske, *From Midshipman to Rear-Admiral,* p. 538.

52 The additional information regarding Chambers's "plucking" in this and previous paragraphs is taken from Stein, *From Torpedoes to Aviation,* pp. 181–98.

53 Van Deurs, *Wings for the Fleet,* pp. 64–65; Senior Aviation Officer [Towers] to SecNav (Bureau of Operations), 18 December 1912, GB-418.

54 At the time, soloing marked the end of training; [Chambers?], "The Development of Naval Aviation" and "Naval Aviation at Guantanamo Bay," both undated, Chambers Papers; Reynolds, *Admiral John H. Towers,* pp. 56–63; Van Deurs, *Wings for the Fleet,* pp. 79–82. Like Towers, Mustin initially saw possibilities for the airplane in extending naval gunfire. Like Cunningham, Mustin was an enthusiast before joining naval aviation; John Fass Morton, *Mustin: A Naval Family of the 20th Century* (Annapolis, Md.: Naval Institute Press, 2003), pp. 65–81.

55 "List of Officers Who Have Taken Flights . . . ," undated but probably mid-to-late 1913, Chambers Papers; Reynolds, *Admiral John H. Towers,* p. 59.

56 Towers to Ellyson, 20 February 1913, Towers Papers. Towers was still assisting Chambers in Washington.

57 Senior Aviation Officer [Towers] to Officer in Charge of Aviation, "Weekly Report on Aviation," 15 March 1913, Towers Papers; Van Deurs, *Wings for the Fleet,* pp. 82–87, 93–94, 103–104.

58 Fiske, *From Midshipman to Rear-Admiral,* pp. 538–39.

59 [Bristol?], memorandum for the Aide for Operations, "Development of Aeronautics," undated but probably December 1913, ONA, 1-14-½, seems to be Bristol's recommendations for actions to be taken. [Fiske to SecNav?], memorandum, "Development of an Aeronautic Service in the Navy," 30 December 1913, ONA [1-14-1?], seems to be Fiske's recommendations to SecNav for action. [Fiske?], press release, "Naval Aeronautics: Air Craft Will Take Their Place in the Fleet," 31 December 1913 ONA, 1-14-3.

60 Daniels assigned Fiske to the Naval War College in July 1915 to get him out of Washington. Stein, *From Torpedoes to Aviation*, p. 195.

61 Press notice, "Report of a Naval Board on Aeronautics," 10 January 1914, ONA, 58-14; Archibald Turnbull and Clifford Lee Lord, *History of the United States Naval Aviation*, Literature and History of Naval Aviation (Manchester, N.H.: Ayer, 1971), pp. 33–34.

62 Daniels to Towers, 3 January 1914, ONA, 2-14-1.

63 Bristol to Commanding Officer [hereafter CO], USS *Mississippi* [Mustin], 7 January 1914, ONA, 10-14. At the time, no one was sure whether Pensacola would be the permanent home of naval aviation.

64 Bristol to Towers (via Mustin), 6 January 1913, ONA, 13-14.

65 Morton, *Mustin*, pp. 81–101.

66 [Bristol] to Aide for Personnel, 6 January 1913, plus 5 enclosures, ONA, 8-14.

67 Smith to CO, Flying School [Towers], 10 March 1914, ONA, 255-14.

68 Barnett to Commander in Chief, Atlantic Fleet [hereafter CINCLANTFLT], 3 February 1914, 16721-86:1; and CINCLANTFLT to Aide for Operations, 14 February 1914; both SecNav GC.

69 Two planes were in good shape, and one was questionable—it and the fourth were brought along for spare parts. *Birmingham* was the flagship of a torpedo-boat squadron commanded by William S. Sims.

70 CO, USS *Mississippi* to CINCLANTFLT, 19 May 1914, ONA, 1037-14.

71 Mustin to Bristol, 14 May 1914, ONA, 611-14; [Bristol?], "Memorandum for Secretary," 29 May 1914, ONA, 693-14.

72 Towers to Bristol, 3 August 1914, ONA, 1028-14; Reynolds, *Admiral John H. Towers*, pp. 84, 89.

73 Reynolds, *Admiral John H. Towers*, pp. 89–105. The ONA correspondence also contains many of Towers's letters from London.

74 For USS *North Carolina*, see Morton, *Mustin*, p. 96; Mustin to Bristol, 11 July 1914, ONA, 904-14.

75 Mustin to Bristol, 1 August 1914, 1027-14; Bristol's reply, 6 August 1914, 1049-14; Mustin to Bristol, telegram, 6 August 1914; Bristol's reply of same date, 1051-14; Mustin to Bristol, 5 August 1914, 1060-14; Bristol's reply, 17 August, 1060-14; Herbster to Bristol, telegram, 6 August 1914; Bristol's reply, 8 August 1914; all ONA. Turnbull and Lord, *History of the United States Naval Aviation*, p. 44; Van Deurs, *Wings for the Fleet*, pp. 115–17.

76 Van Deurs, *Wings for the Fleet*, pp. 115–17; Morton, *Mustin*, pp. 96–101.

77 Morton, *Mustin*, p. 103.

78 Bristol to CO, USS *North Carolina* [Oman], 13 August 1914, ONA, 1082-14.

79 [Bristol?] to the Aide for Operations, 16 October 1914, ONA, 1460-14.

80 Oman to SecNav, telegram, 19 August 1914, ONA, 1106-14.

81 Mustin to Bristol, 24 August 1914, GB-449.

82 Office of Naval Aeronautics to Office of Naval Intelligence, 4 September 1914, ONA, 1189-14.

83 Van Deurs, *Wings for the Fleet*, p. 125.

84 Press release, 15 April 1915, ONA, 1222-15; press release, 26 April 1915, quoting a letter from Daniels to the president of Williams College in response to a query from the latter, ONA, 1697-15; Bristol to Daniels, 4 March 1916, ONA, 995-16. The three aircraft were Burgess-Dunne pushers. Despite aviators' requests for tractor machines, Bristol believed that pushers were the better military design; Mustin to Bristol, telegram, 11 March 1915, ONA, 764-15.

85 "Terms of the Office of the Chief of Naval Operations," *Naval Historical Center*, www.history.navy .mil/.

86 [Benson?], 8 July 1915, ONA, 2434-15. The reorganization was made official by Daniels in his memorandum of 12 October 1915, 26983-566 ½, SecNav GC.

87 The position of Chief of Naval Operations (CNO) was considerably weaker when it was established than it is now. Robert William Love, Jr., ed., *The Chiefs of Naval Operations* (Annapolis, Md.: Naval Institute Press, 1980), pp. 4–7.

88 U.S. Navy Dept., press release, 1 July 1915, ONA, 2557-15.

89 Bureau of Ordnance to Office of Naval Aviation, 30 October 1915, 4407-15; SecNav to Commandant, Pensacola, 4 September 1915, 3397-15; U.S. Navy Dept., press release, 10 November 1915, 4500-15; Director of Naval Aviation [Bristol] to the Burgess Co., 24 July 1915, 2730-15; Commandant, Pensacola [Mustin] to BuNav, 16 August 1915, 3126-15; CNO to BuC&R, 1 December 1915, 4621-15; all ONA.

90 Bristol to Herbster, 2 March 1916, ONA, 938-16; Van Deurs, *Wings for the Fleet*, pp. 117, 136.

91 Turnbull and Lord, *History of the United States Naval Aviation*, p. 59.

92 McKean to CNO, 10 April 1916, ONA, 4156-16.

93 Van Deurs, *Wings for the Fleet*, pp. 151–52.

94 Aide for Material [McKean] to CNO, 8 June 1916, ONA, 2382-16.

95 Reynolds, *Admiral John H. Towers*, pp. 106–107.

96 Ibid., pp. 150–52; Bristol to Mustin, 30 June 1915, ONA, 2320-15.

97 Mustin to CNO, radiogram, 12 June 1916, ONA, 2505-16. See also note 82, above.

98 Van Deurs, *Wings for the Fleet*, pp. 142, 155–56.

IV *Riverine Operations of the Danube Flotilla in the Austro-German Romanian Campaign of 1916*

MICHAEL B. BARRETT

At three o'clock in the afternoon of 27 August 1916, the traffic stopped on the Austrian-Romanian border. It took a while to register with the guards, because Romanian soldiers initially stopped the flow twenty kilometers from their side of the border. Austrian gendarmes and customs officials first noticed things were amiss when scheduled trains failed to appear. They duly reported this troubling development to their headquarters, knowing and dreading what it meant. They did not have long to wait; shortly after nine o'clock, word came back from the border crossings that trains entering Romania were being fired on.[1]

Two hundred miles to the south, on the Danube River, the war started a half hour later, at 9:30 PM, with a torpedo fired from a well concealed Romanian torpedo boat lying off Ramadan Island, in the harbor of the Romanian city of Giurgiu. The torpedo streaked across the river to where vessels from the Austrian Danube Flotilla lay at anchor at the Bulgarian city of Rustchuk. Aimed at *Bosna*, the flagship of the flotilla, the torpedo missed, hitting instead a nearby barge of fuel and coal, which exploded, broke in half, and sank as flames from the burning fuel engulfed the anchorage. At first the Austrian sailors suspected a torpedo, but when no further activity ensued they concluded that the fire had started due to spontaneous combustion or carelessness. But at 10:30 word came from army headquarters that Romania had declared war.[2]

For the entire flotilla to remain at the open anchorage at Rustchuk was out of the question. A flurry of signals and radio messages set vessels in motion, and the flotilla's 1st Division weighed anchor and headed upriver for the safety of the Belene Channel at Sistov. The departing craft, invisible in the dark, stole safely out of Rustchuk. When dawn broke, an observer would not have been faulted for thinking he had stepped back fifty years in time, for the craft puffing and chuffing upriver were museum pieces that resembled the monitors of Flag Officer Andrew Hull Foote or Admiral David Farragut, those "cheese boxes on rafts" whose appearance on the rivers of the Confederacy had inevitably heralded the arrival of a Union army. Only machine guns and radio masts visibly differentiated the craft from those of the American Civil War.

The resemblance was neither superficial nor coincidental. Impressed with the manner in which the monitors had facilitated successful campaigns deep in the heart of the South, the Austro-Hungarian navy had deliberately copied the design. Each sporting a turret with a single gun of approximately five-inch (120-mm) caliber and some smaller twelve-pounder guns, *Maros* and *Leitha,* laid down in 1865, had entered service in 1878 and promptly participated in the occupation of Bosnia-Herzegovina. The next forty years saw the flotilla gain in numbers and size.[3] By 1914, on the eve of war in Europe, the flotilla numbered some six monitors, some with howitzers and turrets mounting twin five-inch guns, designed to slug it out with enemy vessels and shore batteries. The monitors had armored protection for the gun positions as well as along the waterline. Four additional monitors came off the ways in 1914 and 1915, but owing to the loss of *Temes I* in 1915 the flotilla numbered nine at the start of the 1916 campaign. The original monitors carried complements of fifty-seven men and had a speed of 7.5 knots; the final vessels had crews of 105 men and could attain thirteen knots. In addition, there were patrol boats carrying machine guns and small cannon designed for reconnaissance and for engaging infantry and small watercraft. Armed steamers were envisioned if war came; like the patrol boats, they would be armored against rifle fire and were to tow barges and carry troops. They could also protect civilian shipping. Mining craft were constructed to lay mines and sweep them, as well as to set up barricades and take down enemy ones. Logistical vessels and tugs carried everything necessary for self-sufficiency. Hospital barges took care of the wounded, while headquarters vessels had sleeping quarters for the staffs and support elements, as the monitors were too cramped to accommodate any but their complements.[4]

Ironically, the Austrian monitors never engaged in the envisioned ship-to-ship combat; of the Dual Monarchy's potential riverine enemies, Serbia had no vessels and Bulgaria joined the Central Powers in 1915. Romania did have a river flotilla, but technically it sided with the Central Powers until 1914, and an inept strategy when it entered the war on the Triple Entente side in 1916 wasted its assets. Nevertheless, the Austrian Danube Flotilla saw plenty of action fighting enemy shore batteries and assisting with river crossings in the campaigns against Serbia and Romania; the monitor *Temes I* is credited by many with firing the first shot of the war, at Belgrade on 28 July 1914.[5] More importantly, the monitor flotilla played a critical role in the Romanian campaign, thwarting a Romanian crossing of the Danube. Had that crossing succeeded, Field Marshal von Mackensen's diversion in the Dobrudja beginning in September 1916, which stunned the Romanians and transferred the initiative in that campaign to the Central Powers, might have had a very different ending, leaving the Central Powers overextended on a front longer than the entire previous eastern front at the end of tenuous lines of communication at the farthest reaches of the Austro-Hungarian Empire.

The Danube Theater

The Danube River theater was important for two reasons: it delineated for the most part (starting in the west at the Iron Gate and ending at Kalimok, where the river passed into purely Romanian territory) the border between Romania and Bulgaria (an ally of the Austro-Hungarian Empire) and was hence the likely place of military operations between the two nations, at least initially; also, it was the main avenue of trade for southeastern Europe in a region bereft of rail lines and bridges. From Kalimok the border ran overland southeast across the Dobrudja region to the Black Sea at Varna. Between Belgrade in Serbia and the Black Sea, a distance in excess of five hundred miles, only one bridge crossed the Danube—the recently opened King Carol Bridge at Cernavodă, carrying Romania's commerce via a rail line from its only seaport (Constanza) to the capital at Bucharest. The river constituted the major highway of southeast Europe. Before the war hundreds of barges had plied its waters between Romania and the Central Powers, carrying the rich natural resources of Wallachia, namely, petroleum products and agricultural goods. When the war began, over a million tons of grains, vegetables, and coal purchased by the Central Powers sat in these barges, virtually all in Romanian harbors and seized by Romanian armed forces.[6]

In general, once clear of the narrow and turbulent Iron Gate on the border with Serbia, the Danube slows appreciably and widens. What high land and bluffs exist on the Romanian side are some ten to fifteen kilometers inland and north from the river channel; thus a low, swampy area with ponds and lagoons forms the Romanian floodplain. On the Bulgarian side of the river, the hilly extensions of the Balkan Mountains usually come right to the river's edge, presenting that side of the river with formidable banks and high bluffs. Just beyond Silistria the Danube turns north, flowing in that direction to Braila, where it again turns east and flows into the Black Sea. At the mouth of the Danube, there is a delta with three main channels. The southernmost, the sixty-three-kilometer-long Sulina Channel, is the normal one for shipping, as deep-draft vessels cannot use the other two.[7]

The Danube suffered from low water in the summer, narrowing the navigable channel. Ordinarily the Romanian Hydrologic Service buoyed the river during low-water season (starting around 1 June) and pulled the markings when the ice came, usually in late November.[8] The Romanians did not perform this function in 1916, so the Danube Flotilla had to rely on lead-line soundings as it negotiated the river.

Crossing the Danube was not hard—armies had passed over it since antiquity—but crossing the river under fire was another thing. The locations suitable for the purpose were few and well known, and a resolute defender with modern artillery could thwart any attempt.[9]

Initial Operations

The monitors played an essential role in the Balkans from the beginning of the war, but our attention must turn to 1916 and Romania. The Austrian high command anticipated the eventual entry of Romania into the war on the side of the Entente and had moved the flotilla to the lower Danube in late 1915, after the fall of Serbia. The Austrians moved into several Bulgarian harbors, principally Lelek, now that Bulgaria was a member of the Central Powers, and conducted reconnaissance along the Danube. They acquired excellent, detailed knowledge of Romanian fortifications, barricades, minefields, and artillery defenses.[10] As Romania's attitude became more questionable, the Austrians placed the flotilla under the operational control of Army Group Mackensen, the senior Central Powers headquarters in the region. In the event hostilities erupted, Field Marshal von Mackensen directed, the flotilla was to secure its anchorage facilities and destroy enemy harbors and rail yards, while establishing mine barriers across the Danube to deny the Romanian flotilla use of the river. To that end, a mine barrier, designed to be detonated by an observer, was prepared near Lelek.[11]

The onset of hostilities on 27 August caused the flotilla, as we have seen, to scatter to safe anchorage at the Belene Channel, where Persin Island divided the river into two channels and hid the southern one, the Belene Channel, which ran for several miles along the Bulgarian side of the river. Eventually the channel emerged and rejoined the Danube at Sistov, a Bulgarian city facing north across the river toward its Romanian counterpart, Zimnicea. Aware of the advantage of this cover, the Austrians had designated Belene as their main base in case of hostilities and had begun stockpiling bridging equipment there for a possible river crossing. The 1st Monitor Division arrived early on the 28th. The mining craft steamed in later, having left Rustchuk at five that morning, after mining the river. Finally, late in the day, the 2nd Monitor Division made its way in, carrying barges of oil, coal, and grain taken from the Romanians at Giurgiu. The division had waited until daylight, then steamed across the river, captured the barges, and shelled the city, setting the oil and grain storage areas, as well as the harbor, on fire. Much farther upstream at Kladovo, the monitor *Almos* dispatched several patrol boats that night to run a gantlet of enemy fire at the Iron Gate and to safety in the harbor at Orsova, but the trip was too dangerous in the dark for the monitor. Dawn saw *Almos* bombarding the Romanian city of Turnu Severin, destroying a cavalry barracks, silencing shore batteries, and setting afire rail yards and storage facilities before transiting the Iron Gate to Orsova.[12] Over the next several days the monitors, operating in groups of two and accompanied by the smaller patrol craft, undertook cutting-out operations against the various Romanian ports, seizing cargo barges and destroying what they could not make off with.[13]

September proved quiet. The Austrians blocked off the western entrance to their anchorage at Belene with a minefield and reinforced their facilities, especially with antiaircraft weapons, as the Romanians tried to bomb the flotilla on an almost daily basis—without much luck. At the end of the month came a long-sought operation against Corabia, a river port thirty miles west of Belene where, rumors abounded, the Russians had an anchorage. Besides eliminating that menace, the expedition promised to permit the Austrians a chance to respond to enemy artillery bombardments and reinvigorate the fighting spirit of the sailors, who had begun to feel penned up in the Belene Channel.[14] II Monitor Group, consisting of the monitors *Sava* and *Inn,* the armored steamer *Samson,* and some patrol boats, left Belene in fog at 5:15 AM on 29 September. Exiting the west entrance to the Belene Channel and heading upriver, it immediately came under fire from Romanian shore batteries. Returning fire, the Austrians passed unscathed. Beyond Nikopol they linked up with two patrol boats *(Viza* and *Barsch)* sent ahead to scout the channel for mines. Fog, a narrow channel, and poor sounding led to the grounding of *Sava,* but *Samson* pulled it off without damage. At Corabia, reached around noon, *Inn* advanced into the lower harbor and took under fire shore facilities, while *Sava* moved above the town and sent the patrol boat *Viza* into the harbor to make sure it was free of obstacles. Once *Sava* got the all-clear signal, it entered the harbor, where the Russians had their anchorage, and promptly reduced the enemy defenses to rubble with its 120-mm guns. It later silenced an enemy field artillery battery, firing from a distance of 3,600 meters. *Samson* arrived and towed away nine partially loaded Austrian and German grain barges. Three Russian vessels (including a two-stack coastal steamer) and numerous smaller craft went to the bottom. Although the shelling lasted over two hours, the city of Corabia was spared; not a shell landed on it. The townspeople nonetheless panicked; the amazed Austrians watched as Red Cross flags appeared from windows, in apparent confusion with white flags. Some humor was added when a motorized barge, fleeing with nine completely naked people, including two women, ran aground on an island opposite the harbor entrance. The Austrian flotilla left around four o'clock in the afternoon, after rounding up its prizes. On the return voyage, it encountered a few timid volleys and a few near misses from the artillery opposite the entrance to the Belene Channel.[15]

The Romanian Danube Crossing

At ten o'clock the morning of 1 October, an alarming telegraph arrived at the flotilla headquarters: "This morning at 0400 the enemy crossed the Danube at Rjahovo with three companies [of infantry]. Two heavy howitzers and two 90mm field guns already en route."[16]

By noon six battalions had crossed to the Bulgarian side of the river, and there were clear signs the enemy had started to construct a pontoon bridge. The Romanians had stolen a move and taken the Central Powers completely by surprise.

The river crossing should not have come as a surprise, for the Romanians had crossed the Danube in their 1913 invasion of Bulgaria.[17] Both sides had recognized the value of the Dobrudja region (historically, the coastal strip of southeastern Romania and northeastern Bulgaria)—simply stated, neither side could risk crossing the Danube unless its Dobrudja flank was secure. The Romanians had planned to advance there with a combined Russo-Romanian army corps, the appearance of the Russians being designed to deter the Bulgarians from declaring war.[18] Mackensen moved immediately, however, and his unexpected routing of the 150,000 Romanian and Russian forces in Dobrudja caused panic in Bucharest and shook the Romanian high command.[19] King Ferdinand relieved the chief of the general staff, Gen. Vasile Zottu;[20] he also replaced the commander along the border with Bulgaria, Gen. Mihail Aslan, with Gen. Alexander Averescu (1859–1938), his top field commander. Averescu, who had led the 2nd Army into Transylvania, characteristically sought to rectify the impending calamity with a bold move: transferring the impetus of the Romanian offensive from Transylvania to Bulgaria to meet the threat there, crossing the Danube, and advancing into the Dobrudja right into the rear of Mackensen's army, cutting the Germans' line of communications. Ordering a halt to operations in Transylvania, Averescu began moving forces to the south and planning for the river crossing.[21] The Romanians committed an army corps with three divisions to the assault, the first wave crossing in boats without initial opposition at four in the morning from Flamanda on their side to Rjahovo on the Bulgarian side. Mackensen's 3rd Bulgarian Army was caught flat-footed and had advanced too far into the Dobrudja to render immediate help, throwing the responsibility into the lap of Gen. Robert Kosch's VII Corps in Sistov. Kosch had few assets, but he had two unique ones, which he immediately ordered into action: aircraft and the Danube Flotilla.[22]

The aircraft arrived first, around noon, and bombed and strafed both the troops waiting on the shore and soldiers attempting to erect a bridge. The few Romanian aircraft made the mistake of trying to defend the bridge site by circling over it, leaving the initiative to the Germans, who attacked at will, killing over two hundred officers and a thousand soldiers. The Romanian ground forces watched in impotent fury. The bombs seriously wounded Lieutenant Colonel Popovici, the engineer in charge of the bridging. General Lambru, commander of the 21st Division, took over the construction efforts. Lambru estimated that the German attack cost his advance four hours—the bridge was completed by seven in the evening, as opposed to three that afternoon.[23] The loss of those hours was to prove fatal.

The flotilla commander, Capt. Karl Lucich, sent a mine expert, Commander Paulin, overland to Rjahovo to determine the best location from which to launch floating mines against the bridge. Meanwhile, III Monitor Group *(Bodrog* and *Körös),* under Commander Masjon, two patrol boat sections, a mining squadron, and the German motor launch *Weichsel* raised steam and departed in two sections for Rjahovo, the patrol boats leaving at seven o'clock that evening and the rest at nine. Masjon had orders to destroy the bridge and bridging material, along with bringing under fire, and preventing a withdrawal by, the units that had crossed over. The departure times allowed for an arrival at or close to dawn. The river near the crossing site was shallow; in fact, flotilla craft had not been able to pass the area as late as August owing to shallow water. The many sandbars and shoals shifted constantly, requiring approaching vessels to sound the depth, thus ruling out a night approach by the monitors. The Austrians also feared, with ample justification, mines and obstacles placed in the river upstream of the bridge. Further, the river was narrow, restricting both maneuvering and the number of vessels that could approach closely. Finally, a daylight approach offered visibility to adjust fire.[24]

A fierce storm slowed the progress of the Austrians, both the vessels making their way to Rjahovo and Commander Paulin's efforts at launching floating mines (the winds blew all of them back on shore).[25] The storm also wreaked havoc with the bridge construction. Rain and lightning scattered the engineers, broke the bridge three times, and rendered passage over it impossible until early the next morning.[26] At 3:00 AM, Kosch's headquarters radioed Masjon to inform him that a division had crossed over and that "attacking and destroying the bridge was of decisive importance." At eight the patrol boats *Barsch* and *Viza* arrived at Rjahovo and approached to within two hundred meters of the bridge, driving off an enemy artillery battery that had recklessly set up along the bank without cover. Ironically, the storm, which had caused such damage to the bridge, raised the water level of the Danube to the point where the Austrian patrol boats could cross the dam the Romanians had constructed several kilometers upstream of their bridge. The patrol boats opened fire with machine guns and small cannon, their shrapnel shells inflicting many casualties and scattering enemy infantry. Romanian artillery zeroed in on the Austrian vessels, and a direct hit on the bridge of *Barsch* took out its steering, killing three sailors and wounding five. Having expended all their ammunition and unable to launch floating mines owing to the height of the waves, the boats withdrew.[27]

At 10:30, the monitors *Bodrog* and *Körös* arrived, circling three kilometers upstream from the bridge. Blocked from coming closer by the Romanian dam, the two began a steady bombardment with their 120-mm guns, ignoring a hail of fire delivered by Romanian field-artillery batteries from both sides of the river. It became clear, however, that the monitors' guns would not shatter the bridge, so Masjon considered trying to cross the dam and ramming the bridge. He backed off when he realized the bridge was higher than the deck of his vessels, which meant the turrets of the monitors would make contact, and there was a likelihood the turret guns would snag on the bridge, trapping the Austrian vessel. Both sides continued their shelling, with *Bodrog* taking five hits and having to run behind Taban Island to effect temporary repairs to a stuck turret. *Körös* kept up the fire until enemy shells severed steam lines, blinding everyone on the bridge. Its conning officer unable to see, the vessel ran aground momentarily on the Romanian side of the river. Finally, the onset of darkness, the exhaustion of the crews, and the discovery that the Romanians had launched floating mines forced the monitors to leave the scene. Both vessels later that night returned to the Belene base.[28]

While III Monitor Group slugged it out with the Romanians, I and IV Groups (under Lieutenant Commander Wulff) had departed from Belene towing barges with ammunition, coal, and bunker fuel. Enemy shore batteries opposite the east end of the Belene Channel on Ginghinarelle Island holed the coal barge, forcing I Group to run for cover to make repairs, while IV Group dared not risk shells hitting the fuel barge and waited until nightfall to head downstream. The two groups arrived at Rjahovo during the morning of 3 October. They discovered that the Romanians had repaired the previous day's damage to the bridge and that enemy troops were streaming across it—but they were marching back to the Romanian side! Army Group Mackensen had discovered from a captured Romanian colonel that General Averescu had ordered a retreat and had even countenanced abandoning his artillery on the Bulgarian side of the river if necessary. Mackensen frantically directed that the bridge be destroyed at all costs to thwart the enemy retreat. His staff suggested using fireships if necessary.[29]

I and IV Monitor Groups had brought good weather with them, and *Szamos*, some three kilometers upstream near Taban Island, released a number of floating mines around 10:00 AM on 3 October. So did the patrol boat *Compó*. An hour later came a series of mighty explosions, ripping three enormous gaps in the bridge. Joined by *Leitha*, the two monitors kept the remnants of the bridge under fire until dark, preventing the Romanians from making repairs and escaping. As night fell, I Monitor Group relieved IV Group. I Group had brought along two empty barges, partially flooded, to ensure low profiles, and filled with explosives. It released the barges and heard five large explosions an hour or two later, but darkness prevented it from ascertaining the damage.[30] Later that night, around eleven, came word that Bulgarian-German forces had taken Rjahovo. At 1:00 AM a radio message indicated that the Romanian monitor flotilla was heading upriver, north of Turtucaia. At four, orders came from VII Corps to complete the destruction of the bridge and of any related material left on the shoreline, and then to head for the barrier at Kalimok.[31] The darkness prevented the Austrian monitors from navigating the channel in the dark to Kalimok, and by midday it was clear that the news about approaching Romanian monitors was false. The flotilla attempted to return to the base at Belene.

Ginghinarelle Island

A nasty surprise awaited the flotilla upon its return. At the east opening of the Belene Channel to the Danube lay Ginghinarelle Island, a low-lying landmass one kilometer wide and four long, behind which on the Romanian side of the river stretched impenetrable swamps and marshes for several kilometers before reaching high ground at Fantanele. The Romanians had established artillery at Fantanele, but their bombardment of the Belene base had done little damage, because Persin Island blocked direct observation. The Romanian occupation of Ginghinarelle at the end of September rectified that failure, allowing partial viewing for artillery spotters. The Romanians promptly protected their position by laying mines in the opening of the Belene Channel and placing an infantry company and two artillery batteries on Ginghinarelle. The Austrians decided to drive the Romanians off the island, but their infantry could not cross safely until the artillery on Ginghinarelle, as well as that at Fantanele, was silenced. That mission fell to II Monitor Group (monitors *Inn* and *Sava*), along with a ten-centimeter artillery battery already on Persin Island. After a day of bombardment by the two monitors and the German artillery, a combined force of German infantry and Austrian combat engineers overran the island on 8 October, capturing six guns, 130 prisoners, and related equipment. The flotilla's minesweeping detachment then cleared the channel, allowing the entry of I and III Monitor Groups, which had had to wait at Lelek after their successful operations against the Romanian bridgehead at Rjahovo.[32]

The Austro-German Danube Crossing, 23 November 1916

Even before the start of the war with Romania, both the Austrian and German high commands had envisioned crossing the Danube with a force from Bulgaria under the command of Field Marshal von Mackensen. To that end, the Austrians had moved their bridging equipment from depots in Hungary to the Belene Channel base in early August 1916.[33] The Austrians wanted to cross the Danube at the onset of the war, but the Germans, who called the shots, vetoed that plan until both the Dobrudja flank was secure and the German 9th Army, under General von Falkenhayn, had successfully crossed the Transylvanian Alps.[34] The Danube crossing would bring Bucharest under concentric attack from two directions, with Falkenhayn advancing on the enemy capital from the northwest and a German-Bulgarian army coming from the south. General Kosch's VII Corps, the senior German headquarters in Mackensen's Danube Army, had the mission of conducting the crossing. Kosch was an excellent choice; units under his leadership had already made a successful crossing of the Danube in the recent Serbian campaign.[35] His mission for the flotilla was succinct—

protect the flanks of the crossing and provide artillery support. III Monitor Group, temporarily at Lelek, sailed back upriver to protect the right flank of the crossing, while I Group guarded the left. IV Group provided artillery support for a feint at Samovit, designed to draw Romanian attention.[36]

The operation began at 6:30 in the morning of 23 November and proceeded relatively smoothly, interrupted only by the dense fog, not by the enemy. Captain Lucich, on *Temes II,* anchored in the middle of the crossing zone but with hardly any enemy opposition to the crossing he had little to do other than to watch the ferries and motorboats ply back and forth in the fog across the river, carrying the infantry. *Enns,* charged with protecting the troops landing in Zimnicea, simply came alongside the city quay and blew away the customhouse, ending any resistance from that point. By noon on the 24th, three divisions had crossed from Bulgaria to Romania, and a day later (the 25th) the Austrians had thrown a bridge across the Danube. After LII Corps had crossed the river and headed for Bucharest, command and control of the flotilla passed directly to Army Group Mackensen.[37]

Later in the month, on the 27th, III Monitor Group assisted the Bulgarians in crossing the Danube from Rustchuk to Giurgiu. Once ashore, the Bulgarians constructed a pontoon bridge, finishing it around 4 December. Austrian engineer units assisted. At this time, the river craft of the Romanian navy, which the Bulgarians had been unable to locate for three months, miraculously appeared, and in good operating order. They proceeded with the systematic plundering and burning of ports and towns on the Romanian side of the river from Giurgiu to Turnu Severin. The Austrians intervened several times to stop the senseless destruction. II Monitor Group helped corner the 1st Romanian Infantry Division at the juncture of the Olt and Danube Rivers. Pursued across Wallachia from Orsova by Colonel Szivo's brigade, the Romanians could not cross the river and had to surrender.[38]

Breaching the Kalimok Barrier and the Final Advance

As Mackensen's Danube Army moved northeast toward Bucharest, his logisticians wanted to send ammunition barges downstream to ports where intact rail lines crossed the river. The field marshal ordered "mines cleared with all means as fast as possible; progress reports daily at 1800 [6:00 PM]."[39] This touchy work fell to Lt. Cdr. Georg Ritter von Zwierkowski, head of the mine-clearing detachment.[40] The chief obstacle lay at Kalimok, on the former Romanian-Bulgarian border, where a system of impediments consisting of contact and observer-detonated mines and concrete and metal-tipped wooden pilings, with barriers on top of them, all interwoven with 3.5-inch steel cables, effectively blocked traffic. Even the barge *Anny,* which had ripped through the Romanian pontoon bridge at Rjahovo, had floundered against this massive bulwark.

Zwierkowski initially told Mackensen's headquarters that the work would take thirty or forty days; in the event, he opened a channel within a week. Zwierkowski's sailors, assisted by engineer troops, started the gargantuan task on 11 December, and by the 17th a small channel hugging the Romanian bank was clear to Oltenita. The flotilla moved there on the 18th and then to Silistria on the 24th. By the end of the month Zwierkowski's force had cleared the river of mines as far as Hirsova, a distance of 257 kilometers, earning for him the coveted and rare Military Maria Theresa Medal.[41] By January the flotilla had advanced to Braila, opening the Danube to the Central Powers as far as the Siret River. Southeast of Braila, Zwierkowski mined the Danube so the Russians could not enter it from the Black Sea. By that time, ice had formed on the rivers, and most of the flotilla was withdrawn to Hungary for maintenance. The 1916 campaign had ended with the Central Powers having effectively knocked Romania from the war.

Conspicuously missing in action from the 1916 campaign was the Romanian river flotilla, whose absence raises the question of why. When the war began, the Romanian flotilla lay at Hirsova, a fact that necessitated an immediate decision once hostilities erupted. The flotilla had to be moved to one side or the other of the Kalimok barrier before the latter was sealed. With Mackensen's forces marching into the Dobrudja on 1 September, defending that region had priority; thus the Romanian vessels remained north of the barrier, unable to provide assistance to their own river crossing or to threaten the Austro-German one, an operation that sealed Romania's fate.[42] Consequently the Austrian Danube Flotilla had free run of the southern border, where its vessels provided valuable artillery support to the German Danube crossing and safeguarded critical shipments of supplies after the crossing. Its most important mission, however, clearly came with the opportunity to interrupt the Romanian crossing at Rjahovo, where it excelled.

NOTES   1 For the Romanian order to close the border, see
War Ministry, Great General Staff, Order no. 2765,
for Headquarters, I Army Corps, Bucharest, 13 August 1916, in *Romania in razboiul mondial 1916–
1919* (Bucharest: Ministerul Apararii Natjionale,
Marele Stat-Major, serviciul istoric, 1934–46), annex, vol. 1, doc. 103, pp. 254–55; Arthur Freiherr
Arz von Straussenberg, *Zur Geschichte des Grossen
Krieges 1914–1918* (Graz: Akad. Druck- u.
Verlagsanstalt, 1969), p. 108ff. An immediate report
went that night to the Austrian army high command. See Österreichisches Staatsarchiv (ÖStA),
NFA, AK1/k11, 1AOK, op. 343/24, 27 August 1916.

2 Olaf Richard Wulff, *Österreich-Ungarns
Donauflottille in den Kriegsjahren, 1914–1917* (Vienna: L. W. Seidel, 1918) [hereafter *Donauflottille in
den Kriegsjahren*], pp. 173–76. Wulff commanded
the flotilla for two weeks in September 1914, as well
as the monitors *Temes I, Temes II, Bodrog,* and
Enns, and one of the monitor divisions for two
years. Published in the last year of the war, this volume covers 1914–16 and is much more detailed
than his later work, *Die österreichisch-ungarische
Donauflottille im Weltkriege, 1914–18: Dem Werke
"Österreich-Ungarns Seekrieg, 1914–18"* (Vienna,
Leipzig: W. Braumüller, 1934) [hereafter *Donauflotille im Weltkriege*], pp. 82–84. A Romanian account, while admitting the attack was a failure,
claimed that three torpedo boats actually attacked
the flotilla. The Austrians never saw any boats or
any more torpedoes. See Constantin Kiritescu,
*Istoria razboiului pentru intregirea Romaniei 1916–
1919,* trans. A. Razu (Bucharest: 1922), chap. 2, section on "Attacking the Austro-Hungarian Fleet at
Rusciuk," available at 1914-1918.invisionzone.com/
forums/.

3 All Austro-Hungarian monitors were named after rivers within the Dual Monarchy: *Maros, Leitha, Körös, Szamos, Bodrog, Temes (I* and *II), Inn, Enns, Bosna,* and *Sava.*

4 All in all, the flotilla consisted of some ten monitors, twelve patrol boats, several minesweepers and mine-layers, and nine assorted logistical vessels. Wulff, *Donauflotile im Weltkriege,* pp. 11–12; for a list of the vessels and armaments, pp. 260–61.

5 Ibid., p. 249; Anthony Sokol, *The Imperial and Royal Austro-Hungarian Navy* (Annapolis, Md.: Naval Institute Press, 1968), p. 92. Also Heinz Steinrück, "Das österreichisch-ungarische Donauflotille im Weltkriege" *Militärwissenschaftliche und technische Miteilungen,* nos. 1/2 (1928), pp. 11–18.

6 ÖStA, DF, 1052-1500, Executive Committees of the Three Central Grain Purchasing Combines to the Austrian War Ministry, no. 14652, 28 September 1916, pp. 5–29.

7 Wulff, *Donauflotille im Weltkriege,* p. 10.

8 ÖStA, DF, 300-800, KuK Kreigsministerium, Marinesektion, 1853, 25 March 1916.

9 Oskar Regele, *Kampf um die Donau: Betrachtung der Flussübergänge bei Flamanda und Sistow* (Potsdam: L. Voggenreiter, 1940), p. 42.

10 ÖStA, AOK, OOK, Ru Gruppe/k 550, Reconnaissance Report of Romanian Fortification on the North Side of the Danube, Col. v. Brosch, 20 June 1916. This is a detailed, fourteen-page report, with maps. The Romanians had worked feverishly on the river's defenses since early 1916. Cf. Brosch's report with that from the Austrian military attaché in Bucharest, ibid., DF 3-800, Evid. Bureau des kuk GS, B 150/1, mid-December 1915–mid-February 1916; Wulff, *Donauflottille in den Kriegsjahren,* p. 168; Steinrück, "Das österreichisch-ungarische Donauflotille im Weltkriege," p. 56.

11 Rudolf Kiszling, "Darstellung der Teilnahme der dem Oberkommando Mackensen unterstellten k.u.k. Truppen und der Donauflotilla am Feldzüge in der Dobrudscha, Donauübergang bei Sistow und Vormarsche nach Bukarest," ÖStA, MS1/Wk Ru 1916–1919 [hereafter Donauflotilla am Feldzüge in der Dobrudscha, Donauübergang bei Sistov und Vormarsche nach Bukarest], pp. 4–5. Most of Mackensen's forces were Bulgarians, facing the Entente Army of the Orient, led by French general Maurice Sarrail.

12 Wulff, *Donauflottille in den Kriegsjahren,* pp. 178–82. *Almos* did not have sufficient power to overcome the current at the Iron Gate until its crew, in midstream and in view of the enemy, jettisoned twenty-five tons of coal. See Steinrück, "Das österreichisch-ungarische Donauflotille im Weltkriege," p. 57.

13 Wulff, *Donauflottille in den Kriegsjahren,* pp. 185–87.

14 The German LII Corps, which had operational command over the Danube Flotilla, gave permission for the operation on 28 September, the day after Army Group Mackensen's operations chief, Col. R. Hentsch (1870–1918), came under enemy fire while visiting Belene. See ibid., p. 188. The official report

confirms Wulff; ÖStA, DF, KuK DF Kommando, Res. 1416, Combat Report, 29.9-9.10.1916.

15 ÖStA, DF 1359, II Monitor Group, op. 18, Action against Corabia, 3 October 1916; KuK DF Kommando, Res. 1416, Combat Report, 29.9-9.10.1916, pp. 1–5. Pages 190–92 of Wulff, *Donauflottille in den Kriegsjahren,* have photographs of this raid.

16 ÖStA, DF, KuK DF Kommando, Res. 1416, Combat Report, 29.9-9.10.1916, p. 5.

17 The Romanians crossed unopposed in four locations, with the largest crossing of three army corps led by then–crown prince Ferdinand at Corabia. Austrian observers admired the technical skill of the engineers. See Regele, *Kampf um die Donau,* pp. 35–36.

18 As the price for joining the Entente, Romania had demanded 150,000 Russian troops for a campaign in the Dobrudja, plus an allied offensive against Bulgaria launched from Salonika led by the allied Army of the Orient. This and the other Romanian demands were exorbitant. The give-and-take (mostly take by Romania) can be traced in The National Archives (United Kingdom): various reports from the British ambassador to Romania, Sir George Barclay, in FO 371, folders 2606 and 2707, 1916. The allies eventually agreed to a show of force from Salonika to tie down the Bulgarian armies there, while Russia sent an army corps (weak divisions) to the Dobrudja.

19 Kiritescu, *Istoria razboiului pentru intregirea Romaniei 1916–1919,* chap. 2, sec. 5, "Days of Emotion and Reflection."

20 Zottu had completely discounted in his mobilization planning any Central Power advance from the south. Worse, he had predicted that even if the Bulgarians crossed the Danube, they would not have the strength to move on Bucharest. See Romania's War Plan, Plan "Z" in *Romania in razboiul mondial,* annex 1, "Chapter 2," doc. 43, pp. 111–12. Zottu had also come under suspicion for treason; he committed suicide in November 1916.

21 "Memoir Concerning the Situation and the Dispositions That Are Supposed to Be Taken on the 15th of September 1916," *Romania in razboiul mondial,* annex 2, doc. 1, pp. 3–6; document 2 is the operations order (no. 852, 19 September) from the high command, ordering a switch from the offensive to the defensive in Transylvania. Ernst Kabisch, *Der Rumänienkrieg 1916* (Berlin: O. Schlegel, [c. 1938]), p. 51; and Regele, *Kampf um die Donau,* pp. 59–60. Kiritescu, *Istoria razboiului pentru intregirea Romaniei 1916–1919,* chap. 2, secs. "General Averescu's Criticism" and "Review of the Operation Plan," gives the best account of the confusion in the Romanian high command. The same source, under "General Averescu's Offensive," describes the Romanian strategy.

22 ÖStA, DF, KuK DF Kommando, Res. 1416, Combat Report, 29.9-9.10.1916, pp. 5–6.

23 Commander 3rd Army to Commander, Army Group South, 1 October 1916, doc. 19, pp. 38–39; V Army Corps, op. 347, 2 October 1916, doc. 21, pp.

39–40; both *Romania in razboiul mondial,* annex 2; Regele, *Kampf um die Donau,* pp. 77–78. Also Kiritescu, *Istoria razboiului pentru intregirea Romaniei 1916–1919,* chap. 2, sec. "Crossing the Danube."

24 ÖStA, DF, KuK DF Kommando, Res. 1416, Combat Report, 29.9-9.10.1916, pp. 6–7.

25 Kiszling, "Donauflotilla am Feldzüge in der Dobrudscha, Donauübergang bei Sistov und Vormarsche nach Bukarest," p. 8.

26 Masjon radioed back that his visibility was zero, and he had to stop his vessels. See ÖStA, DF, KuK DF Kommando, Res. 1416, Combat Report, 29.9-9.10.1916, p. 7. The Romanians said the bridge swayed fifty to a hundred meters laterally and pitched up and down some six to ten meters; Kiritescu, *Istoria razboiului pentru intregirea Romaniei 1916–1919,* chap. 2, sec. "Crossing the Danube," and V Army Corps, op. 347, 2 October 1916, annex 2, doc. 21, pp. 39–40.

27 ÖStA, DF, KuK DF Kommando, Res. 1416, Combat Report, 29.9-9.10.1916, pp. 8–9.

28 Ibid., pp. 9–10. *Körös* had taken twelve direct hits; Hermann Schmidtke, *Völkerringen an der Donau* (Berlin: Alfred Marschwinski, 1927), pp. 75–77. For the Romanian perspective, see Kiritescu, *Istoria razboiului pentru intregirea Romaniei 1916–1919,* chap. 2, sec. "Crossing the Danube."

29 ÖStA, DF, KuK DF Kommando, Res. 1416, Combat Report, 29.9-9.10.1916, pp. 11–14. Averescu called off the operation on the night of 2–3 October; Kiritescu, *Istoria razboiului pentru intregirea Romaniei 1916–1919,* chap. 2, sec. "The Retreat."

30 ÖStA, DF, KuK DF Kommando, Res. 1416, Combat Report, 29.9-9.10.1916, p. 14.

31 Ibid., p. 15.

32 Ibid., pp. 19–25. Also KuK DF Kommando, II Monitor Group to k.u.k Donauflotilla Commander, Combat Report, Res. 21 op. 9, October 1916. This report has, as enclosures, the II Monitor Group operations order for the undertaking, along with a map. For an eyewitness account of the storming of the island, see Oskar Regele, "Aus das Kriegestagebuch einer österreich-ungarischen Pionier-Feld-Kompanie," in *Im Felde Unbesiegt. Erlebnisse im Weltkrieg erzählt von Mitkämpfern,* ed. Gustav von Dickhuth-Harrach (Munich: J. F. Lehmanns Verlag, 1922), vol. 2, pp. 170–71. Regele commanded the 2nd Company, 5th Austro-Hungarian Pioneer Regiment. Cf. Wulff, *Donauflottille in den Kriegsjahren,* pp. 206–208, for photographs of captured soldiers and materiel. Also, Kiritescu, *Istoria razboiului pentru intregirea Romaniei 1916–1919,* chap. 2, sec. "The Retreat."

33 Kiszling, "Donauflotilla am Feldzüge in der Dobrudscha, Donauübergang bei Sistov und Vormarsche nach Bukarest," p. 3.

34 Erich von Falkenhayn, *Der Feldzug der 9. Armee gegen die Rumänien und Russen, 1916/17. Erster Teil: Der Siegeszug durch Siebenbürgen. Zweiter Teil: Die Kämpfe und Siege in Rumänien* (Berlin: E. S. Mittler & Sohn, 1921), pp. 6–8, and *Die Oberste Heeresleitung 1914–1916* (Berlin: E. S. Mittler &

Sohn, 1920), pp. 236–37. There is considerable debate over who originated this plan, with both the Falkenhayn and Ludendorff camps claiming credit. Cf. *Ludendorff's Own Story, August 1914–November 1918* (New York: Harper, 1919), vol. 1, pp. 295–96, and Georg Wetzell, *Kritische Beiträge zur Geschichte des Weltkrieges; von Falkenhayn zu Hindenburg-Ludendorff. Der Wechsel in der deutschen Obersten Heeresleitung im Herbst 1916 und der rumänische Feldzug. Beiheft z. 105 Jahrgang d. Mil. W. Blattes* (Berlin: E. S. Mittler & Sohn, 1921).

35 Kosch (1867–1942) led X Army Corps in the Serbian campaign and then at Verdun until August 1916, when he was sent to take command of the newly organized LII Corps in Sistov, Bulgaria, and was promoted to lieutenant general.

36 ÖStA, MS1/Wk Ru 1916–1919, Bericht [Gruppe Generalmajor Gaugl] beim Donauübergang, 23 November 1916, pp. 1–2; Kiszling, "Donauflotilla am Feldzüge in der Dobrudscha, Donauübergang bei Sistov und Vormarsche nach Bukarest," p. 14.

37 Kiszling, "Donauflotilla am Feldzüge in der Dobrudscha, Donauübergang bei Sistov und Vormarsche nach Bukarest," p. 16; [German Infantry Division von der Goltz] I op. 235, Operation Order for the Crossing, 19.1.1916; KuK Pioniergruppe Oberst Mjk, no. 310 [operation order for the Austrian engineers conducting the crossing], 21 November 1916; after-action report from same headquarters, op. 338, 23 November 1916; Regele, "Aus das Kriegestagebuch einer österreich-ungarischen Pionier-Feld-Kompanie," p. 172; Schmidtke, *Völkerringen an der Donau,* pp. 85–89.

38 Ibid., pp. 16–17; Wulff, *Donauflottille in den Kriegsjahren,* pp. 238–40. For an eyewitness account of the pursuit across Wallachia, see Bernhard Bellin, *Sturmtruppe Picht: Ein Erinnerungsblat aus dem Kriege gegen die Rumänen im Jahre 1916* (Berlin: Verlag Tradition Wilhelm Kolk, 1929).

39 Wulff, *Donauflotille im Weltkriege,* pp. 111–14.

40 Zwierkowski (1873–1932) did not understand the word "no." Born in Poland, after an undistinguished career in the Austro-Hungarian navy he was given in 1912 a "tombstone promotion" to lieutenant commander and pushed out. He tried to return to the navy when war broke out, but it would take him only at his permanent rank of lieutenant. He instead joined an Uhlan (light cavalry) regiment(!), but he somehow worked his way back to the navy, ending up at Orsova in late 1915, clearing the Serbian section of the river of mines to enable shipment of ammunition to Turkey. Fearless, he personally steered the tiny minesweeping vessels in their searches. After the war, he joined the Polish navy, retiring in 1927. Carl von Bardolff, Oskar von Hofmann, and Gustav von Hubka, *Der Militär-Maria Theresien Orden: Die Auszeichungen im Weltkrieg, 1914–1918* (Vienna: Verlag Militärwissenschaftliche Mitteilungen, 1943).

41 Ibid.; Wulff, *Donauflotille im Weltkriege,* p. 114, and *Donauflottille in den Kriegsjahren,* pp. 238–54.

42 Kiritescu, *Istoria razboiului pentru intregirea Romaniei 1916–1919,* chap. 2, sec. "The Fight at Arabagi."

V *"There's Nothing a Marine Can't Do"*
Publicity and the Marine Corps, 1911–1917

HEATHER PACE MARSHALL

Visiting his local library in 1916, Sgt. Frank Stubbe was disappointed to discover that he was the first person to borrow Richard Collum's *History of the United States Marine Corps* since 1904. For Stubbe this experience made manifest the public's ignorance about the Corps. As a recruiter, he struggled not only to convey the message that the Marine Corps even existed but also to convince people that it was a "good" organization.[1] Stubbe was not the first to recognize this problem. In 1911 the U.S. Marine Corps Recruiting Publicity Bureau began issuing booklets for potential recruits, setting forth the Corps's perennial problem: the public only had a "vague idea" what Marines did.[2] Still, the bureau appeared to console itself with the belief that at least people recognized the Marine "as being a man who is thoroughly onto the job, and lets it go at that."[3] Rather than seeking to convey to the public what mission it fulfilled, the Corps wished to emphasize the quality of service it provided and its ability to carry out any assignment. Countless newspaper articles proclaimed the variety of tasks that Marines could accomplish. One paper even hyperbolized, "There's Nothing a Marine Can't Do."[4] Between its establishment in 1911 and World War I, the bureau did everything it could think of to reach the public. A journalist at the time might have summarized the bureau's activities with the headline, "There's Nothing That the Publicity Bureau Won't Try."

The Corps's approach to publicity had begun decades earlier. After the Civil War, a handful of officers sought to create an image for the institution by producing a written history. They claimed, inaccurately, that the Marine Corps was the oldest military service in the United States and stressed its rich traditions.[5] With the Publicity Bureau's establishment in 1911, the efforts of Marines to make themselves known to the American public became institutionalized and increasingly cohesive and effective. Unable to claim an exclusive mission, the Corps sought to convince the public that it was an elite institution. This outward focus had critical ramifications internally. The themes the bureau discussed and debated enabled the strengthening and solidification of the Corps's larger institutional identity.

Two trends worked to encourage the Marine Corps to curry public favor. First, the institution faced another of its frequent existential crises in 1908, when

President Theodore Roosevelt issued Executive Order 969. The order terminated the assignment of Marines as policemen aboard naval vessels. Congressional resistance to the order temporarily ended threats to the Corps, but some Marines probably believed that the institution needed broader support above and beyond that of Congress.[6] The Corps's increased manpower requirements in the wake of the Spanish-Cuban-American war also necessitated the expansion of its recruiting base.[7] As a result the institution shifted away from an ad hoc method of recruiting to a more permanent one. Recruiters would also depart from a heavy reliance on classified ads, which often consisted of formulaic requests for volunteers, and focused on practical benefits, such as pay and the prospect of travel.

With the Publicity Bureau's establishment, the Corps's recruiting efforts became formalized.[8] The bureau served as a central clearinghouse for the production of posters, recruiting pamphlets, and other materials.[9] Hand in hand with the acquisition of more effective means to reach the public were major changes in the message the service wanted to communicate. Rather than simply advertising as they had in the past, Marines actively courted journalists, to obtain favorable coverage of their institution and its activities.[10] Publicity replaced advertisements as the Corps's primary recruiting tool. The Marine Corps adopted a business model of recruiting. As Sgt. Clarence Proctor noted, successful businesses focused less on "giv[ing] notice" and more on shaping public opinion.[11] The Corps could achieve this goal most effectively by making clear what distinguished its product from others.[12] It had to demonstrate its superiority not only to its primary competitors, the army and navy, but also to civilian employers.[13] Marines seized on every opportunity to demonstrate the institution's strengths.[14] Like civilian advertisers, who sought to carve out market niches for their products, the bureau struggled to determine the best way to increase familiarity with an institution that confused the general public no end.[15] The *Recruiters' Bulletin,* a monthly publication of the bureau that discussed recruiting and publicity matters, took every opportunity to recount the public's ignorance. One recruiter told of a prospect who arrived at a Marine recruiting station only to announce contradictorily that he "want[ed] to be a soldier" and yet would "rather be a submarine [*sic*] than anything else."[16] Simultaneously, the Corps sought to expand its focus from its traditional recruiting area on the Atlantic seaboard to the entire nation.[17] While developments in transportation like automobiles might enable recruiters to reach untapped markets, they did not ensure that people would be aware of the Marine Corps's existence, much less want to enlist in it, when recruiters arrived.[18]

To persuade the public of the institution's merits, the bureau launched a "comprehensive" campaign designed to ensure that people became just as familiar with the Corps as they were with the army and the navy. The bureau sent press releases to thousands of newspapers, "embroidered" just enough to ensure that newspapers would want to publish them.[19] By doing so the Corps wanted to convey the message that "every old Tom, Dick, and Harry isn't eligible to enter its ranks."[20] Historian James D. Norris has identified the use of "superlatives" as a common tendency among advertisers who had yet to determine how to distinguish their products from those of their competitors.[21] Making vague suggestions about the Corps's selectivity was far easier than explaining why the institution should be considered elite.

Like professional advertisers, the bureau began seeking a trademark, or what might today be considered "branding," to make a Marine easily recognizable.[22] One recruiter believed that the public needed to latch onto a standard image associated with the Corps. He suggested the figure of the "Hiker," which to him seemed "emblematic of an ideal Marine—attractive, rough and ready, prepared, and commanding respect."[23] This recruiter's vision of the model Marine linked the institution to its more recent expeditionary service on shore rather than its history of service aboard navel vessels. The phrase "soldiers of the sea" was more popular within the bureau, however. It allowed the Corps to distinguish itself from the army and the navy while stressing the versatile nature of its duties. The bureau reinforced this theme with the concept of an opportunity for "two in one" service, which, ideally, would provide the recruit with more variety than the other services could. It also hoped the idea of "double service" would appeal to those seeking adventure.[24] From the bureau's perspective, it was "much more satisfactory to be a Marine than a bluejacket," because a Marine was always "charging gallantly into something or other, and the papers at home talk about you."[25] Of course, newspapers mentioned the Marines so frequently because of the bureau's success in disseminating its articles.

While many of the bureau's practices coincided with the emergence of modern advertising in the United States, the Corps stopped short of fully adopting Madison Avenue's practices. In 1912 Congress had thwarted the institution's early hopes of using a professional advertising agency, in order to save money.[26] Perhaps as a result, the Corps's approach to publicity did not always mirror commercial advertising. A professional advertiser's suggestions published in the *Bulletin* troubled one Marine.[27] The advertiser had advised the bureau to de-emphasize the possibilities of war and focus instead on "opportunity."[28] In response, Sgt. George Kneller expressed his distaste for what he saw as misrepresentation. While Kneller had no problem with pointing to the practical applications of the Corps's training in an incidental way, he very much opposed the advertiser's suggestion to avoid any mention of the "cannon and the uniform." Kneller believed this approach would require recruiters to "practice a form of hypocrisy and resort to subterfuge."[29] His opinion coincided with the rhetoric among recruiters that in the long run honesty profited the Corps. Recruiters preferred a smaller number of top-quality men more likely to complete training over a large number of recruits likely to suffer high attrition.[30] Contributors to the *Bulletin* repeatedly stressed the value of being straightforward with candidates to ensure that they understood what military service entailed.[31] They also deliberately held out the lure of challenge. As one Marine wrote, life in the Corps was "not a bed of roses."[32] Still, one recruiter, taking this analogy one step farther, argued that at least the Corps had fewer "thorns" than any other branch.[33] Becoming a Marine might not be easy, recruiters suggested, but overcoming the challenges the institution offered would provide the recruit with long-term benefits. Faced with impending quotas, no doubt some recruiters eschewed the approach so popular in the *Bulletin*. Overall, though, the discourse of challenge helped reinforce the bureau's claim that the Corps was an elite military institution while perhaps saving it money in the short term.

The bureau suggested hyperbolically that to join such an institution required something akin to physical perfection. Of course, all military institutions maintain certain physical requirements. Marine recruiters, however, linked the purportedly elite status of the Corps to the physical qualities it required. These traits drew on such currents in larger society as social Darwinism.[34] As one sergeant rhymed, Marines were the "best of men / That Uncle Sam can get, / And if you're not perfect in eye and limb / You'll be rejected, you bet!"[35] The importance the Corps placed on high standards reinforced its corporate identity as an elite institution while playing to society's image of the ideal man.[36] After the Corps rejected a talented marksman because he was missing several fingers, a bureau press release explained that not only would the recruit have experienced difficulty while drilling but his hand would "look bad."[37] Image had grown as important to the Marines as reality.

The bureau held recruiters to similarly high standards and encouraged them to strive to improve their social status and economic standing.[38] A recruiter's experience differed in many respects from that of most other Marines. The average recruiter could and did often spend years in one location. Many recruiters worried they would lose the stability they had acquired after years of more itinerant service.[39] The bureau held up the lifestyle of recruiters as a model for what a recruit could achieve by serving in the Corps. One press release highlighted Sgt. Maj. James Deaver's acquisition of a significant fortune as an example of how a Marine could enter the service with "no capital" and through his "own efforts" make something of himself. It described how Deaver had saved his money carefully and invested it wisely.[40] The suggestion that the Corps could make a man "better" reinforced the sense of belonging to an elite institution even as it offered a recruit the sense that the service provided a road to self-improvement.[41]

In this vein, the Corps promised a viable path for enlisted Marines to be commissioned as officers.[42] This prospect, along with the bureau's rhetoric of domesticity, resonated with Americans seeking ways to improve their positions in society.[43] The Corps strongly resisted any suggestions that it was designed to reform reprobate characters or offer a last resort for the unemployed.[44] A "crack military body" was no "dumping ground for incorrigibles," one newspaper's headline informed its readers; the subsequent article sought to counter the notion that the Corps accepted moral delinquents.[45] The institution sought only those who would work to "maintain" the Corps's high reputation. Recruiters, Sgt. Louis Zanzig argued, had a responsibility to ensure they selected the recruits most likely to identify with the Corps. Given its purportedly "wonderful" history, the Corps could "afford to be particular."[46] In this way the bureau made an "emotional" appeal that corresponded with the approach of American advertisers in the first decades of the twentieth century.[47] At the same time, its recruiters stated their desire to choose recruits who would maintain the institution's corporate identity.

The bureau did not just stress that recruits might become officers. It also broke down some of the traditional hierarchical divide between officers and enlisted men. Perhaps because many recruiters constituted the elite of the Corps's enlisted ranks, officers and enlisted Marines appear to have intermingled more within the bureau than they did in the Corps as a whole. One *Bulletin* image showed bureau Marines of various ranks exchanging jokes at a dinner held in honor of a sergeant who had been selected to become an officer.[48] Over time the bureau's culture seems to have imprinted itself on the institution's broader corporate identity. The bureau certainly took steps to describe the Corps as the most democratic military branch. One article suggested that the "cast [*sic*] system" so prevalent in the army and the navy might explain why they, unlike the Marine Corps, struggled to obtain recruits.[49] Another article even connected the assertion that the Corps was the "finest" and "most efficient" branch to the idea that it was the most democratic.[50]

The leeway given to recruiters also encouraged a more democratic culture, especially in the pages of the *Bulletin*. Often in charge of their own recruiting subdistricts, enlisted Marines contributed their recruiting experiences and ideas to the *Bulletin* and, in the process, helped mold the Corps's identity in a forum largely free from the influence of the Commandant and headquarters.[51] Sgt. Norman Shaw, for example, faulted officers for suggesting uniform changes that he believed would erase important aspects of the Corps's history. He also praised Marines who refused to imitate the army's uniform changes.[52] Occasionally the *Bulletin*'s editor at the time, Maj. Albert McLemore, would interject a dissenting opinion. Other officers, however, sometimes moved to support an enlisted Marine's idea in opposition to McLemore. In one debate, a major backed Sgt. Louie W. Putnam's suggestion to add current news articles to recruiting signs as a means of encouraging more people to stop and read the signs.[53] Likewise, in one case even the critical comments of the editor and a commentator could not deter another sergeant from writing a second article elaborating on his ideas for improving the Corps's uniform.[54] Other officers wrote to commend enlisted Marines for the ideas they had submitted to the publication.[55] The *Bulletin* provided a forum for officers and enlisted Marines to debate policies openly.

Some of these suggestions shaped the institution as a whole, especially its practices and ceremonies. One tradition attributed to enlisted Marines was that of rendering salutes to Civil War veterans, an initiative of Sgt. Edward Callan.[56] Many of these ideas sought to ensure that Marines remained connected to their institution. The Commandant quickly adopted the proposal that Marine retirements be celebrated with more "ceremony."[57] The Corps also efficiently implemented Sgt. Leslie C. McLaughlin's suggestion that all honorably discharged Marines be presented with pins upon leaving the service.[58] Recruiters believed that ensuring the goodwill of retiring Marines would help secure future recruits in their home communities.

The *Bulletin* not only provided a forum for discussing how to obtain recruits but also fostered the Corps's identity. As the service's first institutional magazine, the *Bulletin* filled a particular need. Beyond its pragmatic purpose, it encouraged recruiters and Marines in general to identify emotionally with their institution. One ramification of the *Bulletin*'s success was the realization of the need for service magazines for all Marines, not just recruiters.[59] One sergeant expressed his approval, noting he was tired of reading national military publications only to find the Corps relegated to a small section.[60]

In providing a forum for discussion of historical and other matters, the *Bulletin* also helped solidify some of the Corps's traditions. Capt. Frank Evans, for example, noted that of all the services the Corps was the only institution to have its own "song," "The Halls of Montezuma." He decried the fact, however, that so many different versions of the song circulated among Marines. The tendency of Marines to modify the song after each expedition, he claimed, only aggravated the problem.[61] Hoping to "standardize" the lyric, Evans suggested purging those verses containing "undignified or bombastic wording." That the song, at least by 1914, stated that the Marines were "the finest ever seen" suggests how the bureau's rhetoric might have seeped into the Corps's institutional identity at large. Over time the song was referred to more frequently as a "hymn," exemplifying the extent to which the bureau stressed a corporate identity verging on the spiritual.

Just as individual enlisted recruiters made important contributions to debates within the bureau, they had some room for initiative in conveying the Corps's image to the public. The bureau encouraged recruiters to reach out to journalists in their communities. These efforts often enabled the Corps to secure favorable and free publicity.[62] Over a five-month span, one sergeant's efforts to win publicity for the Corps resulted in the publication of sixteen articles in a small Missouri town. Such efforts afforded recruiters an opportunity to end the perennial confusion about what purpose a Marine served. One officer met with reporters on an individual basis to limit factual errors. As a result, some recruiters believed they finally were making progress in educating the public about their institution.[63]

Small, local newspapers were not alone in favorably receiving the bureau's publicity efforts. Metropolitan newspapers and magazines gladly used the articles they received from the bureau.[64] Moreover, many editors responded favorably when queried about the quality of the articles. Publications with wide circulations, including the *New York Herald*, the *New York Tribune,* and the *New York Journal,* used the bureau's releases. A few editors, however, expressed concerns that the Corps might be deviating from straightforward journalism. The city editor of Washington, D.C.'s *The Star*, for example, pointed out that the element of "propaganda" evident in some stories tended to undercut the "good human interest" of the stories.[65]

A willingness to try just about anything characterized the bureau's approach to public relations. The office issued a number of articles, ranging from the humorous to the serious, detailing why potential recruits had been rejected.[66] One story recounted how William James had been about to be sworn into the Corps when he saw a cat and began screaming in fear.[67] James's subsequent rejection by the Marines helped to remind the reader that the Corps could afford to be selective, while entertaining the reader with a humorous incident. William James's irrational fear of a harmless cat demonstrated that he was not a "real man" and thus unworthy of becoming a Marine.[68]

Marine posters had stated the desire to recruit "men" since the nineteenth century, but the addition of the word "real" in the twentieth century suggested the need for men to prove themselves. Similarly, Marine officials explained how men with "artistic temperaments" were more likely to desert.[69] Recruiters had flexibility in devising solutions for applicants deficient in other areas. Minnesota recruiters even opened a "night school" for physically qualified recruits who had not received enough education.[70] But a recruit either met the desired standard of masculinity or he was not fit to be a Marine.

As the possibility of involvement in World War I began to seem more likely, the Corps struggled to remain competitive as the army's manpower needs increased substantially and both the army and navy began to implement practices similar to the bureau's.[71] In response Marines unleashed a wealth of creative ideas to bring their institution into the limelight. While some ideas verged on the outlandish, many represented the Corps's traditional determination to do more with less. On one occasion, a party of Marines set out with journalists in tow to rid the New Jersey coast of sharks that had been terrorizing swimmers.[72] The outing did not result in any shark deaths; however, the Associated Press wire account of the excursion reached North Carolina, where one recruiter found himself besieged with applicants interested in joining the Corps to participate in similar expeditions.[73] Another recruiter ignited a debate throughout Boston. After hearing a Civil War veteran be-moan the public's ignorance of the national anthem, the recruiter had a discussion with a Boston journalist regarding the possibility of writing an article on the sub-ject. When the article's publication prompted further discussion, the recruiter took advantage of public interest to pass out five thousand small cards with the anthem's lyrics on the front and an abbreviated history of the Corps on the back. Marines dis-tributed all of the cards in less than an hour.[74]

When it came to releasing articles to newspapers, the bureau was just as creative. It appears to have written some articles to spark pride in local residents. After the Corps issued a list of those Marines who had obtained expert marksmanship rat-ings, the bureau released a skeleton article for recruiters to edit as they saw fit to in-clude names of local Marines.[75] One article cited the "many interesting experiences and adventures" of Oral R. Marvel, who was stationed in China. The article stressed that his officers considered his qualifying as a marksman as "little short of marvel-ous," given that he was "scarcely more than a recruit." In the future, they "ex-pect[ed] him to break many marksmanship records." That two other Marines located in different cities received almost identical commendations in print, how-ever, suggests that Marvel's actions were not quite as exceptional as the article por-trayed. Other articles mentioned local Marines' relatives, perhaps seeking to rectify the traditionally negative images of enlisted servicemen by demonstrating their hometown ties to presumably respectable citizens.[76] The bureau referred to these articles as "flimsies," designed to allow individual recruiters to "hang a local con-nection to them."[77]

By the time the United States declared war on Germany in 1917, the Corps had po-sitioned itself to obtain the types of recruits it wanted, train them, and ensure their presence overseas in a land war that was atypical of its previous experience. The Corps's attention to wartime publicity reaped postwar dividends. By 1918, the bu-reau could rest easy, in the assurance that the public had a positive image of the Corps's wartime contributions. Rather than being associated with any particular duty, "Marine" conjured up visions of indomitable, elite fighters. This image helped to justify an institution perched uncomfortably and vulnerably between the navy and the army.

A side effect of the Publicity Bureau's efforts was the crystalization of an identity for the Marine Corps. Recruiters and other Marines helped to develop an image of the Corps as an institution of elite fighters capable of any mission. The *Bulletin* en-abled Marines of disparate ranks to enhance and solidify the Corps's traditions and practices. By the time Marines arrived on the battlefields of World War I, they would be practiced at seizing on any opportunity to ensure they received publicity for their efforts.

President Harry Truman once described the Marine Corps's publicity machine as something akin to the best propaganda efforts of the Soviet dictator Joseph Stalin.[78] His comments can probably be understood in reference to his experience as an army officer during World War I. If he shared the common opinion of army officers at the time, he would have believed the Corps to be a master of self-promotion at the expense of its sister services. The tools the institution had honed over almost a decade proved invaluable when it came time for Marines to demonstrate their worth in a way that would resonate across the United States. If the bureau's efforts ensured that the Corps would be featured in newsprint across the country, Marines would work to ensure that its exploits during World War I were written in indelible ink.

NOTES The author would like to thank Dr. Alex Roland for his many suggestions. She is also grateful for the support of her husband, Maj. John Marshall, and her parents, Temple and Cecilia Pace.

1 Sgt. Frank Stubbe, "Wilkes-Barre Opinions," *Recruiters' Bulletin* [hereafter *Bulletin*] (January 1916), p. 14.

2 For one of many examples of the bureau's frustration and attempts to rectify this ignorance, see "Setting Them Right," *Bulletin* (December 1915), p. 16.

3 U.S. Marine Corps Recruiting Publicity Bureau, *U.S. Marines: Duties, Experiences, Opportunities, Pay,* 2nd ed. (New York: Chasmar-Winchell, 1912), p. 3.

4 "There's Nothing a Marine Can't Do," *Columbus Daily Enquirer,* 13 November 1916, p. 8.

5 I discuss this process in further detail elsewhere. See, for example, "'Telling It to the Marines': Constructing and Using the Corps's Early History, 1875–1935" (paper presented at the annual meeting for the Society for Military History, Manhattan, Kansas, 18–21 May 2006).

6 Later Marines certainly recognized the importance of public support. See "Words of Praise from Chicago," *Bulletin* (December 1914), p. 2.

7 The Corps increased more than fivefold between 1896 and 1916, from 2,676 Marines to 15,630. Robert Heinl, *Soldiers of the Sea: The United States Marine Corps, 1775–1962,* 2nd ed. (Baltimore, Md.: Nautical and Aviation, 1991), pp. 610–11.

8 Capt. H. C. Snyder "established" the bureau; see "The Publicity Bureau: Its Equipment and Activities," *Bulletin* (February 1917), p. 1. Sgt. James F. Taite credited Maj. A. S. McLemore for the success of the bureau in "Publicity, Etc.," *Bulletin* (January 1915), p. 9. In 1907, recruiters in Chicago had established a small publicity office that provided press releases to the public, presaging the birth of a structure that could combine the Corps's dual needs for publicity and recruiting; see Robert Lindsay, *This High Name: Publicity and the U.S. Marine Corps* (Madison: Univ. of Wisconsin, 1956), p. 9.

9 For example, the Corps printed a calendar for distribution. Sgt. Joseph Ascheim, "A Good Way to Get Names for the Publicity Bureau," *Bulletin* (March 1915), p. 2.

10 Sgt. William H. Green, "Small Town Recruiting and Some Suggestions for Recruiters," *Bulletin* (August 1916), p. 12; Lindsay, *This High Name,* p. 9. Like civilian advertisements of the period, the Corps's nineteenth-century advertisements were "modest" in scope and scale; James D. Norris, *Transformation of American Society, 1865–1920* (New York: Greenwood, 1990), pp. 12–13.

11 Sgt. Clarence B. Proctor, "Advertising and Recruiting: Some Publicity Bureau Help," *Bulletin* (October 1916), p. 6.

12 Important works on advertising include Timothy Jackson Lears, *Fables of Abundance: A Cultural History of Advertising in America* (New York: Basic Books, 1994); Roland Marchand, *Advertising the*

American Dream: Making Way for Modernity, 1920–1940 (Berkeley: Univ. of California Press, 1985); Stephen Fox, *The Mirror Makers: A History of American Advertising and Its Creators* (New York: William Morrow, 1984); Daniel Pope, *The Making of Modern Advertising* (New York: Basic Books, 1983); Pamela Walker Laird, *Advertising Progress and the Rise of Consumer Marketing* (Baltimore, Md.: Johns Hopkins Univ. Press, 1998); and Stephen Harp, *Marketing Michelin: Advertising and Cultural Identity in Twentieth-Century France* (Baltimore, Md.: Johns Hopkins Univ. Press, 2001).

13 Norris, *Transformation of American Society, 1865–1920,* p. 22.

14 See, in particular, the images included in *The Marines in Rhyme, Prose, and Cartoon* (New York: U.S. Marine Corps Recruiting Publicity Bureau, 1914).

15 Norris, *Transformation of American Society, 1865–1920,* p. 48.

16 "Wanted to Be Submarine," *Bulletin* (December 1914), p. 11.

17 For the importance of railroads, see Norris, *Transformation of American Society, 1865–1920,* pp. 3–4.

18 For commentary about general public ignorance, see Sgt. L. W. Ahl, "An Idea for Producing Better Recruiting Results," *Bulletin* (January 1915), p. 10, and Capt. C. S. McReynolds, "Odds and Ends from Musty Files with Apologies to the *Recruiters' Bulletin,*" *Bulletin* (January 1917), p. 5. McReynolds believed that the public was ignorant of all military branches, particularly the Marine Corps.

19 For contradictory numbers on how many articles it released, see "More Room for Publicity Bureau," *Bulletin* (January 1915), p. 16; and "Our Press Department," *Bulletin* (November 1915), p. 12.

20 Capt. Frank E. Evans, "First Aids to Publicity," *Bulletin* (November 1914), p. 2.

21 Norris, *Transformation of American Society, 1865–1920,* p. 26; Richard A. Foley, "The Superlative in American Advertising," *Printers' Ink,* 2 January 1919, pp. 57–58.

22 For a discussion of trademarks or branding, see Nancy F. Koehn, "Henry Heinz and Brand Creation in the Late Nineteenth Century: Making Markets for Processed Food," *Business History Review* 73 (Autumn 1999), pp. 361–62.

23 "Standardizing Our Advertising," *Bulletin* (July 1916), p. 20.

24 Cpl. Percy Wiess, "Service and Study: Marines Can Learn While They Earn," *Bulletin* (January 1917), p. 6; "The Recruiting Signs," *Bulletin* (February 1917), p. 20; "The Recruiting Situation," *Bulletin* (June 1916), p. 16.

25 "Spokane Reporter Converted: Prefers Marines Because of Their Picture Books," *Bulletin* (March 1916), p. 5.

26 Lindsay, *This High Name,* p. 11.

27 The *Bulletin* was first published in November 1914.

28 Clifford Bleyer, "Stimulating Recruiting Suggested by an Advertising Expert," *Bulletin* (December 1916), p. 13.

29 Sgt. George Kneller, "Straight from the Shoulder: Handling of the Recruiting Question," *Bulletin* (February 1917), p. 4.

30 Sgt. Louis F. Zanzig, "Good Advice from Indianapolis," *Bulletin* (December 1914), p. 13; "Quality before Quantity in Final Standing Consideration," *Bulletin* (October 1916), p. 8.

31 "Editorial," *Bulletin* (December 1914), p. 8; Sgt. Thomas McCrum, "A Few Suggestions from an Old Recruiter to Beginners," *Bulletin* (March 1915), p. 6; Sgt. Frank Stubbe, "Some Wilkes-Barre Viewpoints," *Bulletin* (September 1915), p. 19.

32 While it would be difficult to prove a definite link, the Corps drew on this theme in the 1970s. A popular recruiting poster depicting a drill sergeant yelling at a recruit stated, "We didn't promise you a rose garden." See Allan R. Millett, *Semper Fidelis: The History of the United States Marine Corps* (New York: Free Press, 1980), p. 613. For another use of this phrase see Bishop Rhinelander, "The Baccalaureate Sermon," in *University of Pennsylvania: Proceedings of Commencement, June 19, 1918* (Philadelphia: Univ. of Pennsylvania, 1918), p. 29.

33 Sgt. Norman F. Hatcher, "Thorns and Roses," *Bulletin* (August 1916), p. 22.

34 Timothy Jackson Lears stresses the Anglo-Saxon emphasis on physical perfection common in advertising; Lears, *Fables of Abundance,* pp. 169, 172. Also see Paul A. Kramer, "Empires, Exceptions, and Anglo-Saxons: Race and Rule between the British and United States Empires, 1880–1910," *Journal of American History* 88 (March 2002), pp. 1315–53. Numerous stories informed readers of the Corps's strict standards for enlistment; see "Only 3 Percent Able to Pass Marine Test," *San Jose Mercury News,* 3 January 1917, p. 3.

35 See, for example, Capt. Frank E. Evans, "The Lure of the Fighting Man," *Bulletin* (July 1915), p. 2.

36 For this ideal in the United States see John F. Kasson, *Houdini, Tarzan, and the Perfect Man: The White Male Body and the Challenge of Modernity in America* (New York: Farrar, Straus, Giroux, 2002).

37 "His Trigger Finger Made No Difference," *Wilkes-Barre (Pa.) Times,* 30 August 1916, p. 6.

38 The *Bulletin* abounds with lighthearted stories about recruiters and their families; see "Marjorie's Madness," *Bulletin* (November 1915), p. 19. Some recruiters appreciated the quality of family life that recruiting duty in the Corps enabled. Sgt. L. C. McLauchlin compared the Marine Corps's provisions for married recruiters favorably to those of the army in "Spokane Letter," *Bulletin* (December 1914), p. 2.

39 For humorous commentary on this fear, see "Adios Trabajo," *Bulletin* (April 1915), p. 15; and "The Bulletin Appreciated in the Western Division," *Bulletin* (December 1914), p. 11.

40 "With $100,000 Deaver Retires from Marines," *Charlotte (N.C.) Observer,* 26 November 1915, p. 9.

41 For the idea that the Corps could improve a man, see Gus R. Fisher, "Too Old to Be a Marine," *Bulletin* (July 1916), p. 14; and "A Recruiter's Varied

Experiences," *Bulletin* (December 1914), p. 16. For a recruit who enlisted for this reason, see "He Came Down from Alaska to Enlist," *Bulletin* (January 1917), p. 22.

42 "Corporal Miller, of Lehman, May Be Made Lieutenant," *Wilkes-Barre (Pa.) Times,* 3 August 1916, p. 8. One recruiter even suggested that it was better to be a private in the Corps than an officer in another branch; see Sgt. C. W. Herzog, "The Truth Counts," *Bulletin* (January 1915), p. 13.

43 Norris, *Transformation of American Society, 1865–1920,* p. 47.

44 "Wants No Rum Hound: Marine Corps Not Refuge for Dipsomaniacs," *Wheeling (W. Va.) State,* 11 August 1916, p. 9; "Explain the Service to Everybody," *Bulletin* (January 1915), p. 13.

45 "Only Real Men Can Hope to Join Uncle Sam's Carefully Trained Marine Corps," *Wilkes-Barre (Pa.) Times,* 13 April 1916, p. 7. This approach also overlapped with Progressive ideas regarding morality within military institutions. See, for example, Nancy K. Bristow, *Making Men Moral: Social Engineering during the Great War* (New York: New York Univ. Press, 1996).

46 Sgt. Louis F. Zanzig, "How to Obtain Good Men," *Bulletin* (March 1915), p. 18. Lt. Arthur J. Burks expressed a similar idea in "Selling the Corps," *Marine Corps Gazette* 9 (June 1924), p. 115.

47 Norris, *Transformation of American Society, 1865–1920,* p. 44.

48 *Bulletin* (April 1918), p. 25.

49 "The U. S. Marine Corps: An Object Lesson of Democracy in the Military," *Wilkes-Barre (Pa.) Times,* 27 November 1916, p. 8.

50 "Distinguishing Emblem for Recruiters," *Bulletin* (December 1914), p. 14. For the suggestion that the Corps was "a little better" than the other branches because its "officers [were] closer to their men, looking out for their welfare," see James F. J. Archibald and Berton Braley, "Soldiers and Sailors, Too," *Collier's,* 16 May 1914, p. 12.

51 "'Tis Not for Gold We're Here," *Bulletin* (November 1916), p. 16; Sgt. John F. Cassidy, "School for Recruiters at Recruit Depot Is Suggested," *Bulletin* (May 1916), p. 6.

52 Sgt. Norman M. Shaw, "A Plea for Big, Yellow Chevron," *Bulletin* (September 1915), p. 4.

53 "The Bulletin Appreciated in the Western Division," p. 11; Sgt. Louie W. Putnam, "Various Suggestions and Comments," *Bulletin* (August 1916), p. 22.

54 "The Distinguishing Emblem for Recruiters," *Bulletin* (February 1915), p. 7.

55 Capt. William Brackett, "Sgt. Katcher Has Right Idea," *Bulletin* (October 1916), p. 22; Capt. Frank E. Evans, "Carrying the Message," *Bulletin* (May 1915), p. 4.

56 "Military May Honor Veterans of Civil War with Officer's Salute," *Morning Olympian,* 9 June 1916, p. 1.

57 Sgt. John F. Cassidy, "Lack of Publicity," *Bulletin* (June 1915), p. 5.

58 "Honorable Discharge Buttons," *Bulletin* (February 1917), p. 3.

59 "New Marine Corps Publication," *Bulletin* (June 1916), p. 16. All recruiters received a copy of the *Bulletin.* The bureau also distributed enough copies so that one in twenty Marines would receive one, counting on individuals to share copies. "Distribution of *Bulletin,*" *Bulletin* (November 1918), p. 24.

60 Stubbe, "Some Wilkes-Barre Viewpoints," p. 9.

61 Capt. Frank E. Evans, "'The Halls of Montezuma': Call for All Versions of Song," *Bulletin* (February 1916), p. 7. Evans's article seems to have inspired the bureau to take action. See "Favorite Song of the Marines," *Wilkes-Barre (Pa.) Times,* 25 February 1916, p. 12. Today the Corps is known as the only institution to have a "hymn" rather than a song. By 1914 more Marines were beginning to refer to the song as a hymn; see, for example, "'Marines' Hymn' Recalled," *Charlotte (N.C.) Observer,* 26 April 1914, p. 4.

62 "They Know and Won't Tell," *Bulletin* (June 1916), p. 16.

63 Capt. William E. Parker, "The Recruiting Officer and the Newspaper," *Bulletin* (June 1915), p. 16.

64 See, for example, "Blushing through Our Tan," *Bulletin* (October 1916), p. 16.

65 "Press Bureau Checks Up and Receives Some Wonderful Replies," *Bulletin* (August 1916), p. 10.

66 For more lighthearted articles, see "Take Him," *Idaho Statesman,* 17 January 1916, p. 5; and "Ford Jokes Reach Marine Corps," *Charlotte (N.C.) Observer,* 20 December 1915, p. 6.

67 "Afraid of a Cat[:] Rejected as Marine," *Columbus Daily Enquirer,* 5 February 1917, p. 1.

68 "Only Real Men Can Hope to Join Uncle Sam's Carefully Trained Marine Corps," p. 7.

69 "Tapering Fingers Mean Anything but Stability," *Idaho Statesman,* 28 August 1916, p. 3.

70 "Young Men Study for Entry into Marine Corps," *Montgomery Advertiser,* 10 December 1916, p. 2.

71 For suggestions regarding the better quality of the Corps's recruiting material, see "Spokane Reporter Converted," p. 5. The army's methods lagged behind the Corps's; see "Army Officers Get Advertising Instruction," *Printers' Ink,* 2 January 1919, p. 86.

72 Sgt. W. W. Sibert, "Down North Carolina Way," *Bulletin* (16 August 1916), p. 28. For newspaper articles about the expedition, see "Expert Shark Hunters Organize for Crusade," *Montgomery Advertiser,* 21 July 1916, p. 10.

73 Sibert, "Down North Carolina Way," p. 28.

74 Sgt. B. J. Doherty, "Newspaper Publicity Up Boston Way May Help You," *Bulletin* (May 1916), p. 4.

75 "Another Luzerne County Boy Makes Good with Marines," *Wilkes-Barre (Pa.) Times,* 7 February 1916, p. 2.

76 See, for example, "Louis Harvey with Marines," *Grand Forks (N.D.) Herald,* 19 September 1915, p. 6.

77 "Attention! Everyone!," *Bulletin* (November 1915), p. 24.

78 Quoted in Lindsay, *This High Name,* p. 3.

VI *Arms and the Man*
Some Approaches to the Study of British Naval Communities Afloat, 1900–1950

BRUCE TAYLOR

"Of arms and the man I sing." So begins the *Aeneid*, Virgil's allegory of war and duty. This paper endeavors to trace out some approaches to researching another iteration of men under arms—that of the Royal Navy afloat in the first half of the twentieth century. Its aim is to offer a framework within which researchers can address one of the sternest challenges in the field, that of reconstructing the social history of a warship community. The thoughts and conclusions contained here have come out of prolonged research on the life and functioning of the battle cruiser HMS *Hood*, in many respects an unusual ship, given its fame and status, but in others all too typical with regard to the problems facing those researching the subtle and complex world of shipboard life.[1]

A naval community afloat is no more fixed than the vessel that encloses it. It is the fate of a ship's company to be scattered by recommissioning or the vagaries of war after no more than a few years. Also, with very few exceptions, the ship itself is destined to succumb to changes by dock yards and to the efforts of the breakers, to the violence of the enemy, or to the will of the ocean. Naval life afloat is welded in discipline, tradition, and war and yet susceptible to annihilation in a matter of seconds; it is its transient yet lasting quality that affords it much of its fascination—short in time but rich in memory. As institutions go, a ship and its community are therefore characterized by an unusual degree of impermanence, their physical forms and manifestations by destruction that is often almost total. Not for them the continuities of the regimental mess, archive or museum, or for that matter the persistence of the navy itself, though the advance of oceanographic technology makes it one of the ironies of naval history that sinking is now a surer way of saving a vessel for posterity than practically any other. Despite the lingering questions surrounding its loss, HMS *Hood,* sunk in 1941, is more tangible, through the discovery of its wreck in 2001, than could have seemed possible thirty years ago.

From a documentary point of view, this impermanence means that a ship's own archive, from the wardroom wine book to the engine-room oil registers, is likely to be dispersed and most probably destroyed. While not lacking, the surviving official documentation of so great a vessel as *Hood,* for twenty years the flagship of the

Royal Navy, rarely extends beyond operational matters and technical issues.[2] Of the ship's functioning and evolution, of its internal affairs and ongoing morale, there is little in official collections from any part of its career. *Hood* experienced the suicide of its first lieutenant in June 1939 and what appears to have been a mutiny of sorts in December 1940, but one would never know it from the Admiralty documentation housed in The National Archives at Kew in London.[3] *Hood,* of course, was shattered within the space of a few minutes, but it is unlikely that its archive would have fared any better had it survived to be scrapped, since the position seems in respect to be no different for other ships in this period or before. This is not to be wondered at, since naval authorities tend to concern themselves with the internal affairs of a vessel only in respect of officer promotion or should its morale or condition affect its operational viability.

The sort of material on which a social historian might feed is therefore rarely encountered in official sources, and all attempting "total histories" of warships in all their richness of context, structure, and character must gird themselves for prolonged research among widely scattered sources. For here lies the central challenge to any who would write the social history of a warship: where they survive at all, the majority of records illuminating life on board are the product of individuals and are held in private hands, though increasing numbers are becoming available to researchers through archival deposit and on the internet. The interpretation of this material and what it may tell us of the nature of the authors' attachments to their ship as individuals or as members of a particular grouping forms the backdrop to this paper, a reminder that the culture and community of a warship are even richer and more imposing in their order and design than the structure that encloses them.

So, where to begin? The answer, perhaps, is to start by framing the history of the vessel under review in a detailed chronology. This can be built up relatively simply from the registers of Royal Navy ships' movements or in greater detail from the surviving deck logs of submarines or fighting ships of cruiser size or larger.[4] The next step is to form a picture of the naval day, the four-hour watch system that provided the rhythm of its routine, day in and day out for years on end.[5] Equally important is to draw a clear distinction between peace and war, the one always in expectation of the other. It is sometimes said that the life of a peacetime navy is comparatively uneventful. Certainly it lacks the emotional voyage that only battle can bring, but likewise is it spared the deadening routine that is the chief characteristic of war at sea, against the backdrop of sleep deprivation and fear of the unknown and the unexpected, the sense of a grinding monotony that only catastrophe might interrupt. On the other hand, the Second World War in particular brought numbers of civilians into the closed world of shipboard life, both in the wardroom and on the lower deck, people destined to change that world forever and be transformed in their turn by the realities of their service.

Having fixed the unit in time, the researcher is ready to turn to its fabric. One of the features of naval history generally, and ship biography in particular, is that it requires of its practitioners an unusually firm grasp of the immediate physical and technical environment of their subject if they are to do it justice. In this respect those who study naval communities have been well served by the focus on technical matters that has increasingly characterized naval interest and naval publishing over the last thirty or forty years. Who, for instance, would not find their research enhanced into a third dimension by a volume from the remarkable Anatomy of the Ship series launched by Conway Maritime Press in 1982, or the ShipShape series produced by Chatham Publishing between 1997 and 2003?[6] Failing these or their like, the researcher may turn to the huge deposit of ships' plans held by the National Maritime Museum at Woolwich and begin to appreciate the scale of the enterprise from each stroke of the draftsman's pen. The plans impress now for their scale, just as the finished article impressed for its immensity, for the power and consequence vested in it, and for that particular warship aesthetic refined by naval architects in the first decades of the twentieth century.

This sense was never better evoked than by the journalist V. C. Scott O'Connor, who accompanied *Hood* on the ship's world cruise of 1923–24, which announced it as the greatest warship afloat: "*Hood* . . . moved upon her course, like the stars themselves, without a sound or murmur. Upon her quarter-deck one stood, for all her greatness, very near the sea. Above its smooth levels there rose, as if to remind one of the ship's dread purpose, her colossal turrets, the long straining muzzles of her guns, like ghosts of Armageddon, her tiers of decks."[7]

But the fabric of a ship is one thing, its operation quite another. To be afforded a plan or photograph of a fifteen-inch turret is not, alas, to be given any significant idea of its functioning, though as with ship design and structure generally, there is an increasing fund of material on weapons systems and sensors, such as radar.[8] However, such sources rarely provide any impression of the impact of such systems on those who operated them, the monstrous power of the guns, the searing heat of the engine spaces. This is important because to study a ship in detail is to be made aware that certain items of equipment acquired characters all their own, characters intimately associated with those given responsibility for serving or maintaining them. Can any member of *Hood*'s engineering department have thought of the boiler room fan flats without thinking also of Chief Mechanician Charles W. Bostock, whose proudest possession was a certificate from the Netley mental asylum stating that he was entirely sane?[9] Or imagine the turrets without the "qualified ordnancemen," or "turret rats," long-service able seamen with no interest in promotion but sufficient guile to leaven their work with those illicit pleasures that made life bearable? The navy, mindful of the disasters at Jutland, might issue stringent rules against smoking in the turrets, but these could hardly stop a man from lighting up in the working chamber or discourage an ordnance artificer from puffing, on a pipe, his way through his morning turret inspection.[10] Nor, for that matter, could it stop Able Seaman "Tubby" Barney, a Scot, from slaking his thirst with a ruinous cocktail of white spirit and Pusser's lime juice after a hard morning's work.[11] In the way of this or any other navy, its work coexisted with the lives of those who made it what it was.

Equally, much as a vessel's career may be traced in official or private sources or its fabric divined from plans and published material, the tenor of its shipboard life is far harder to follow or reconstruct in its network of command structures, unit organization, and personal relations. A warship was nothing if not a community of communities, of groups of men divided into departments, messes, watches, tricks, and working parties yet parts of a highly evolved organization centuries in the making. Not without reason did Adm. Lord Chatfield, captain of the battle cruiser *Lion* during the Great War and First Sea Lord from 1932 to 1938, describe the management of fleets and ships as a "national art," one that prompted a succession of manuals outlining ideal forms of shipboard organization during the period under review.[12] Like John Roberts's Anatomy of the Ship volume on HMS *Hood,* it is hard to imagine studying that ship without reference to Capt. Rory O'Conor's *Running a Big Ship on "Ten Commandments,"* published in 1937, the author having served as *Hood*'s executive officer from 1933 to 1936. That the Royal Navy was recognized for its expertise in what might be called ship husbandry is shown by the fact that *Running a Big Ship* was translated into both French and Italian before the outbreak of war.[13]

Although the tendency of most of these manuals is to describe ship organization in holistic terms and from above, any making a detailed study of the operation of a vessel will find it the aggregation of groups of perhaps ten or twenty individuals who in turn reflected the wider organization of the ship itself by specialization and, of course, rank, with all that this implied. Throughout its myriad spaces, decks, and compartments, dozens of such communities performed their duties and lived their lives with varying degrees of competence and enthusiasm, from the Double Bottom Party to the Royal Marine Band and the staff of an admiral. The men who constituted them came to know each other intimately in their work and leisure, their days and nights, as much ashore as afloat. Through their character and society the ship acquired that distinctive quality that set it apart from all others, causing its men to remember it with varying degrees of fondness, equanimity, or loathing for the rest of their lives.

This brings us to one of the key issues in ship biography, the question of relations between officers and men. In the deferential society of early twentieth-century Britain, a majority of men held their officers in awe, not only for reasons of rank and social status but also for their education and command of language. For their part,

too many officers continued to respond to this deference with tactlessness border-
ing on disdain, much as they respected the skill, tenacity, and resourcefulness of
those under their command. Something of this innate condescension is captured in
the journalist Filson Young's memoir of Christmas at sea during his interlude in
Lion over the winter of 1914–15. Here he recalls the traditional round by the ship's
senior officers of the mess decks, in this case seasonally decorated by their inmates
for Vice Adm. Sir David Beatty and his staff:

> What was more remarkable, and not a little touching, was that men living such a life of un-
> changing routine and toil, cramped and crowded, poised insecurely between life and death,
> should think it worth while to add to their labours by building up for such a brief moment
> these childish structures of decorative rubbish. It was eloquent of the need there is in every
> heart to make festival at some time or other, and surely eloquent also of that enviable gift,
> one of the best which the bluejacket possesses, of making something out of nothing, of being
> happy with little, and of constructing out of the material of daily toil a bright-hued fabric of
> pleasure.[14]

Although the Invergordon mutiny of 1931 ushered in a significant change in officer attitudes, there can be little doubt that arrogance and thoughtlessness lay at the
root of much disgruntlement and disaffection on the lower deck. In most instances
the men could draw on a subtle and evolved language to express their disgust or dis-
appointment at those given command over them. A tone of voice, a nuance of body
language, a show of reticence all spoke volumes to those on the receiving end. Adm.
Sir Frank Twiss captures this perfectly in recalling a botched maneuver made by
him while commanding his first ship, the frigate *Porlock Bay:*

> With a nasty rending noise the stanchions bent and broke and then, in one of those mo-
> ments of utter silence which usually follow disaster, I heard a sailor's voice from somewhere
> aft, "Away stanchions." I never forgot that cry. It said everything the Ship's Company
> thought of their new Captain: cack-handed, no ship handler, spoiling our nice ship, not
> what we expected of you, Sir, not what we look for at all.[15]

There were moments, however, when extreme aggravation called for more direct means of communication. Shoddy or listless work, mass leave-breaking, and
desultory performances in fleet sporting events were sure signs of poor morale and
failing leadership. By contrast, the officer whose men called him a "gent" was being
paid their very highest compliment, and there was little they would not do for him.
Adm. Sir Reginald Bacon has this memory of Cdr. Sacheveral Darwin, with whom
he served in the battleship *Alexandra* in the early 1880s:

> One morning, after we had been in commission some months, he slipped coming down a
> ladder, and broke his knee-cap, which necessitated his going to hospital. Christmas Day
> came, and in the afternoon his two boy messengers were sent by the crew up to the hospital
> with a basket containing something from each of the men's messes to show that he had not
> been forgotten. A rare mark of affection from a crew.[16]

But most were glad to keep their distance and generally had as little contact with
officers as possible. Nowhere is this attitude more exquisitely captured than in the
following exchange between Midn. George Blundell, then in command of *Hood*'s
first picketboat, and his Westcountry coxswain. The year is 1924.

I have often reflected on what a lot the petty officers tactfully taught me on how to behave. One day we landed a number of officers just after lunch: the ship's company was still at work. On return I asked the coxswain (Jeffreys was his name; he was a darling man) "What do the men think of the officers going ashore in working hours?" Jeff looked at me with that "three badge" twinkle in his eye. "Lor' bless you, Sir," he replied, "We likes to see them out of the way." I have never forgotten that wise remark.[17]

Officers, of course, took a very different perspective on relations with the men, though these varied depending on the type of vessel concerned; plainly, discipline and polish were less pertinent among the picked and highly trained men in the confines of a submarine or destroyer than they were in a battleship, with a thousand compartments and many hands to keep from idleness. For most officers, guardians of a great tradition, relentless work and supervision served not only to restrain the unruliness and aggression that made the British sailor the formidable man he was but also to harden him against the day when the sea or the enemy might mete out more than irksome labor or petty discipline. Naturally, the navy had mechanisms to relieve the tensions that inevitably arose, including the elaborate "Crossing the Line" ceremony and, more frequently, the risqué inversions of rank, gender, and sexual orientation represented in the "S.O.D.S. operas" with their wry and frequently mordant commentaries of shipboard life, events, characters, and morale.[18]

Evidently, much of this experience remains locked in the mind, fated to slip quietly into oblivion unless coaxed out by time or providence. This is why—where still possible—contact with veterans is so valuable to any study of a naval community, giving the researcher the opportunity less to identify the salient features of life afloat or the highlights of a ship's career or commission than to put these into the perspective of its daily atmosphere and routine, to gauge the tenor of its life, and to appreciate the extent to which incidents were blips in an existence that for many was characterized more by boredom and drudgery than by excitement or zeal. For the source material that survives, in whatever form it is transmitted—letters, diaries, memoirs published or otherwise, oral histories, film, or direct contact with veterans—many obstacles and pitfalls remain where its interpretation is concerned. To read the memoirs of an officer and a rating of the same commission (or, generally, cruise, in American parlance) is to appreciate the gulf-like gap in outlook and prospects separating the two sides. There was mutual respect, collaboration, and a degree of comradeship in adversity, but to pretend that any ship was truly "of one company" is to ignore the fundamental realities of service afloat.

Both then and since, the opinions expressed are invariably bound up in the assumptions and realities of class that continue to characterize British and particularly English society generally. The views range from morbid bitterness and disgust among ratings to suppositions among senior officers of harmony and satisfaction that existed among only a small proportion of ratings. Between these extremes are memoirs offering penetrating insights into the life and atmosphere of the ship from both ratings and officers. Inevitably, much of this material reflects the very decided opinion, prejudice, or agenda of its author, either at the time or later. Those using it must therefore be careful to draw a distinction between opinions reflecting personal experience and those that can be taken as representative of the views of a wider community of men, between those written at the time and those that are the products of memory, more reasoned and ordered in their perceptions but less accurate to the moment in their detail or emotional tone.

Then there is the matter of confidentiality and withholding of information alluded to just above. The "Silent Service" (that is, the submarine arm), whose members set down and publish their memoirs less frequently and less candidly than do those of the other armed services, yields its secrets only with the greatest reluctance. The sense of a world apart that only those who lived it can share or understand remains strong. Beyond this, service in a ship usually implies a bond of loyalty and attachment to be broken only by death. In writing on such an emotive subject as HMS *Hood*—sunk with huge loss of life in an episode that has come to represent the Calvary endured by the Royal Navy in the Second World War—one cannot fail to become aware of the amount of information, inevitably concerning its less agreeable aspects and episodes, that was and is known but can neither be revealed nor admitted. This of itself has something to say about the mentality of those under review, about the values of the community in which they served, and the self-perception of the navy of the time and since. Nor is this mentality confined to veterans, and so to bring a subject under close and dispassionate scrutiny is to risk raising the ire of those who, for reasons that have more to do with the present than the past, would rather the gilded image of the Royal Navy be left untarnished.

A warship community is of course part of a wider institution—a navy—which in its turn is an expression of the government that directs and supports it and the culture and society from which it emerges. No ship community can therefore be abstracted from the wider context of events, and the first half of the twentieth century saw far-reaching changes in British society that are accurately reflected in the Royal Navy.[19] Even with a visionary genius like Sir John Fisher at the helm, the speed of technological change in the first years of the century largely outpaced the ability of the Royal Navy to assimilate it, and for various reasons the service was unable to make good its many advantages during the Great War. The inability of the navy to deliver a knockout blow to the High Seas Fleet at Jutland or prevent the shelling of towns along the east coast of England or the slaughter of British merchantmen in 1917 was a blow to a service steeped in the tradition of Nelson and diminished its prestige in society at large. Then in 1921 came the "Geddes Axe," which beached a third of its officer corps and contributed to poor officer morale for the rest of the decade. The postwar years also produced a pronounced reaction against technical specialization and technology generally—the "materialists," as its practioners were known—which was long suspected to have blunted the offensive capabilities of the navy. Among other things, this resulted in concerted steps to reduce the influence of naval engineering and even in a disparaging of gunnery officers in some quarters. Meanwhile, a profound nostalgia among certain senior and retired officers for the service of their youth prompted a movement for the restoration of sail training in the Royal Navy, a scheme Admiral Chatfield was at pains to quash on becoming First Sea Lord in 1932.[20] All this against the backdrop of ongoing debate as to the worth of the battleship and the holiday on capital-ship construction, which was extended in 1930—issues central to the perpetuation of the navy as an effective force.

The Royal Navy also found difficulty in adjusting to social and economic change. On the lower deck the settlement of 1919 had brought sailors' pay above the breadline, but the failure of the navy to recognize the profound social upheaval brought on by the Great War, its neutering of entities set up to represent lower-deck grievances, and a series of inept and ill-advised pay cuts led to the Invergordon mutiny in 1931.[21] Gone were the "crews of lithe, active, catlike men of poor education but giants in muscle and pluck" who had characterized the navy until the turn of the twentieth century.[22] Reflecting more stringent qualifications for entry and improvements in education on a national level, the Royal Navy was now receiving men of much broader formation and aspirations than had been the case before the Great War—men who found little outlet for their ambitions in the navy. By the late 1920s the legion of sailors promoted to petty officer during the war was acting as a bar to advancement for younger men, many of whom represented much more suitable candidates for higher ratings. As one sailor recalled, "It was explained to us by the odd older members of the crew—a lot of whom were survivors of the wartime fleets, now drastically reduced—[that they] only put up with the poor conditions and pay to avoid the mass unemployment that awaited them if they did not achieve Pension Age."[23]

Then there were those for whom cynicism was the ultimate lesson of their experience: "Of the others, survivors of the previous generation, most were tough old nuts with nothing to lose, their Good Conduct badges having gone to the wind many a time, and toughened up by periods of detention. [Together, this] made for a tough old navy that required tight control."[24]

Needless to say, few officers were under any illusions as to the type of man they were dealing with here. Capt. Francis Pridham of *Hood* made no bones about it:

> There are of course various kinds of "black sheep." The chap who is "grey black" through his own foolishness, gets drunk on shore and makes himself a noisy nuisance, is no great anxiety. The really "black" ones, the Bolshies, the coarse, the lecherous and the surly gaol bird are the dangerous ones. I have no compunction in saying that the risk we run in carrying this type justifies us hounding him down, and out, when we find him out. The Navy is not a reformatory.[25]

Invergordon provided a stark revelation of the administrative deficiencies under which the Royal Navy had been laboring since the end of the Great War and showed the Admiralty to be disconnected from both the officer corps and the lower deck. Nonetheless, the 1930s brought on a profound change of approach and leadership at the top. In shipboard life this was reflected in a renewed emphasis on the divisional system of warship organization (refined by Cdr. William James and Capt. W. R. Hall in the battle cruiser *Queen Mary* immediately before the Great War) and in improved training and promotion prospects for talented ratings. Mindful of the political militance of many of the older men it had traditionally recruited as stokers from the industrial north of Britain, the navy turned to younger men from the south to staff the engineering departments of its ships, though at some cost to shipboard organization, as separate messes had to be established to keep new recruits from their older shipmates.

The 1930s also saw an easing of the tensions that had traditionally characterized relations between marines, stokers, and seamen, the product of a broader outlook among those joining the navy and greater efforts at integration on the part of their divisional officers. The popularity of shipboard lending libraries and wide interest in advanced courses are telling indicators of the sort of men being drawn to a naval career. This against a decline in traditional shipboard crafts like fancy rope work and even in the number of those taking their rum rations; in 1934 less than a quarter of those eligible on *Hood*'s lower deck elected to do so, though financial considerations no doubt had a bearing on this figure.[26]

Meanwhile, the worsening diplomatic situation ushered new ships, new technology, and new ideas into the navy. As recruitment gathered pace in the late 1930s, the navy's commitments during the Abyssinian crisis of 1935 and then the Spanish Civil War disrupted both its training regime and the ordered sequence of the naval year, with its rotation of fleet exercises, training, competition, refitting, and leave.[27] Then came the Second World War, which drafted hundreds of thousands of reservist officers and "hostilities-only" ratings into the service, with all the logistical and training requirements this brought in its train.[28] The great influx of volunteers and conscripts did not begin until 1940, but once they started arriving in numbers the atmosphere afloat changed perceptibly. For the regulars of the peacetime navy it was no doubt an exasperating yet fascinating spectacle. Here were men, drawn from every walk of life, thrust in time of war into the unforgiving and largely closed world of the lower deck of the Royal Navy. Some wilted under the pressure, but curiosity and mutual respect caused many unlikely friendships to be struck up. As technology assumed an ever greater role in naval operations and attrition thinned the ranks of career officers, the navy came increasingly to rely on the Royal Naval Volunteer Reserve and the Royal Naval Reserve to bridge the gap.[29] There were tensions, of course, as reservist officers brought their breezy approach and technical expertise into the conservative environment of the peacetime service, but the navy would never be the same again.

This brings us to perceptions, first those of the navy and then ours as historians. Although firm conclusions are hard to come by and generalization is a risky proposition, it is always useful to speculate on the extent of individuals' or a group's attachment to the ships in which they sail or the navy in which they serve, of their allegiances by rank, specialization, or geographical origin—or lack thereof. Equally, in an institution that routinely separated men from home for very extended periods, the nature of a sailor's attachment to the land is an important indicator of his relationship to the parent institution. By the 1930s the navy had long since ceased to be a world of bachelors, and in 1934 nearly 40 percent of *Hood*'s company were married, while 30 percent had dependent children—part of the wider family of a ship's company, a part whose existence was first acknowledged by farsighted officers like Rory O'Conor.[30]

Most, however, remained married to the service and its culture, and at its best the navy, among both its officers and men, was a community or set of communities in which it was sufficient for a man to feel that he had earned the respect of his peers and could be counted as one of them in the fullest sense—enough to believe that in extremis the moment might come when they laid down their lives for you and you might do likewise for them. Courage, fortitude, and loyalty—in Toynbee's memorable phrase "nonetheless virtues for being jewels set in blood and iron."[31] At its worst that community was a sullen and cynical rump imbued with the darker sides of naval life, of skulking, thievery, bullying, and sexual predation, and in the case of officers characterized by timeservers, failures, and nonentities, those who, in Captain O'Conor's words, lacked "the spark of leadership, . . . the ability to organise, and the will to carry things through."[32] Such a world was discovered by Ordinary Seaman George Melly on being drafted to HMS *Argus,* once an aircraft carrier and by then an accommodation ship at Chatham. It is July 1945:

> The *Argus,* as I soon discovered, was a den of skivers, misfits and lunatics, a floating, tethered thieves' kitchen. Our Captain, an elderly and scrawny religious maniac risen from the ranks, seldom left his cabin and could be heard, during the night watches, loudly declaiming the more bloodthirsty passages from the Old Testament. Despite his age and length of service, he was still, and understandably, a Lieutenant. The rest of the ship's company were all involved in a conspiracy to remain exactly where they were, tucked snugly away, a cosy and corrupt community dedicated to mutual aid.[33]

Finally, we come to the contrast between our perceptions and concerns as historians and those of the individuals under review. To question a veteran about life afloat is to grasp the extent to which disparity of experience is matched by a gulf in priorities. Few veterans of *Hood* therefore have—or had—very much interest in precisely how it was sunk. Rather, they imagine sheets of flame enveloping men and spaces intimately known and nostalgically recalled. Abstracted from the tactical and strategic realities that exercised their superiors and animate their historians, they remember the comradeship, the sense of hardships shared that made all things bearable and set the navy apart from every other walk of life—the community evoked here by Leading Seaman Leonard Williams of *Hood:*

> Here we lived together as a giant family. We knew each other's failings and weaknesses, and liked each other in spite of them. We slept in close proximity, in swaying hammocks. We even bathed together in the communal bathrooms. In fact we lived candidly with one another, accepting the rough with the smooth. This sharing and living together forged a comradeship which one can never find in civilian life. Nor was the ship herself left out of our lives, for everything we did was for her. On our smartness, the way we dressed, in fact everything we did depended our ship's efficiency rating in the fleet. She was our constant task mistress. While we could, and often did, call her all the rough names under the sun when things went wrong, heaven help those, not of our company, who tried to do the same. This is the team spirit we miss when we leave the service, for it is something very fine. Something which, through countless ages, has scaled the highest mountains, fought and won hopeless battles.[34]

The re-creation of such a community in all its splendor and misery, in its terror and ennui, its structure and subtlety, has rarely proved enticing to historians, who in taking on any such project must resign themselves to the possibility, even the likelihood, of only partial success after much labor. While few would dispute the centrality of the human dimension of life afloat in naval studies, until a larger body of research is available to permit of comparison between ships and navies, the dominant impression of such communities must remain more firmly rooted in the realm of fiction than of history, and of arms more than men.[35]

NOTES   My thanks to Dr. Nicholas Lambert, Prof. Jon Sumida, and Prof. Christopher McKee for their kindness and encouragement in connection with this paper—and also to Deborah Eppolito, to whom it is lovingly dedicated.

1 See Bruce Taylor, *The Battlecruiser HMS* Hood: *An Illustrated Biography, 1916–1941* (London: Chatham, 2005). See also Capt. John Wells, *The Royal Navy: An Illustrated Social History, 1870–1982* (Stroud, Glos., U.K.: Alan Sutton/Royal Naval Museum, 1994); Henry Baynham, *Men from the Dreadnoughts* (London: Hutchinson, 1976); Christopher McKee, *Sober Men and True: Sailor Lives in the Royal Navy, 1900–1945* (Cambridge, Mass.: Harvard Univ. Press, 2002); Ronald H. Spector, *At War at Sea: Sailors and Naval Combat in the Twentieth Century* (New York: Viking, 2001); John Reeve and David Stevens, eds., *The Face of Naval Battle: The Human Experience of Modern War at Sea* (St. Leonards, NSW, Australia: Allen and Unwin, 2003); Kenneth Poolman, *The British Sailor* (London: Arms and Armour, 1989); and G. G. Connell, *Jack's War: Lower-Deck Recollections from World War II* (Manchester, U.K.: Crecy, 1995).

2 It can be summarized as follows. There are two voluminous collections of technical papers relating to its fabric, together with the transactions of the boards of enquiry held into the sinking. On the operational side, there are over twenty years of deck logs, a collection of papers concerning the world cruise of 1923–24, and brief reports on the involvement of the ship's detachment in the Norwegian

campaign in April 1940 and of the ship itself at the shelling of the French fleet at Mers el-Kébir in July of that year. Where the ship's internal affairs are concerned, the material is limited to several medical officers' journals and assorted papers concerning disciplinary issues, including the Invergordon mutiny. For references see Taylor, *Battlecruiser HMS Hood*, p. 250.

3 Ibid., pp. 121, 195.

4 The registers of ships' movements are archived in the Naval Historical Branch of the Ministry of Defence, Portsmouth. Ships' logs are held in The National Archives at Kew, but those of miscellaneous or smaller vessels, including destroyers, were disposed of in the early 1970s.

5 See, for example, Taylor, *Battlecruiser HMS* Hood, pp. 232–34.

6 Both series owe their existence to Robert Gardiner, editor in chief of, successively, Conway Maritime Press and Chatham Publishing.

7 V. C. Scott O'Connor, *The Empire Cruise* (London: Riddle, Smith, and Duffus, 1925), p. 37.

8 See, for example, Norman Friedman, *Naval Firepower: Battleship Guns and Gunnery in the Dreadnought Era* (Annapolis, Md.: Naval Institute Press, 2008); and Derek Howse, *Radar at Sea: The Royal Navy in World War 2* (London: Macmillan, 1993).

9 See Taylor, *Battlecruiser HMS* Hood, p. 46.

10 Ibid., p. 87.

11 Ibid., p. 46.

12 Admiral of the Fleet Lord Chatfield, *The Navy and Defence* (London: Heinemann, 1942), p. 219. The chief manuals of shipboard organization are, chronologically, Capt. W. W. Hewett, *Order Book for Executive Officers of the Royal Navy*, 2nd ed. (Portsmouth, U.K.: Gieve, Matthews, and Seagrove, 1900; first published 1894); Cdr. Sir Robert Arbuthnot, *Commander's Order Book for a Mediterranean Battleship* (Portsmouth, U.K.: Griffin, 1900); Capt. Christopher Cradock, *Whispers from the Fleet: A Seamanship Story Book*, 2nd ed. (Portsmouth, U.K.: Gieve, Matthews, and Seagrove, 1908; first published 1907); Cdr. the Hon. R. A. R. Plunkett, *The Modern Officer of the Watch*, 5th ed. (Portsmouth, U.K.: Gieve, Matthews, and Seagrove, 1913; first published 1908); Capt. A. D. Pound, *Man-of-War Organisation* (Portsmouth, U.K.: Gieve, Matthews, and Seagrove, c. 1910); Cdr. W. M. James, *New Battleship Organisations and Notes for Executive Officers* (Portsmouth, U.K.: Gieve's, 1916); A Watch-Keeper [Lt. Cdr. B. V. Sturdee], *Five Minutes to One Bell: A Few Hints to Junior Watch-Keepers Together with Some Remarks on the Duties of a Destroyer First Lieutenant* (Portsmouth, U.K.: Gieve's, c. 1918; first published c. 1914); Cdr. Russell Grenfell, *A Cruiser Commander's Orders* (Portsmouth, U.K.: Gieve's, 1933); and Capt. Rory O'Conor, *Running a Big Ship on "Ten Commandments" (With Modern Executive Ideas and a Complete Organisation)* (Portsmouth, U.K.: Gieve's, 1937).

13 Rory O'Connor [*sic*], *Service intérieur (Running a Big Ship on Ten Commandments)* (Paris: État-Major Général de la Marine, 1938); and Rory O'Conor, *I "dieci Comandamenti" per governare una grande nave* (Rome: Tipo-Litografia dell'Ufficio di Gabinetto del Ministero della Marina, 1938).

14 Filson Young, *With the Battle Cruisers* (Annapolis, Md.: U.S. Naval Institute, 1986), p. 144.

15 Adm. Sir Frank Twiss, *Social Change in the Royal Navy, 1924–1970: The Life and Times of Admiral Sir Frank Twiss, KCB, KCVO, DSC* (Stroud, Glos., U.K.: Alan Sutton/Royal Naval Museum, 1996), p. 111.

16 Adm. Sir Reginald H. Bacon, *A Naval Scrap-Book. First Part: 1877–1900* (London: Hutchinson, c. 1925), p. 50.

17 Capt. George Blundell, memoirs, vol. 3, anecdote 3, p. 6, Imperial War Museum, Department of Documents, 90/38/1.

18 S.O.D.S. stands for Ship's Own Dramatic Society, or Ship's Operatic and Dramatic Society.

19 See Capt. Stephen W. Roskill, *Naval Policy between the Wars* (London: Collins, 1968–76); Vice Adm. Sir Louis Le Bailly, *From Fisher to the Falklands* (London: Institute of Marine Engineers, 1991); and Christopher M. Bell, *The Royal Navy: Seapower and Strategy between the Wars* (London: Palgrave Macmillan, 2000).

20 Admiral of the Fleet Lord Chatfield, *It Might Happen Again* (London: Heinemann, 1948), pp. 54–59.

21 Anthony Carew, *The Lower Deck of the Royal Navy, 1900–39: The Invergordon Mutiny in Perspective* (Manchester, U.K.: Manchester Univ. Press, 1981).

22 Bacon, *Naval Scrap-Book*, p. vi.

23 Fred Coombes, typescript memoirs, Imperial War Museum, Department of Documents, 91/7/1, p. 42.

24 Ibid.

25 *Lectures on Mutiny*, part 1, *Prevention*, p. 8. Author's collection.

26 See Taylor, *Battlecruiser HMS* Hood, p. 231.

27 Ibid., pp. 75–79.

28 Brian Lavery, *Hostilities Only: Training in the Wartime Navy* (London: National Maritime Museum, 2004).

29 Brian Lavery, *In Which They Served: The Royal Navy Officer Experience in the Second World War* (London: Conway Maritime, 2008).

30 See Taylor, *Battlecruiser HMS* Hood, p. 231.

31 Arnold J. Toynbee, *A Study of History* (Oxford, U.K.: Oxford Univ. Press, 1939), vol. 4, p. 640.

32 O'Conor, *Running a Big Ship on "Ten Commandments,"* p. 149.

33 George Melly, *Rum, Bum and Concertina* (London: Weidenfeld and Nicolson, 1977), p. 57.

34 Leonard Charles Williams, *Gone a Long Journey* (Bedhampton, U.K.: Hillmead, 2002), p. 141.

35 Prominent examples of fictional re-creations of shipboard life are C. S. Forester, *The Ship* (London: Michael Joseph, 1943); Nicholas Monsarrat, *The Cruel Sea* (London: Cassell, 1951); and Alistair MacLean, *H.M.S. Ulysses* (London: Collins, 1955).

VII Ostfriesland, *the General Board of the Navy, and the Washington Naval Treaty*
A Relook at a Historic Sinking

JOHN T. KUEHN

This paper revisits the historic sinking of the German dreadnought battleship *Ostfriesland* in Chesapeake Bay after World War I by Army Air Corps bombers. Few events have been surrounded with so much hype and myth. According to a heroic version of events, William "Billy" Mitchell demonstrated conclusively the obsolescence of battleships, and by extension navies, by sinking a modern dreadnought with his bombers. The opposite view holds that the sinking of a moored vessel of questionable seaworthiness in fine weather with no crew to "fight" it proved nothing about the efficacy of airpower against naval power.

The real story, as usual, is more complicated, and this essay hopes to explore some of these complexities, including those that have been obscured by overheated historical approaches. In particular, this investigation will examine how the General Board of the U.S. Navy reacted to data collected by representatives of the Bureau of Construction and Repair who submitted detailed after-action reports on the various Army Air Corps tests. If one does this, one finds that the General Board took the evidence gathered from *Ostfriesland* and other ordnance tests so seriously that it decided to use the scrapping clause of the Washington Naval Treaty as an opportunity to test further the efficacy of airpower and the survivability of battleships. The General Board found that the reality differed greatly from the hype and committed itself to a practical program of battleship improvement within the confines of the Washington Naval Treaty and based on solid evidence and analysis.

Before discussing the physical evidence, the context of a conflict between Gen. Billy Mitchell and the General Board must be provided. Each side had very good reasons to be resentful of the other. In the summer of 1919 Mitchell related the following to a credulous congressional audience: "We believe that if we are allowed to develop essentially air weapons . . . that we can carry the war to such an extent in the air as to make navies almost useless on the surface of the waters. The Navy General Board, I might say, agree with me on that." This testimony found its way into the records of the General Board, whose members most certainly did not agree with General Mitchell. Their protest was so vociferous that Secretary of War Newton D. Baker was forced to write a letter to the secretary of the navy the following October stating, "A careful perusal of the record of this hearing indicates that General Mitchell was not justified in the conclusion which he reached."[1] It is almost certain that Baker and John J. Pershing (who had commanded the American Expeditionary Force, now held the rank General of the Armies, and would in 1921 be appointed Chief of Staff of the Army) were not so circumspect and restrained when they talked with Mitchell about the matter. So began a feud within a feud, the feud between Mitchell and the General Board—a feud whose climax occurred with the sinking of a German dreadnought.

In order to understand why General Mitchell concluded that the General Board agreed with him we must go back to April of the same year, when General Mitchell and Gen. C. T. Menoher (Mitchell's nominal superior) testified before the General Board as it debated the "development of naval aviation policy," specifically the need for an aviation institution organic to the navy and separate from the army. The General Board was itself a relatively young organization, having been created by the secretary of the navy by executive fiat only in 1900, as a sort of incognito naval general staff. It was composed of about a dozen senior captains and admirals (with a junior officer as secretary) and included the Chief of Naval Operations (CNO) and the Commandant of the Marine Corps as permanent ("ex officio") members until 1932. Its official role was advisory in nature, but it had more or less become the senior policy-making body in the navy and provided the last word on ship and fleet design. At the time of Mitchell's testimony, the membership included the most senior admirals on active duty. Often the senior member present was in fact the most senior officer in the navy. (This was before the CNO position developed into the service chief for the navy under Adm. Ernest King in World War II.)[2] The other key element needed to understand Mitchell's testimony to the General Board involves its unique hearing process. The General Board gathered information on various topics before rendering "advice" to the secretary of the navy through formal, secret hearings. Additionally, this secret testimony was transcribed and maintained for future reference in the writing of recommendations for the secretary of the navy, often encompassed in General Board studies referred to as "serials."[3] Today, Mitchell's release of information from the hearing might be regarded as a violation of the rules governing classified information.

The topic of naval aviation was of great interest to the navy's senior leadership and the General Board in particular. In March 1919 the board held hearings on recent gunnery tests using airborne spotters and the battleship *Texas*. These hearings had impressed the General Board with the potential value of naval aviation. On 3 April 1919 Mitchell and Menoher testified, along with several key members of the nascent Directorate of Naval Aviation (later reorganized as a new Bureau of Aeronautics—BuAer for short). Among these officers were many of the "pioneers" of naval aviation—John Towers, Henry C. "Hank" Mustin, and Kenneth Whiting. The rules for these hearings were very liberal for a military organization. The board tolerated a considerable amount of informality and often made a point not to interrupt or contradict witnesses in order to get as broad a scope of testimony as possible.[4]

The senior admiral present that day was the former fleet commander (1913–14), Rear Adm. Charles Badger. Badger deferred the conduct of the meeting to Adm. Charles G. Winterhalter, former commander of the Asiatic Fleet. Winterhalter established a congenial atmosphere and deferred to Mitchell and Menoher, as the following passage demonstrates: "I have outlined in general what our immediate needs are, and will be very glad if you will, in your own way, handle this subject."[5] The starting point for the discussion was the navy's acquisition of a number of Sopwith aircraft for training and testing out concepts. Mitchell's first words were confrontational: "My opinion in regard to the employment of an air service, as a general proposition, is to get what material the people who are using it desire for their work. The airplanes mentioned will be shot down as fast as they go up against an enemy."

When Admiral Winterhalter stressed that the planes were simply for training, Mitchell remained adamant: "We would shoot [them] down immediately." This exchange might cause one to conclude that the primary enemy of the United States, in Billy Mitchell's mind, was its navy.[6]

Mitchell may have gained the impression that the General Board agreed with him because it politely listened to him. The most direct evidence came after about seven pages of testimony, most of it by Mitchell. "My opinion is you can make a direct attack on ships from the air in the future," claimed Mitchell. Winterhalter agreed, but such agreement did not equate to concurrence that navies are "almost useless." Rather, it was a simple recognition that airplanes can attack ships. This line of questioning led to a proposal for some testing. Winterhalter, putting himself in Mitchell's shoes, mused out loud about his own sense of the current vulnerability of ships to attack from the air: "You gentlemen [of the Army Air Corps] ought to feel very much encouraged about the condition of surface vessels at the present time. They are most vulnerable to attack from the air. There is now more weight in vertical armor than in horizontal armor."

Mitchell responded immediately, "We can try a good many things out around Chesapeake Bay." At this point Mitchell may have stopped listening and come to his mistaken conclusion that it followed from this discussion that the General Board agreed navies were "almost useless." Winterhalter went on to stress that he agreed that testing was necessary "to find out what your methods of attack are so we can find them out to meet them." The navy wanted to do the testing to improve its surface vessels' defenses against prospective future enemies—not against the Army Air Corps. However, given this exchange, one can understand why someone with Mitchell's personality—headstrong and egocentric—might mistake common courtesy with complete agreement. Winterhalter later asked Mitchell whether it might not be a good idea for the army to assign a "liaison" officer to "join our aviators here"—that is, at all the hearings associated with naval aviation. Mitchell agreed that this was a good idea.[7]

Thus it must have been a bitter surprise to Mitchell to be rebuked by his own service secretary at the instigation of the General Board (and Navy Secretary Josephus Daniels). Lost in all the hype was the board's recommendation to its boss advocating the further aggressive development of naval aviation ships, planes, and organizations "capable of accompanying and operating with the fleet in all waters of the globe."[8]

In the meantime, forceful voices lent themselves to the cause of the development of aviation within the navy. In 1919 Adm. William Sims returned from his wartime command of the naval forces deployed to aid the allies in the Great War. He was assigned to the Naval War College and reopened that institution (closed temporarily during the war) in July. A longtime advocate of reform, Sims was a committed "battleship admiral" who was as yet unconvinced of the value of carrier aviation. He proceeded to test rigorously the use of aircraft in the college's curriculum, during its periodic war games. By January 1921 he had become an advocate of a separate naval air service within the navy and had even begun to consider aircraft carriers as capital ships that would displace the battleship from its perch as the centerpiece of the battle fleet.[9]

Meanwhile, another key personality had become convinced of the value of naval aviation and of the need for the navy to have a strong organization in charge of it—Capt. William Moffett, an officer with political connections. In December 1918, while in command of the battleship *Mississippi*, Moffett had observed as Towers and Mustin demonstrated the effectiveness of gunnery spotting by naval aviation; Towers and Mustin then converted him to their cause. Moffett had his congressional contacts urge the Navy Department to appoint him to succeed Capt. Thomas Craven as Director of Naval Aviation and to recommend that the job be upgraded to an admiral's billet. The navy was already leaning in the direction of assigning Moffett, since he was considered a "battleship officer." In March 1920 Moffett was appointed to the job, and in July the billet was upgraded by Congress to the directorship of a full-up navy bureau, with accompanying admiral's rank. One must understand that for an organization to have the status and name of "bureau" was a very big deal in those days—it meant that the institutional navy believed naval aviation had a promising future.[10]

Ironically, the same month that Moffett was appointed chief of the navy's newest bureau, Mitchell finally got his chance to test out his ideas about aviation making navies "almost useless" against a bona fide dreadnought battleship—SMS *Ostfriesland*. As part of the armistice agreement signed in November 1918, the

United States was authorized to take possession of several warships of Germany's former High Seas Fleet, including *Ostfriesland*.[11] On 12 July 1921, the same day Congress passed the law establishing BuAer, *Ostfriesland* and the light cruiser SMS *Frankfurt* departed from their moorings in New York Harbor under tow, bound for Chesapeake Bay.[12] Mitchell and the secretary of the navy, Josephus Daniels, had been engaged in a public debate about the effectiveness of land-based bombers against battleships. Daniels reputedly responded to Mitchell's proposal to test his ideas against the battleship *Iowa* by saying, "I'm so confident that neither Army nor Navy aviators can hit the Iowa when she is under way that I would be perfectly willing to be on board her when they bomb her!" Deadlines established by the allies for destruction of the German vessels after the war and congressional pressure orchestrated by Mitchell (whose father had been a senator from Wisconsin) resulted in the new administration's directing a new secretary of the navy, Edwin Denby, to accede to the tests in July 1921.[13]

Mitchell's goals for the test contrasted sharply with those of the navy. Mitchell meant to prove the concept that airplanes could sink battleships. Once this was established he hoped it would provide the momentum for his drive to establish an independent air force by causing Congress to act legislatively. Additionally, in proving that the navy had no proper appreciation for the potential of airpower, he could claim that any naval component for airpower properly belonged within the new independent service he hoped to establish. This reflected what the British had done with their Fleet Air Arm, which was controlled, mainly through budgetary means, by the Air Ministry and the Royal Air Force.[14] On the navy side, the goals were more modest: to study and collect data on the effect of bombs of various sizes on ships of various sizes, study German warship design, and take the lessons learned and use them to design less vulnerable warships.[15]

Mitchell prepared his pilots for these tests as if he was preparing for actual combat. For him the tests were the moral equivalent of war.[16] However, his target was not at all what it was painted in the popular press to be—the latest and greatest in unsinkable dreadnought technology. *Ostfriesland* was no spring chicken. It had been launched in 1909 as a first-generation German dreadnought, built in response to Sir John "Jackie" Fisher's "dreadnought revolution," in the course of what had been to that point the most expensive peacetime arms race in the history of warfare. The ship had managed to survive the battle of Jutland in 1916 but was almost sunk before reaching port by a British mine. *Ostfriesland* finished out the war much as did the rest of the High Seas Fleet, mostly in port, with its material condition degrading. It was not at Scapa Flow (where most of the German fleet had scuttled itself) and was turned over to the U.S. Navy in April 1920.[17]

The navy, as was its habit, assigned an officer of proven experience and competence from its Bureau of Construction and Repair to take charge of the preparations of *Ostfriesland* for the test—Cdr. (later Adm.) Alexander Hamilton Van Keuren. He was to inspect the vessel and collect data in order to do what Admiral Winterhalter had emphasized two years previously—figure out how to make warships, especially battleships, less vulnerable to attack from the air. Van Keuren found *Ostfriesland* in poor material condition. Many of its watertight hatches and scuttles were so damaged that they had to be secured with Manila ropes for the voyage down to Chesapeake Bay. Van Keuren's report clearly indicated that the ship was lower in the water than it should have been and that it contained brackish water in its bilges and tanks. Hull vents that should have been above the waterline were now at the waterline and so were secured to prevent even more water from entering the ship.[18]

By the time *Ostfriesland* reached the Virginia Capes for further examination on 16 July, Van Keuren observed a "slight list to port." Additionally, he found hatches and manholes open to the machinery spaces. His most important finding, though, was that the ship had taken on even more water during its transit, which raised real concerns in his mind about the overall watertight integrity of the ship. He ended his paragraph entitled "Water in Ship" as follows: "A slow leakage was taking place which became more serious later on when anchored outside [Lynnhaven Inlet] in rough water." On 18 July the ships were towed out to the "Experimental Grounds" test site in Chesapeake Bay. By 20 July, before the first round of bombing, Van Keuren observed that *Ostfriesland* had settled another foot into the sea, which convinced him that it was slowly sinking. Also, its port list was now more pronounced, at two degrees.[19]

The first round of bombings, against other ships prior to 20 July, went well. *Frankfurt,* a submarine, and a destroyer were all sent to the bottom through the cumulative efforts of navy, Marine, and army aviators. On 20 July it was *Ostfriesland*'s turn. The big news that day was that *Ostfriesland* remained afloat, despite the delivery of five 1,100-pound bombs in an unauthorized low-level raid by Mitchell's flyers (using compasses supplied by the navy). The nominal purpose of the tests was to test the effectiveness of level medium-to-high-altitude bombing. Mitchell was furious and made the decision to use his specially built 1,800-pound bombs the following day—he needed a big media event. Nonetheless, the 20 July bombing had caused serious damage to *Ostfriesland,* although Van Keuren's examination of the ship, slowly sinking after the bombing, states nothing about the deployment of a boarding party to keep it afloat, as do some accounts. (Perhaps these accounts confuse Van Keuren's inspectors with a damage-control boarding party.) Van Keuren believed that the day's bombing had accelerated the process by which the ship was filling: it was now down by the stern over four feet, with large quantities of water in its engine rooms, bilges, and "dead pockets." Its port list was now three degrees. He was so concerned it might sink during the night that he had the old battleship *Delaware* stationed alongside—to what purpose his report does not say. One might presume Van Keuren meant for *Delaware* to stand by in order to send another party aboard to make final observations, the better to determine how and why the ship sank, one more time before it went down.[20]

Mitchell had one more chance to prove his point, and his actions immediately prior to the final day of bombing reflect his anxiety: a change in the bomb load and a personal briefing to his pilots. Prior to the army bombers' arrival, Van Keuren had observed that *Ostfriesland* was now down by its stern over eight feet, almost double from the day before, and that it had settled overall another two feet into the Chesapeake. The first five planes, carrying the lighter 1,100-pound bombs, went in and scored two hits. The second wave, also with 1,100-pound bombs, after hits were scored, was sent back to Langley, Virginia, while Van Keuren and his team went aboard to assess the damage. The army aviators, who had been recalled in mid-run to allow the inspection, per the rules, dumped their bomb loads not far from the navy ships observing the test, in a dangerous display of juvenile pique. Van Keuren's observation is worth quoting in its entirety from the report, for what it tells us: "There was no free water in any holds or compartments that we entered on the days immediately preceding bombing nor any signs of strained bulkheads. As remarked before, however, I felt sure the ship was slowly taking water all the time from the time she anchored on the experimental grounds, and this may have been spreading slowly to bunkers through the inner bottom or 2nd skin."

Nonetheless, the beat-up German dreadnought remained stubbornly afloat. The navy was prepared to sink it with the fourteen-inch guns of the dreadnought *Pennsylvania* if it remained afloat after flight operations were secured. Finally, Van Keuren noted that several of the watertight hatches had been jarred open but that there was no time to resecure them, probably due to the unexpected arrival of General Mitchell for one last bombing run.[21]

Mitchell had decided on one more run with his heaviest bombs (which had not been used in the first runs), and he led the charge personally in the lead aircraft. This time Mitchell and his aviators ignored the rules and the recall signals after the first hits, delivering 1,800-pound bombs one after the other. Van Keuren and his team were thus denied the opportunity to collect further data on the ship's now certain sinking. *Ostfriesland* began to settle rapidly by the stern, something the famous photograph of its final moments shows quite clearly. After twenty-one minutes, *Ostfriesland* turned turtle and disappeared into the water, first standing almost on end with its bow in the air. Mitchell sent his final bomber in to drop its load on the bubbling water where it had once been. He then flew a victory pass over the "enemy" navy ships.[22]

A picture is worth a thousand words, and Mitchell had gotten his, despite his violation of the rules and the questionable circumstances surrounding *Ostfriesland*'s demise. Mitchell was exultant, as were those who favored drastic naval disarmament in

Congress. Senator William Borah trumpeted that "the experiment off the Virginia coast demonstrated . . . that the battleship is practically obsolete."[23] The more sober Van Keuren came away with a different set of conclusions, which he cataloged in a secret report and forwarded to the General Board on 30 August 1921. He believed that the test clearly showed "that a crew aboard could have easily kept the ship almost free of water." He also observed "that but for the initial water in the ship, the damage inflicted by bombs would not have sunk the ship, and that gun fire would have had to be resorted to accomplish this end." These comments, being secret and not meant for public consumption, give us good reason to believe that Van Keuren was rendering an objective professional opinion as a naval construction engineer. Van Keuren summarized for the board the following larger recommendations:

- Eliminate or strengthen any areas of contact with the outside sea.
- Develop shrapnel-type antiaircraft ordnance.
- Develop aircraft carriers with fighters to shoot down bombers.
- Develop new tactics and maneuvers to defeat bombers, to shoot them down before they reach the battle line.
- "Since the shots that miss are the shots that count in this new form of warfare, we must see that the least possible number of shots are fired by hostile airplanes and that those that are fired go very wide of their mark."

The last opinion perhaps influenced the General Board the most in terms of battleship design. It must have also been gratified to see Van Keuren support its own earlier decision to convert *Jupiter* into the aircraft carrier *Langley*. During the hearings the previous February, Admiral Badger had led a General Board discussion on "characteristics of airplane carriers" that considered using the design of the planned new battle cruisers, displacing thirty-five thousand tons with the latest boilers and electric drive, as the hulls for big, fast aircraft carriers for the fleet. Clearly the General Board appreciated the potential of naval aviation.[24]

Before Van Keuren's report arrived, though, the Harding administration had already acted, sending out its invitations to a naval disarmament conference to meet that November in Washington, D.C. Harding and Secretary of State Charles Evans Hughes wanted to defuse tensions in the Pacific and halt the postwar naval arms race among Great Britain, Japan, and the United States. It seemed possible that the battleship would fare poorly and perhaps even be abolished, along with the submarine, as a naval weapon. Meanwhile, Mitchell had very much overplayed his hand after his great moment. In particular, he had alienated airpower advocates inside the navy that might, under different circumstances, have supported his bid for an independent air force—particularly Adm. William Moffett and Cdr. John Towers. Towers, especially, would prove instrumental in keeping naval aviation inside the navy during the critical period of the Morrow Board and its report in 1925. Within his own service, Mitchell was repudiated by none other than General Pershing in the report of the Joint Board on the tests, which characterized the battleship as "still the backbone of the fleet."[25]

In the meantime the General Board prepared for the Washington Naval Conference. The technical experts provided by the active-duty naval officer corps to the conference included Capt. William V. Pratt (an Admiral Sims protégé) and Adm. W. L. Rodgers. Both were sitting members of the General Board, and Rodgers was in fact its senior member.[26] The General Board recommended that Hughes propose a fleet equal in size to that of the British and twice the size of that of the Japanese. Hughes rejected the General Board's position and instead made his sweeping proposals to declare a "Capital Ship Building Holiday" and fix tonnages to which the three major naval powers would scrap, down to a ratio of $5:5:3$ for the capital-ship fleets of the United States, Great Britain, and Japan, respectively. Much written about the Washington Naval Conference has missed that Hughes preempted any discussion of the abolition of battleships in the seemingly liberal proposal actually to decommission and scrap them. To get the Japanese to agree to this numerically "inferior position" the Americans also traded away, in article 19 of the Washington Naval Treaty, the right to develop naval bases further in the Philippines and Guam.[27]

Two other articles of the treaty, which resulted from intense negotiations during the conference, reflected the direct impact of the *Ostfriesland* sinking and Van Keuren's recommendations to the General Board. It is worth emphasizing that a copy of his report was placed specifically in the naval aviation files that were used to write General Board studies for the secretary of the navy in August 1921, *prior* to the conference. The importance of aircraft carriers was reflected in article 9 of the treaty, which made allowance to convert as many as two thirty-three-thousand-ton battle cruisers targeted for scrapping into aircraft carriers *(Lexington* and *Saratoga)*. As mentioned previously, the General Board had already proposed the idea of using the existing battle-cruiser hull and propulsion designs as the bases for its first purpose-built aircraft carriers, and here was the opportunity to do just that, under the sanction of the Washington Naval Treaty. The treaty failed to limit the numbers of naval aircraft that navies could build to use in concert with their fleets.[28]

The second article of interest here emphasized the General Board's actions vis-à-vis the battleships retained under the terms of the treaty. The Americans and the British—*Ostfriesland* very much in the minds of the former and possibly the latter—ensured the insertion of a special paragraph in article 20 of the treaty allowing weight increases of up to three thousand tons to allow the major powers to improve the defenses of battleships "against air and submarine attack." Pratt testified to the General Board about his own role in the adoption of this proposal at the conference. He told the board that the proposal had been initially the idea of the British naval delegates and that its intent was to allow battleships to keep pace with threats by aircraft and submarines, which were not limited under the terms of the treaty. As a member of the General Board, he had certainly seen Van Keuren's report. This suggests that the *Ostfriesland* experience, especially the comments regarding near misses and watertight integrity, played a direct role in the drafting of this "reconstruction clause." It very much opened the door for the signatory powers, including the U.S. Navy, to continue to improve the survivability of the battleships they retained under the treaty to keep pace with the threat posed by airpower. Two years later, the first major naval spending program passed in Congress since World War I approved the first phase of a battleship modernization program to implement antiaircraft improvements, as well as internal changes to improve survivability against air attacks.[29]

The General Board had also learned that decommissioned battleships, especially of the most modern types, made excellent targets to test weapons development and warship design. Pursuant to this it lobbied the navy secretary and the president for permission to scrap some of the newest battleships in much the same manner they had disposed of the German ships, by the deployment of the newest gunnery and aerial and torpedo weapons against them. The treaty allowed the navy to dispose of one of the ships scheduled for scrapping as a target each year. Given the experience of *Ostfriesland,* the navy was keen on taking advantage of this clause.[30] The battleship *Washington*'s use as an experimental target was immediately proposed. It was the navy's most modern battleship scheduled for scrapping under the treaty. Someone on the board had broached this issue; use of *Washington* for experimentation had been adopted in 22 April 1922 as the board's official policy. Admiral Rodgers stated that he knew "of no reason why we cannot destroy the *Washington* by target practice in the period set by the treaty and be in every respect within the terms of the treaty."[31]

In the event, *Washington* was not the first ship to be disposed of in this way. In 1923 the older *Virginia* and *New Jersey* were bombed and sunk by the Army Air Corps. Service feeling over these tests tended to increase, rather than weaken, the navy's resolve to strengthen the battleship but also beef up its own fleet aviation.[32] The next ships disposed of were the battleships *North Dakota* and *South Carolina.* These ships were altered with the proposed conversion designs in mind, especially *South Carolina.* Results from their use as targets provided needed data to test the blister design for coal bunkers and their deck-protection designs. Valuable data were also gathered on shock protection for gun turrets.[33]

President Calvin Coolidge approved *Washington*'s use as a target in August 1924. The navy secretary had emphasized to him that the tests were experimental and "in the public interest," since the results would be studied "by a board of naval experts" for use in the modernization program.[34] The subsequent tests showed that the navy's design for survivability of its class (the *Tennessee* class) was basically sound. The *Washington* tests, which would not have been held if not for the treaty and the experience of *Ostfriesland,* established the soundness of the navy's continued institutional support for the battleship.

These tests did much to defuse the navy's concern over near misses that had arisen from the *Ostfriesland* and other level-bombing tests, while providing the navy with valuable underwater data to enhance torpedo protection. *Washington* was eventually sunk by fourteen-inch gunfire from *Texas,* which further reinforced the navy's commitment to improve deck protection and lengthen the range of its guns, as permitted by the treaty.[35] Navy leaders' attitudes were both changing and staying the same. Attitudes about the central role of the battleship changed little inside the institutional navy; most navy leaders redoubled their efforts to retain it as the pillar of naval power. However, in maintaining this stance they changed their views in other areas, especially regarding the threat of airpower and submarines. These nontraditional platforms gained importance in the minds of these men, in part due to their dedication to the idea of the survivable, big-gun battleship.[36]

Not only did the tests, particularly on *Washington,* alleviate many of the concerns the General Board had had about the soundness of the design of its most modern battleships, but in the crucible of war these same ship designs would prove themselves against the best that aviation could throw at them. On 7 December 1941 at Pearl Harbor, *Tennessee, West Virginia,* and *Maryland,* ships whose design and damage-control training had been based on and validated by the experience of *Washington,* were hit with bombs and torpedoes from Japan's professional naval aviators. It was a testament, perhaps, to the legacy of *Ostfriesland,* the General Board, and the Washington Naval Treaty that both *Tennessee* and *Maryland* were easily raised from the shallow water of Pearl Harbor and steamed back to the West Coast under their own power for repairs. *West Virginia,* which took an incredible seven torpedo hits in addition to direct hits by armor-piercing ordnance delivered by dive-bombers, showed what a trained and dedicated crew could do to keep a dreadnought from capsizing while under air attack. It too settled to the bottom of Pearl Harbor; its damage was severe, and it was not refloated until six months later. But then this ship too was repaired and would take its revenge on Japan at the Surigao Strait in 1944. Obviously Mitchell's proclamation of the "death of the battleship" was premature. However, as with all things, perhaps in 1921 the battleship became aware of its own mortality.[37]

NOTES 1 Hon. Newton Baker to the Secretary of the Navy, 21 October 1919, General Board Studies, 449 series, record group [hereafter RG] 80, War Department Correspondence, National Archives and Records Administration [hereafter NARA].

2 For a short history of the General Board during this period see John T. Kuehn, *Agents of Innovation: The General Board and the Design of the Fleet That Defeated the Japanese Navy* (Annapolis, Md.: Naval Institute Press, 2008), chap. 3. See also "Developments in Naval Aviation," 3 April 1919, Proceedings and Hearings of the General Board, RG 80, NARA [hereafter PHGB, NARA].

3 Kuehn, *Agents of Innovation,* pp. 15–21.

4 27 March and 3 April 1919, PHGB, NARA. See also Kuehn, *Agents of Innovation,* pp. 15–21.

5 *Arlington National Cemetery,* www.arlingtoncemetery .net/; 3 April 1919, PHGB, NARA. See Kuehn,

Agents of Innovation, chap. 3, for a detailed discussion of hearing procedures and dynamics. Both Badger and Winterhalter were rear admirals, but as fleet commanders they had held temporary four-star rank (admiral).

6 3 April 1919, PHGB, NARA.

7 Ibid.

8 Williamson A. Murray and Barry Watts, "Military Innovation in Peacetime," in *Military Innovation in the Interwar Period,* ed. Williamson Murray and Allan R. Millett (Cambridge, U.K.: Cambridge Univ. Press, 1996), pp. 390–92.

9 Ibid., p. 392; see also Richard Hough, *Death of the Battleship* (New York: Macmillan, 1963), p. 22.

10 Murray and Watts, "Military Innovation in Peacetime," pp. 393–96. Secretary of the Navy, General Order 65 establishing Bureau of Aeronautics, 10

August 1921, attached to GB (General Board) study 1140, 15 August 1922, RG 80, NARA.

11 "Conditions of an Armistice with Germany," *WWI: The World War I Document Archive,* wwi.lib.byu .edu/. See also Williamson Murray, "Versailles: The Peace without a Chance," in *The Making of Peace: Rulers, States, and the Aftermath of War,* ed. Williamson Murray and Jim Lacy (Cambridge, U.K.: Cambridge Univ. Press, 2009), p. 221.

12 Cdr. A. H. Van Keuren, CC (USN), report, "Ex-German Battleship OSTFRIESLAND: Comments on Bombing of," 29 July 1922 [hereafter Van Keuren Report], p. 449, RG 80, NARA.

13 "Fight for Survival: The Battle at Home & the Court Martial of Billy Mitchell," *Home of Heroes,* www .homeofheroes.com/; William D. O'Neil, "Transformation: Billy Mitchell Style," U.S. Naval Institute *Proceedings* (March 2002), p. 100; Harry H. Ransom, "The Battleship Meets the Airplane," *Military Affairs* 23, no. 1 (Spring 1959), pp. 21–27.

14 O'Neil, "Transformation," p. 101. For a concise discussion of the British system, see Geoffrey Till, "Adopting the Aircraft Carrier: The British, American, and Japanese Case Studies," in *Military Innovation in the Interwar Period,* ed. Murray and Millett, pp. 191–226.

15 Van Keuren Report.

16 For an objective short description of Mitchell's preparations, see Lisle Rose, *Power at Sea: The Breaking Storm, 1919–1945* (Columbia: Univ. of Missouri Press, 2006), pp. 26–27. See also Hough, *Death of the Battleship,* pp. 30–31.

17 Gene T. Zimmerman, "More Fiction than Fact: The Sinking of the *Ostfriesland,*" *Warship International* 12, no. 2 (1975), pp. 142–54; Holger H. Herwig, "The Battlefleet Revolution, 1885–1914," in *The Dynamics of Military Revolution, 1300–2050,* ed. Williamson Murray and MacGregor Knox (Cambridge, U.K.: Cambridge Univ. Press, 2001), chap. 7. For Jutland see John Keegan, *The Price of Admiralty* (London: Penguin, 1988), p. 176.

18 Van Keuren Report.

19 Ibid.

20 Ibid.; Arthur Hezlet, *Aircraft and Sea Power* (New York: Stein and Day, 1970), pp. 109–10. See also Rose, *Power at Sea.* This otherwise excellent account states a boarding party was sent aboard *Ostfriesland* to "keep it afloat" (p. 27), but Rose does not cite the authoritative Van Keuren report, which, in this author's opinion, clarifies what the boarding party was doing.

21 Van Keuren Report; Hough, *Death of the Battleship,* pp. 32–33.

22 Hough, *Death of the Battleship,* pp. 34–35. The photo clearly shows *Ostfriesland's* port list and how that accelerated its capsizing and sinking.

23 Hough, *Death of the Battleship,* pp. 34–35; 61 *Congressional Record* (5 August 1921), p. 4708.

24 Van Keuren Report; "Characteristics of Airplane Carriers," 21 February 1921, PHGB, NARA.

25 Ransom, "Battleship Meets the Airplane," p. 22; O'Neil, "Transformation," pp. 101–104. For the Washington Conference, see Kuehn, *Agents of Innovation,* pp. 2, 3, 25–27; and Clark G. Reynolds, "John H. Towers, the Morrow Board, and the Reform of the Navy's Aviation," *Military Affairs* 52, no. 2 (April 1988), pp. 78–84. For General Pershing's view, see *Report on the Results of Aviation and Ordnance Test* (Washington, D.C.: Joint Board, 18 August 1921), p. 7.

26 "Interpretation of Treaty re Modernizing Capital Ships," 17 April 1922, PHGB, NARA. See also Harold H. Sprout and Margaret Sprout, *Toward a New Order of Sea Power: American Naval Policy and the World Scene, 1918–1922* (Princeton, N.J.: Princeton Univ. Press, 1940), pp. 146, 242.

27 George Baer, *One Hundred Years of Sea Power* (Stanford, Calif.: Stanford Univ. Press, 1994), pp. 93–96. See John T. Kuehn, "The Influence of Naval Arms Limitation on U.S. Naval Innovation in the Interwar Period, 1921–1937" (Ph.D. diss., Kansas State Univ., 2007), pp. 77–80.

28 Van Keuren Report. See also Kuehn, *Agents of Innovation,* app. 1, p. 185.

29 "Interpretation of Treaty re Modernizing Capital Ships." The details of modernization allowed under the treaty were contained in the "reconstruction clause," which can be found in article 20, chap. 2, part 3, para. (d); see, again, Kuehn, *Agents of Innovation,* app. 1, pp. 193–94; Sprout and Sprout, *Toward a New Order of Sea Power,* chaps. 8–14. See also Kuehn, "The Influence of Naval Arms Limitation on U.S. Naval Innovation in the Interwar Period, 1921–1937," pp. 143–45, 147–49.

30 GB 449, 4 November 1921, PHGB, NARA. Admiral Taylor of the Bureau of Construction and Repair had in fact made this very recommendation in a letter to the General Board before the Washington Conference had even convened: "If the opportunity should be had to carry out such experiments on fairly modern ships, this . . . would be of great value."

31 Admiral Rodgers to Colonel Lucas, 22 April 1922, GB 438-1, PHGB, NARA.

32 H. B. Grow, "Bombing Tests on the 'Virginia' and 'New Jersey,'" U.S. Naval Institute *Proceedings* 49, no. 12 (December 1923).

33 Norman Friedman, *U.S. Battleships: An Illustrated Design History* (Annapolis, Md.: Naval Institute Press, 1985), p. 186.

34 Secretary of the Navy to the President, 17 November 1924, GB 438-1, PHGB, NARA. Presidential approval was attached, bearing the same date.

35 Kuehn, *Agents of Innovation,* p. 75.

36 Alan D. Zimm, "The U.S.N.'s Flight Deck Cruiser," *Warship International* 16, no. 3 (1979), p. 231. Zimm argues that this dedication, at least in 1930, was perfectly understandable, given the defensive power of battleships versus the capabilities of the aircraft of that day.

37 Samuel Eliot Morison, *The Two-Ocean War* (New York: Little, Brown, 1963), pp. 60–62, 446; *USS West Virginia (BB-48),* www.usswestvirginia.org/.

VIII *"This Temporary Strategical Withdrawal"*
The Eastern Fleet's Wartime African Sojourn

ANDREW STEWART

The African coastline covers in excess of sixteen thousand miles, and at the start of the Second World War there were eighty-eight harbors around the continent that were protected from wind and sea on all sides and that were spacious enough and had sufficient depth to accommodate a considerable number of large, oceangoing vessels simultaneously. At this stage British control extended to 37 percent of the total African coastline, and within this there were a total of thirty-two of these "first-class" maritime ports, a combination of undeveloped and developed natural facilities—most notably Freetown in Sierra Leone and Port Sudan in Anglo-Egyptian Sudan—and a number that had been artificially developed, such as at Simonstown in the Union of South Africa and Takoradi on the Gold Coast.[1] Along the whole of the Indian Ocean coast from central Mozambique northward along Tanganyika and Kenya to the boundary of Italian Somaliland, there were a total of fourteen of these most highly sought-after harbors. Not including East London and Durban, once again in South Africa, there were seven others either under direct British control or within the territory of one of its Dominion partners that faced toward the Indian Ocean. Only two of these were developed, and the depth of the natural harbor in Mombasa was significantly greater than that of Dar es Salaam.

Kilindini in Swahili means "deep water" and is the name given to a harbor lying on the west coast of Mombasa Island, within a large bay; it would subsequently be accepted as the name also of the fleet base established there by the Royal Navy. It was described by one contemporary lecturer as "by far the finest harbor anywhere on the east coast of Africa from the Red Sea to Delagoa Bay."[2] The island of which it forms a part is roughly three miles long by two miles broad, an almost entirely flat mass formed from coral stone, with a European population in 1939 of not much over 1,200 people, water depths nearby of one hundred feet and more, and modern wharves that "vessels drawing 33 feet can come alongside."[3] A report published in a U.S. academic journal three years later described it as lying "within one of the finest deep-water bays of Africa, formed by the drowned lower courses of several converging minor streams."

In the summer of 1925 the British government had purchased for the sum of £350,000 from a "Major Grogan" what up until then had been the privately owned Mbaraki Pier.[4] The following year the Secretary of State for the Colonies and Dominions, Sir Leopold Amery, was asked about the cost for construction work then taking place at the port of Kilindini, to which he replied that the total figure involved in building two deepwater berths was £1,320,957, a figure that did not include the outlay for the major's wharf.[5] By way of comparison, during a much later debate in the House of Commons it was confirmed that the total expenditure on the construction and equipping of Singapore as a naval base and fortress up until the outbreak of hostilities in September 1939 was approximately £18,234,000. Of this figure £3,750,000 had come in the form of grants or gifts from New Zealand, Hong Kong, the Federated Malay States, and the sultan of Johore, and the Straits Settlements government had presented as a gift the site on which the base was built, but even so the Kilindini base was clearly much the cheaper option![6]

As a later detailed review would note, a small military naval base was established at Kilindini at the outbreak of the Second World War, but initially "the calls upon it had been small and well within its resources." These demands entailed the provision of "a measure of" protection for convoys and escorts using the port, along with the maintenance of an examination service, a port war signal station, and a small number of minesweepers and patrol vessels. The coast defenses consisted of just two six-inch coastal guns. There were no antiaircraft weapons, although trenches had been dug against Italian air raids and in some parts of the town bomb and splinter barricades had been constructed. There had also been an air-raid protection system organized and a partial blackout was in force. The shortcomings that existed were, however, made up for by the fact that as a harbor Kilindini had "admirable natural protection." It has a clear view to seaward and a reef that was almost awash at low water and narrowed the approach, making the entrance extremely hazardous to both underwater and surface craft except in daylight, or with navigational aids.[7]

Questions about Kilindini's wartime role had first arisen in February 1940, but at this stage the principal interest seemed to lie not so much in what naval role, however limited, Kenya could play but in who would bear the cost.[8] A detailed investigation was begun by the Admiralty, by sending the commanding officer of HMS *Gloucester* to East Africa to produce a detailed review of how much money was being spent at Kilindini and who should pay—the Kenyan government, the Colonial Office, or the Admiralty.[9] Rear Adm. Ralph Leatham, Commander in Chief, East Indies Station, subsequently reviewing the findings, reminded those involved that all expenditure on the Kenya Royal Naval Volunteer Reserve "is primarily the concern of the respective governments."[10] Concluding with a reminder that the need for economy was more urgent than ever, he was prepared to accept that if the base could not "manage without a female typist and cannot obtain an efficient one for less than £20 a month, I approve this rate of wages."

In the months that followed, war came to East Africa, as the Italian leader, Benito Mussolini, decided the time was opportune to join his Axis partner while there were still spoils to be taken. His attack succeeded in capturing British Somaliland—the empire's first territorial loss—but quickly turned into one of the war's less frequently discussed military disasters. A large Italian naval force played little meaningful role in the proceedings, and when the British Commonwealth force eventually captured the important harbor at Massawa it was littered with scuttled vessels.[11] With the Italian threat removed, attention turned to the growing danger in the Indian Ocean, but there was scant reason to believe that Kilindini's role would be any greater than providing a continuing harbor for convoys and affording limited regional maritime protection. The sudden and tumultuous Japanese thrust that began in December 1941 changed this position dramatically. The Eastern Fleet had been formally constituted that month, amalgamating the East Indies Squadron and the China Squadron, and within three months it had been flushed from its main base in Singapore to Trincomalee in Ceylon, with Adm. Sir James Somerville in command—the fleet's third commander since the initial Japanese attack.[12]

The fleet that Somerville had inherited, the largest yet assembled by the Royal Navy during the war, was split into two tactical units, a fast Force A, under his own command, and a slower Force B. While it might have been large in size—five battleships, three aircraft carriers, seven cruisers, and fourteen destroyers—there was much about this fleet that was cause for concern. When he had taken command he signaled his forces, "So this is the Eastern Fleet. Well never mind. There's many a good tune played on an old fiddle."[13] Privately, he compared his position to that of his "brother Commanders-in-Chief" in the Home and Mediterranean Stations, who were "riding comfortably in the Rolls Royces" while he was "pushing a broken-down Ford with a flat tyre."[14] Four of the battleships were the First World War R-class ships, "old, slow and short of endurance"; one of the carriers, HMS *Hermes*, was small and elderly, while the other two had air and naval crews that lacked training and battle experience.[15] Four of the destroyers (of their own "R class") were also of World War I vintage. The official naval historian would describe the Eastern Fleet as "a force which on paper looked substantial" while noting a battleship group that was possibly "more of a liability than an asset," a weak air element, a lack of shore-based long-range reconnaissance aircraft, the almost complete absence of shore-based air striking forces, and sparsely prepared and equipped main bases.[16] This did not take into account the impact of the first two weeks of April 1942, when Vice Admiral Chuichi Nagumo's Striking Force attacked and destroyed various vessels in and around the waters of Ceylon.[17]

Somerville was a tonic for the Eastern Fleet—"he was bold, witty and outspoken, an admiral with the common touch and, at times, a somewhat Rabelaisian turn of humour,"—but the task facing him was a significant one.[18] His force was intended to deter the Japanese from undertaking large-scale and protracted operations in the Indian Ocean; it was subsequently established that the Imperial Japanese Navy's war plans never contained any provision for such operations, merely for raids, but this was not known at the time.[19] Adm. Sir Dudley Pound, the First Sea Lord, had warned Prime Minister Winston Churchill on 8 March 1942 that Ceylon itself was now also threatened and could succumb in the same way as Malaya had. Its loss would "undermine our whole strategic position in the Middle as well as the Far East."[20] He was not alone in his assessment, and intelligence indicated that an attack on the island could be expected on or about 1 April. Stephen Roskill, in his official history, argues that the decision to include the elderly R-class battleships indicated that the Naval Staff back in Whitehall had failed to realize the true nature of the threat to Ceylon.[21] The eventual Japanese attack on Colombo and raid on Trincomalee, along with the sinking of *Hermes* and a number of other vessels, was the net outcome—one that left Somerville in no doubt that his fleet could not be protected in those waters against an opponent who could bring devastating air attacks to bear. With the secretly prepared base at Addu Atoll, the southernmost atoll of the Maldives—known as Port T—not yet deemed safe, he had little choice other than to send the slower force to its East African redoubt while the faster one steamed to Bombay. He was forced to "lie low in one sense but be pretty active in another—keep the old tarts out of the picture and roar about with the others."[22]

A key individual in the Eastern Fleet was Acting Vice Adm. Sir Algernon Willis, who in February 1942 had transferred to HMS *Resolution* as Vice Admiral Commanding 3rd Battle Squadron and Somerville's second in command. He had previously been Commander in Chief, South Atlantic, with responsibility for convoys passing through that area to the Middle East and for operations against enemy submarines and ocean raiders; before that he had been chief of staff for nearly two years to Commander in Chief, Mediterranean. He would retain this new position for a little over a year before being called back to the Mediterranean, where he would be confirmed in the rank of vice admiral and placed in command of Force H, which would operate in the western basin and prevent the Italian fleet from interfering with the landings in North Africa, Sicily, and Salerno. An obituary by the renowned British airpower historian Dr. Noble Frankland would be generous in its praise, describing him as "one of the least conspicuous and most remarkable figures in our recent naval history," an officer who "seemed indeed always to reach the right decision, though often, it might be argued, for the wrong reasons," but who possessed "a remarkably incisive intelligence and an instinctive judgment which but seldom failed."[23] These were traits that he made good use of throughout his command in East Africa.

Willis was to take charge of "the old tarts," his force consisting of the four R-class destroyers, supported by a number of the more modern destroyers and four cruisers.[24] Somerville thought highly of his deputy—"absolute first class as my second in command and I couldn't have a better one"—and he was soon content to leave the fleet's training to him and his deputies while he focused on the wider issues.[25] Somerville's immediate consideration would be to protect what was known as the "WS" series of fast military convoys, which carried troops and equipment to the Middle East and India.[26] As he wrote back to the Admiralty and Vice Adm. Henry Moore, the vice chief of the Naval Staff, the battle of the Indian Ocean was going to be "primarily a *CARRIER* one, for until the enemy's carriers can be reduced, the battleships can only act as a protective force for ours and not a very effective one until we get something like parity in the air over the sea." This meant that there was little option other than to make a "temporary strategical withdrawal to the west—for it can be called no less—[which] is depressing but very necessary until we can be reinforced."[27] His more immediate task, however, was to prepare for a possible Japanese thrust, which could potentially come as far as the East African littoral.

All ports along the coast were to be defended, since if even one were captured Japanese forces could potentially land and then attempt to seize the larger ports from the landward side. The scale of the attack was initially considered to be one Japanese carrier launching thirty aircraft, a brief bombardment, and small landing forces conducting raids. In the first week of April 1942 this was revised "in light of recent developments Far East." The new estimates were of up to 150–200 carrier-borne aircraft operating from three or four carriers supported by a brief bombardment by fourteen-inch battleships or similar vessels, along with attacks by torpedo and minelaying craft. Accompanying this, it was estimated, would be a force of approximately one brigade equipped to seize and hold a lightly defended base or to "smash and burn facilities."[28] Detailed notes were therefore prepared on all of the strategic coastal positions, but given the scarcity of resources available it was recognized that it would not be possible to defend all of the six hundred miles of British-held coastline. This conclusion was in part based on the absence of coastal railway or road communications, added to which were lessons learned from the Far East campaign that suggested that dispersing what little strength was to hand would be a mistake. As a result it was decided that coastal and antiaircraft guns could be sent to Zanzibar and Berbera, and some equipment would go to the port of Tanga in Tanganyika (considered as a "borderline" risk, despite an Anglo-Indian force having selected it for an amphibious operation in 1914), but Mogadishu and Kismayu in the former Italian Somaliland would have to be left undefended.

In all of the planning Kilindini was held to be "undoubtedly the primary port," for it would not be possible without it "to maintain a force of any size" nor conduct "a defensive campaign of any magnitude." Hence it was agreed that Kilindini would receive the greatest share of resources and become a temporary base for the Eastern Fleet, with the neighboring island of Zanzibar to act as an overflow.[29] It was not just a potential dockyard and repair facility but also a convoy assembly and commercial port. There were also the oil fuel depot, ammunition storage, and aerodrome at Port Reitz, not to mention the cable station. The base could accommodate six capital ships or carriers, two ten-thousand-ton cruisers, and any small number of cruisers and destroyers; by June the total for the largest possible ships had grown by one, with the caveat that if extra buoys and moorings were laid a further four could be accommodated and that Mombasa Old Port could take a flotilla of destroyers in an emergency.[30] But as one contemporary commentator noted, with only small resources and no town of any appreciable size in the vicinity, the process of redevelopment "involved much expansion and elaboration."[31] The defenses remained fairly desperate, however—there still being no antiaircraft weapons, aside from some light machine guns, and only two six-inch coastal defense guns. The permanent garrison consisted of the 16th Battalion of the King's African Rifles, the Mombasa Company of the Kenya Defence Force, and the troops manning the coastal guns. It was hoped that two more six-inch guns would become available during the summer, as well as two 75-mm guns intended to counter smaller vessels.[32]

One American visitor during this period was quoted as referring to Mombasa as "two streets and a hostile population." Still, it was bound for here that the bulk of the commander in chief's staff departed from Colombo, sailing on board HMS *Alaunia* on 24 April 1942 and arriving at Kilindini nine days later, a total of 229 people, which included forty-three officers and a number of women and children. The latter caused special difficulties, as all civilians not employed in essential war work had been evacuated from Mombasa. Some local residents were aggrieved that the new arrivals were allowed to stay when their own family members had not been; tensions were not improved when the naval officers and these "nonessentials" were billeted in three hotels that had been retained exclusively for their use. This relatively small number of additional personnel placed a premium on all other accommodation and created a gulf not just with respect to the local populace but with the previously incumbent naval staff as well. This was the position when on 7 May the commander in chief himself arrived, along with a large proportion of the Eastern Fleet carrying about fifteen thousand officers and men. For the most senior officers, including Admiral Somerville, there was a rather opulent residence; they were given permission by the governor of Kenya to use Government House.

For the remainder of the fleet staff, though, the position was initially fairly dire, with a chronic shortage of accommodation and office space. A decision taken to increase the building program at the base dramatically was entirely justified. Indeed with provision needed on shore for 1,500 personnel, it appears that the possibility was even considered of requisitioning accommodation until new quarters could be constructed—in short, forcibly evacuating the island's civilian population. The suggestion had already been made that the base be effectively turned into a closed military zone. In late April, Gen. Sir William Platt, General Commanding Officer in Chief East Africa, informed the authorities in London that in light of the reports of what had happened in Singapore he and Willis had "agreed that certain categories of useless mouths should be compulsorily removed from Mombasa Island and mainland immediately adjacent now while there is yet time."[33] The proposal instantly secured Churchill's personal endorsement, but as events changed it was not implemented, and in mid-June it was canceled.[34]

In the meantime, emergency accommodation for eight hundred European and seven hundred native dockyard workers was built rapidly, but it was of "a very temporary nature." Most of the sleeping or living huts were built from what appeared to be stone walls but were in fact sheets of Hessian (jute-based cloth, like burlap) plastered on both sides with cement wash, while the roofs were made of corrugated iron or palm thatch. Meanwhile exceptions continued to be made for more "important" arrivals. From late April 1942 an eclectic collection of linguists, analysts, cryptanalysts, wireless operators, and career diplomats was housed in a requisitioned Indian school on the island's rocky northern shore. Attached to the Eastern Fleet's Chief of Intelligence Staff, this small group, based in HMS *Alidina*, was at the forefront of efforts to crack Japanese codes, an operation that had begun at the famed Bletchley Park near London.[35]

The huge number of arrivals created varied social and cultural pressures. Most obviously, considerable strains were placed on the often already expensive supplies, and shortages became common. Those arriving from Ceylon noted that the cost of living was much higher than that in Colombo, commodities generally being 30 percent more expensive. The quantity, and indeed quality, of the local bread available was another cause for complaint; maize meal was having to be mixed with the limited supplies of wheat flour. Perhaps of greatest importance for many was the fact that there were just two local breweries, and they were not able to keep up with demand. The situation later improved with the arrival of supplies of Canadian beer, but there were many cases "of drunkenness and unruly behavior in the streets" as ratings overcame the shortages by drinking neat spirits, not just imported varieties but also the more potent locally brewed version. With no brothels, there were a number of private houses where "men are invited in by the 'ladies,'" most of whom were half-caste Indians or Goans. As a report noted, this meant that "venereal disease is prevalent and on the increase." One positive factor was the African natives, who were described as "simple, docile and easy to govern," particularly as some of them were apt to get drunk on palm wine and liked to smoke bhang, the local name for hashish.[36]

Accounts provided by some people based there at the time reveal it to have been a surprisingly stressful experience. A brewery worker turned naval cook serving on the battleship HMS *Warspite* recorded in his diary that being alongside at Kilindini was "a rather humdrum existence" and that life was "a little less strained when the ships were at sea." Even the latter, however, was not apparently the most interesting sort of activity, with "its sweeps out into the Indian Ocean forever exercising, shooting at targets, and the carriers carrying out dummy air attacks on the ships." Indeed the routine of training, the cramped living conditions, and the generally oppressive heat made him glad when orders came to move back to the Mediterranean.[37] A local policeman who was official censor when the Eastern Fleet arrived in Kilindini wrote of this period, "There were more than 150 Royal naval vessels of all sizes and unusual descriptions anchored deep into Port Reitz and around Port Tudor. At one time we had seven Admirals and two Generals, all with their staff, on the Island. Mombasa was really 'Blood Pressure Corner.' There were high ranking officers everywhere you went and you marched down the main road with your arm extended at a permanent salute."[38]

Cdre. C. G. Stuart had arrived in Kilindini in 12 May 1942 to take command of the base; Somerville had almost instantly promoted him to rear admiral and appointed him as Flag Officer, East Africa and Zanzibar. Writing back to the Admiralty he reported that he had found that the site suffered "from many defects," the main one of which was "the lack of alongside deep water wharfage."[39] There were many other difficulties too, such as a lack of sufficient telephone equipment, not enough officers and ratings or accommodation for them, and a lack even of small craft for general port duties. He wished to impress upon the Admiralty the difficulties of trying to establish a base on an island of about five and a half square miles that had a population of about fifty thousand people. All officers who were to be sent to the base should, he urged, be "reasonably young and energetic; physically fit for the tropics and temperate in their habits." Indeed, the best men were needed and not the "leftovers" if the base were to "assume the importance that is apparently intended." Another key recommendation in his lengthy report was that though the skilled European labor that it proposed be sent should all be civilians, either volunteer or conscripted, they should be "enrolled in the Navy in some appropriate rating and be subject to naval discipline." There were many other problems, "too numerous to mention," but the base staff were "not downhearted." The new commander's assessment, in fact, finished on a most positive note, assuring the authorities in London that the site could be adapted within a reasonably short time following the arrival of a fleet repair ship, skilled workers, and equipment. If the

Admiralty were committed to the idea it would in his view be possible to establish an effective facility on the East African coast.

By the first week of August there was positive news also from Willis, who was able to write Somerville that "the unlocated fleet policy" had proved more successful than he had thought possible back in the dark days of April.[40] He was realistic, though, in his assessment. Despite American efforts in the Pacific, which had "assisted very materially" (the victories at Midway and in the Coral Sea had been won that spring and summer, and the Solomons campaign was about to begin), he did not believe his forces were yet in a position to contain the Japanese main fleet. The Eastern Fleet was still not strong enough to maintain a concentrated covering force and provide ocean escorts for convoys in the face of an attack by "much more than a single cruiser or a couple of armed merchant cruisers." The dilemma with which they were now faced was "the eternal conflict between 'cover,' 'patrol and search,' and 'escort.'" He did not believe that hunting groups would be an effective use of resources, as there was a vast area to cover and results were produced only when there was "some advance information of a raider's intentions." Interestingly, Willis was clearly within the select group of those who were in receipt of intelligence from the ULTRA source, as he suggested that only with "really firm intelligence" such as these signals provided would hunting groups be worth undertaking. His overall conclusion was that at this stage it would not be worth breaking up the "limited covering force in order to strengthen convoy escorts." In short, until such time as his strength improved or the Japanese maritime forces were weakened the British strategy needed to remain an entirely defensive one.

Despite the continuing weakness of the Eastern Fleet's position, the Admiralty was still working on the premise as late as December 1942 that it would ultimately return to Ceylon. The date when this would take place would depend on three "unknowns": the strategic situation; the development of base facilities, particularly defenses, in Ceylon; and, critically, the reinforcement of the Eastern Fleet to enable it to take the offensive.[41] Capt. Donald Macintyre, in his biography of Somerville, wonders about the impact on "so vigorous and forceful an Admiral" of having to keep his force safe by, in effect, deliberately avoiding any naval confrontation with the Japanese.[42] His stay in Government House in Mombasa provided him an opportunity for some measure of rest after an intensive period at sea. Indeed he himself noted that his time ashore "was a welcome change from the hot and cramped quarters on *Warspite*'s bridge and the monotonous ocean day after day."[43] For the admiral, the new base was sufficiently pleasant to allow him "to get the physical exercise he found so necessary," with long daily tramps, bathing, and early-morning rowing in a small boat. It could be said that the Eastern Fleet commander remained personally as active as he could, but the approach he was forced to adopt for his command has perhaps quite rightly been termed "a policy of masterly inactivity."[44] There were, however, more aggressive diversions, such as when in late May 1942 he departed with the fast portion of his fleet for Colombo, carried out a diversionary cruise toward the Andamans, returned to Colombo, and then got back to Kilindini by the end of August. It is far from clear how he would have fared if he had encountered any sizable Japanese opposition, but the cruise offered his force valuable training and experience.[45]

Throughout the second part of 1942 and into the following year, the Eastern Fleet was steadily depleted to provide ships for other theaters, leaving barely enough ships to escort the vital Cape–Suez and Indian Ocean convoys. Indeed, the fleet's status quickly became that of "a trade protection Force," while all efforts continued in the preparation of bases to support the anticipated future offensives back across the Indian Ocean.[46] In the first week of November the admiral and his staff transferred to the cruiser HMS *Birmingham* for passage to Bombay and conferences in New Delhi with Gen. Sir Archibald Wavell, his fellow commander in chief, before flying back to London to meet with Churchill. He was back in Mombasa on 30 December and spent another month at the African base. Further travels followed, culminating in a return to South Africa and one last stop at Kilindini. This marked the end of what his biographer termed a period of "constant shifting from ship to ship and to aircraft," as a final recall home to England followed.[47]

The base he left behind had now become a major hub of maritime activity; where the average number of ships using the port in peacetime had been about forty monthly, in wartime this figure had quickly grown to about a hundred.[48] East African waters, however, continued to pose a threat to the Allied war effort. As late as March 1944 a suspected Japanese submarine was detected operating near the port; two months later a German U-boat became stranded in the Gulf of Aden, and salvage crews were dispatched from Kilindini to recover what equipment they could.[49] Throughout August 1944 there were multiple sinkings of Allied merchant shipping between Mombasa and the Mozambique Channel. A long search of the area was conducted, with the Flag Officer, East Africa taking charge. His conclusion was that three enemy submarines were operating there; a task force was deployed to conduct a more extensive search, although this proved fruitless.[50] The sinking of a Greek vessel in the first week of September led to a note in the fleet's war diary that it seemed likely the submarine involved had "passed close to Kilindini."[51] This was the last such recorded incident. By May 1945 all ships traveling from Durban north were officially doing so unescorted. In reality the threat in these waters had ceased some months before.

With his reference to the fleet-in-being strategy, Sir Julian Corbett emphasized that its essence is "mobility and an untiring aggressive spirit rather than rest and resistance." The fleet has to be kept "actively in being—not merely in existence, but in active and vigorous life."[52] This was critically important for Somerville and Willis, in light of the forces available to them. According to one commentator the fleet they commanded was no match for the Japanese Combined Fleet in the spring of 1942; it was "a rag-bag of a fleet" that was "out-paced and out-gunned on the surface, completely outmatched in the air."[53] The British commanders sought to use what resources they had to the best of their abilities, but it is probably for the best that "the old tarts" never actually found themselves tested by the might of the Imperial Japanese Navy. As for the British base at Kilindini, it ultimately provided an acceptable bolt-hole at a time when there were few alternative options. When the tide of war turned in favor of the Allies, the rationale for its development was reduced. The flirtation with the idea that it might become a major naval base was very much, therefore, a reactive response to a previously unimaginable and humiliating maritime defeat. It did, however, provide a pleasant break for already war-wearied commanders and new drinking opportunities on tropical beaches for ordinary members of the Royal Navy.

NOTES All archival sources are from The National Archives, Kew, unless otherwise stated.

1 George F. Deasy, "The Harbors of Africa," *Economic Geography* 18, no. 4 (October 1942), pp. 325–27.

2 Maj. Sir Humphrey Leggett, "The British East African Territories and Their Strategical Implications," Overseas Empire Transmission, 19 June 1940, in *Journal of the Royal African Society* 39, no. 156 (July 1940), p. 206.

3 Deasy, "Harbors of Africa," pp. 334, 327; Mombasa's depth was recorded at thirty-three feet, while its neighbor was only twenty feet deep; Port Sudan was the deepest port, at some sixty-three feet.

4 "Control of Kilindini Harbour," *Times,* 5 August 1925, p. 14.

5 "Question by Sir F. Wise and Colonel Wedgwood, House of Commons Debate," 8 March 1926, Hansard, vol. 192, c1889.

6 "Question by Sir J. Power," House of Commons Debate, 24 June 1942, Hansard, vol. 380, cc1992-3W. Using "Purchasing Power of British Pounds from 1264 to Present," *MeasuringWorth,*

eh.net/hmit/ppowerbp/, and the retail price index and data for 2008, the approximate adjusted cost for the purchase and construction of the Kilindini base equates to £72,279,093.44; the cost for the Singapore facility would have been £633,301,975.08.

7 Eric Jolley, "An Account of the Development of Kilindini at Mombasa in East Africa as a Naval Base for Eastern Fleet" [hereafter "Development of Kilindini"], Mombasa, 8 October 1942, ADM1/ 13010, pp. 2–29.

8 Henry Moore (Governor of Kenya) to Malcolm MacDonald (Secretary of State for the Colonies), 6 February 1940; head of military branch, minute, 10 April 1940; both ADM116/4567.

9 "The Commanding Officer, HMS Gloucester's Report on Naval Affairs at Kilindini," 23 February 1940, ADM116/4567.

10 "Naval Expenditure in East Africa," Commander-in-Chief [hereafter C-in-C], East Indies Station, 19 June 1940, ADM116/4567.

11 Ashley Jackson, The British Empire and the Second World War (London: Hambledon, 2006), p. 281; Cristiano D'Adamo, "Regia Marina Italiana: Red Sea," Regia Marina Italiana, www.regiamarina.net/.

12 Adm. Sir Tom Phillips had been lost with HMS Repulse and HMS Prince of Wales, after which Adm. Sir Geoffrey Layton had taken command.

13 Cited in Jack Broome, Make Another Signal (London: Kimber Books, 1973).

14 Capt. Donald Macintyre, Fighting Admiral: The Life of Admiral of the Fleet Sir James Somerville (London: Evans Brothers, 1961), p. 205.

15 John Winton, The Forgotten Fleet (East Sussex, U.K.: Douglas-Boyd Books, 1989), p. 20.

16 Capt. S. W. Roskill, The War at Sea, vol. 2, The Period of Balance (London: Her Majesty's Stationery Office [hereafter HMSO], 1956), p. 23.

17 Winton, Forgotten Fleet, p. 21.

18 Ibid., p. 20.

19 Ministry of Defence [hereafter MoD], War with Japan, vol. 1, Background to the War (London: HMSO, 1995), p. 98.

20 Roskill, Period of Balance, p. 22.

21 Ibid., pp. 26–28.

22 Macintyre, Fighting Admiral, p. 22; MoD, Background to the War, vol. 1, p. 98; Roskill, Period of Balance, p. 29.

23 "Admiral of the Fleet Sir Algernon Willis," obituary, Times, 14 April 1976, p. 21; "Sir Algernon Willis," obituary, Times, 24 April 1976, p. 14.

24 Roskill, Period of Balance, pp. 23, 25.

25 Cited in Macintyre, Fighting Admiral, pp. 205, 211.

26 Lt. Cdr. Arnold Hague, RNR (Ret.), "Route to the East: The WS (Winston's Special) Convoys," 2007, Naval-History.Net.

27 Willis to Vice Adm. H[enry] R. Moore, Vice Chief of the Naval Staff, 13 April 1942, Churchill Archives Centre, Churchill College, WLLS5/5.

28 Admiralty to C-in-C East Indies, 14 March 1942, 1442A; Admiralty to C-in-C East Indies, 2 April 1942, 2016A, WO106/5213.

29 Colonel Rolleston, minute, 11 March 1942; "Note on East African Ports," n.d.; MO5, note, 12 March 1942; all WLLS5/5.

30 "Summary East Africa and Indian Ocean Islands," October 1942, WO252/856.

31 Jolley, "Development of Kilindini," p. 1; Admiral to Secretary of Admiralty, 28 September 1943, ADM1/ 13010.

32 MO5, "Note on the Defences of Mombasa," 4 March 1942, WO106/5213.

33 GOC-in-C East Africa to War Office, no. 19203, 22 April 1942, WO106/5213.

34 Admiralty to Deputy C-in-C Eastern Fleet, 11 June 1942, ADM1/12982.

35 Hugh Denham, "Bedford-Bletchley-Kilindini-Colombo," in Codebreakers: The Inside Story of Bletchley Park, ed. F. H. Hinsley and Alan Stripp (Oxford, U.K.: Oxford Univ. Press, 1993), pp. 270–72. They would eventually move with the remainder of the headquarters staff and finish the war in Colombo.

36 Jolley, "Development of Kilindini," pp. 2–29.

37 The Second World War Memoirs of R. B. Buckle (London: Imperial War Museum, ref. 11358, n.d.), pp. 88, 93.

38 "Mombasa Was Base for High-Level UK Espionage Operation," Coastweek (Kenya), n.d., available at www.coastweek.com/.

39 Rear Adm. C. Stuart to Secretary of the Admiralty, 6 June 1942, ADM1/12977. A transcribed copy of the War Diary for this period of the Eastern Fleet's activity can be found at Naval-History.Net.

40 Willis to Somerville, 6 August 1942, WLLS5/5.

41 Military Branch, minute, 2 December 1942, ADM1/ 12977.

42 Macintyre, Fighting Admiral, p. 204.

43 Ibid.

44 Winton, Forgotten Fleet, p. 32.

45 Ibid., p. 214.

46 Ibid., p. 215.

47 Ibid., p. 223.

48 "Summary East Africa and Indian Ocean Islands."

49 "War Diary: March 1944," 2 April 1944; "War Diary: May 1944," 24 June 1944; both ADM199/772.

50 "War Diary: August 1944," 9 September 1944, ADM199/772.

51 "War Diary: September 1944," 14 October 1944, ADM199/772.

52 Sir Julian Corbett, Some Principles of Maritime Strategy (1911; repr. Annapolis, Md.: Naval Institute Press, 1972), p. 214.

53 Richard Humble, Fraser of North Cape: The Life of Admiral of the Fleet Lord Fraser (1888–1981) (London: Routledge and Kegan Paul, 1983), p. 239.

IX *Escort Oilers*
The Untold Story of the Battle of the Atlantic

KENNETH P. HANSEN

ombined escort of convoy operations during the Battle of the Atlantic by the Royal Canadian Navy (RCN) and U.S. Navy was the test bed for the development of underway refueling procedures for convoy escorts. Development of the ability to refuel at sea from merchant tankers played a vitally important part in deciding the ultimate outcome. The story of how this was accomplished and of who played the key roles in it is a great and untold story of the Battle of the Atlantic.

Allied escorts suffered from an operationally limiting lack of endurance during early convoy operations. Intelligence advantages were wasted. Meanwhile, German submarines concentrated in a bottleneck area south of Iceland caused by escort meeting points. This artificial restriction heightened the likelihood of U-boats' intercepting a convoy.

The poor performance of RCN escort groups up to May 1943 has been thoroughly documented. The notion persists that for the nagging problems of Canadian escort inefficiency there was simply no alternative to increasing individual training, advancing equipment standards, and improving group operational cohesion.[1] However, besides these qualitative issues, effective use of operational logistics could increase substantially the number of warships available per convoy. Accordingly, senior U.S. Navy commanders developed the concept of underway replenishment from the bunkers of merchant tankers. The increased fuel supply for escorts allowed the use of speed for tactical advantage and the employment of evasion for operational advantage. This increase in operational and tactical flexibility has not previously been credited for the climactic events of mid-1943, when Allied naval forces were able to assume a more offensive posture in their struggle against German U-boats.

The ability to refuel escorts at sea from commercial tankers was developed principally by Capt. Paul R. Heineman, USN, commander of Task Unit 24.1.3 (known in British and Canadian literature as Escort Group A-3). Captain Heineman adapted the standard U.S. Navy abeam-refueling method and trained Canadian and British escort vessels in the practice. He also brought the potential of underway refueling to the attention of the Commander, North-Western Approaches, Adm. Sir Max Horton. Horton in turn, over the strenuous objections of his senior staff, ordered the adoption of this practice by Royal Navy escort groups.

In 1942, Escort Group A-3 included four *Wickes*-class "flush decker" destroyers: *Schenk, Babbitt, Greer,* and *Badger,* plus the Secretary-class U.S. Coast Guard cutter *Spencer.* The Canadian members included the River-class destroyer *Skeena* and the Flower-class corvettes *Arvida, Bittersweet, Collingwood, Dauphin, Mayflower, Rosthern, Trillium,* and *Wetaskinwin,* as well as the British corvettes *Dianthus, Nasturtium,* and *Wallflower.* Of these, only *Trillium,* commanded by Lt. Philip Cabell Evans, RCNR, escorted every convoy protected by the A-3 group between SC-95 in August 1942 and HX-234 in April 1943. When the group was disbanded, the Canadian units were reassigned into the new C-5 group, and the U.S. Navy and Coast Guard units were dispersed to other assignments.[2]

The destroyer USS *Babbitt* first tested experimental refueling at sea from commercial tankers in June 1942.[3] Captain Heineman recorded that the A-3 group commonly practiced refueling from commercial tankers from August 1942.[4] Lieutenant Evans has been identified as "a retired US Naval officer who joined the RCN and helped instruct it in fuelling at sea."[5] This is incorrect. Evans graduated from the U.S. Naval Academy in 1930, standing fourth in his class, and left the service in 1936.[6] He was forced to leave the U.S. Navy due to night-vision problems.[7] His professional writings make it clear that he had absolutely no practical knowledge of refueling at sea before his time in the A-3 group. Evans's experiences while in command of HMCS *Trillium* are pivotal to the history of Canadian exposure to American operational logistics practices.[8]

Evans published an unsigned article in the January 1943 issue of the *RCN Monthly Review* wherein he described his experiences refueling at sea from commercial tankers.[9] His article reports his joining Task Unit 24.1.3 in August 1942. At the first commanding officers' conference, Heineman, who is described by Samuel Eliot Morison as "one of our best escort commanders," said, "We would of course be prepared to fuel at sea by following the destroyers, using gear to be provided by USCGC *Spencer.*"[10] Evans would write of observing *Babbitt* "repeatedly fueling from one of the convoy oilers, under various sea conditions" during the escort of convoy ON-125 in early September. *Trillium* and Evans soon took their turn. As this convoy was the second that *Trillium* escorted after joining the A-3 group, Evans's comment that "energetic coaxing" from the group commander was required to get him to attempt refueling takes on special significance. Evans's description of events is both comic and startling. It was hardly a success; no fuel was transferred, two hawsers were parted, and *Trillium* lost one of its forecastle bollards.

Captain Heineman kept up the pressure on Evans and the other escort commanders to master the process, and his efforts were eventually successful. During the course of seven convoy-escort operations, ending with ON-156 in January 1943, *Trillium* and Evans became very proficient at refueling at sea. He reports having made thirteen successful refuelings out of sixteen attempts, receiving 297 tons of fuel in the process. The largest amount of fuel transferred in a single operation amounted to fifty-two tons (23 percent of total capacity), which took two hours to accomplish. The key to the entire process was learning to hold station alongside the oiler without the aid of steadying lines.[11]

The amounts of fuel involved were generally small and the rates of transfer low, because the system used a single 2.5-inch canvas "deck wash" hose. Despite the low transfer rate, a great advantage was that the fueling point was moved off the forecastle deck and into the shelter of the ship's waist, making fueling in rough weather feasible.

The difference between the Royal Navy and U.S. Navy approaches to refueling at sea soon began to have significant influences on the conduct of operations and tactics. In a technique devised around 1906, the Royal Navy employed a bronze-metallic hose, in one of three diameters: seven-inch, five-inch, or 3.5-inch.[12] For underway replenishment the receiving ship was towed astern; a capital ship being refueled would customarily tow the oiler.[13] Either a five-inch or 3.5-inch hose was suspended from a 4.5-inch wire towing hawser by a system of supporting straps known as "stirrups." In the stirrup method, destroyers and other minor warships were fitted with 3.5-inch fueling connections. Towing speed in a refueling from a battleship was normally twelve knots; the destroyer was meant to stop its engines. If a higher towing speed was ordered, the destroyer used its engines to reduce the strain on the hawser. The length of the towline was 120, 240, or 360 feet, depending on the weather.[14] The system was complex and took hours to rig.

The stirrup method was notoriously unreliable, due to the heavy and fragile bronze hoses, which were both difficult and complicated to handle. They were also prone to rupturing. The bronze hoses were reputedly tested to a pressure of 150 pounds per square inch (psi), although the normal discharge pressure from the cargo transfer pumps was routinely limited to 75 psi.[15] Even this 50 percent reduction in operating pressure was an inadequate precaution, and ruptures continued to be common. Once a breach occurred, it took hours to repair and return a hose to service. Nevertheless, despite these limitations, the astern method remained the principal means of refueling British warships at sea until the end of the Second World War, though an alongside fuel-transfer method was devised by the Royal Navy in 1937.[16]

In that alongside technique, the aircraft-recovery crane of a battleship or cruiser was used to "boom out" the hose, which was supported by a hose cradle known as a "trough." Destroyers were required to approach to as close as forty to sixty feet to the supplying ship. The trough method could be used only when weather conditions were favorable, and it required expert ship-handling skills. The depletion of a capital ship's fuel reserves and the requirement to remain on a steady course while fueling were regarded as major tactical limitations. The trough method has been claimed erroneously as the precursor of the modern abeam method of refueling at sea.[17] Although useful, this alongside system was always regarded as a secondary method of providing a small "top-up" of fuel to minor warships; it was not used to refuel large warships. The 3.5-inch hose restricted the fuel transfer rate to between eighty to a hundred tons per hour.[18]

An uncelebrated outcome of the famous "*Bismarck* chase" had enormous implications for Allied replenishment operations. After *Bismarck* was sunk, the Royal Navy used decoded German naval signals to intercept the German network of nine widely dispersed supply ships supporting the battleship's sortie, known as Operation RHINE, plus the blockade-runner *Elbe*.[19] Two captured vessels, the auxiliary tankers *Gonzenheim* and *Lothringen,* carried replenishment equipment completely unlike that in their British or American counterparts.[20]

German fuel hoses were made of reinforced rubber with threaded aluminum end fittings that allowed the hoses to be made buoyant by filling with air. Whether used by replenishment ships or U-tankers, the hoses were either boomed out or simply floated down to attendant warships. This made simultaneous replenishment of several ships or submarines possible, even under quite adverse conditions. British analysts immediately recognized the utility of the German hoses, and plans were made to copy and produce them for Royal Navy use for astern replenishment. The hose could now be simply floated astern of the oilers and picked up by the trailing warship. The RFA (i.e., Royal Fleet Auxiliary) *Eaglesdale* conducted trials in March 1942.[21] Until that time, it was considered that refueling using the stirrup method in anything but the calmest conditions was impossible.

The alongside, or abeam, method advocated by Heineman and by Evans in his 1943 article required a shorter length of canvas hose (250 feet) than the astern method, with its floating hose (550 to 600 feet), and instead of a specially manufactured rubber hose, the hose was made of readily obtainable canvas. While Evans acknowledged that fueling from astern, either by the stirrup method or a floating hose, was recommended in the standard Admiralty reference (CB 4080), he pointed out that rubber hoses were simply not available and that manila for towing hawsers was in short supply. Quite sarcastically, Evans wrote in his article, "We are chiefly interested in getting our fuel before the war ends." He described the equipment needed for the American system as, in contrast to either astern method, "simple, cheap and easily obtainable."[22]

Although the astern method of refueling was regarded as easier than the alongside method by the Royal Navy, Canadian escorts had significant difficulty with using it. The archival records are full of reports concerning the ineptitude of RCN escorts at refueling and a plethora of incidents involving ruptured fuel hoses or parted hawsers. During the escort of convoy SC-124, HMCS *Mayflower* inappropriately attempted a refueling from astern of the American escort oiler *Chester O. Swain,* despite the fact the tanker was fitted only for alongside refueling with canvas hoses. After parting the tanker's only manila hawser, *Mayflower* fouled its own screw during an ill-advised attempt to pass a 10.5-inch hawser to the oiler.[23] Another corvette from Escort Group C-3, HMCS *Eyebright,* was detached from the convoy to tow *Mayflower* to Londonderry. Quite late into the war, Canadian escorts were accused of being "ignorant of the instructions, . . . not following instructions from the escort oiler, . . . being unable to keep station, . . . being unfamiliar with the transfer [process], . . . and not having equipment ready."[24]

In December 1943, Capt. M. F. Wilson of the Admiralty Trade Division wrote to Rear Adm. Leonard W. Murray, RCN, commander of the Northwest Atlantic Area, in an attempt to provide advice on Canadian refueling problems.[25] The problem in the RCN seemed to be that many commanding officers did not appreciate that the manila line was not intended to be used as a towline, as had been done (though with wire hawsers) before the war using the stirrup method. Canadian warships continued generally to ignore procedures laid down in the Admiralty Book of Reference BR 853, *Procedure for Oiling at Sea by the Buoyant Hose Method,* a fact that drew the ire of Captain Wilson and eventually of the Canadian Naval Board. A letter from the secretary of the board to Admiral Murray stated, "The main cause of misunderstanding is as you say faulty communication, and the need for so much communication is very largely due to the BR either not being studied sufficiently or not being complied with."[26] Despite this prodding, Admiral Murray was unable to effect significant improvement and the complexities of the astern refueling method continued to challenge the seamanship skills of his neophyte commanding officers.

Damage to refueling gear became so widespread that on 21 January 1944 Admiral Murray signaled, "As the services of escort oilers may be vital to the ocean escorts, ships of the Naval Escort Force are not to refuel in SC or HX convoys [i.e., eastbound to the United Kingdom] except in cases of absolute necessity."[27] Two days later, the Admiralty placed further restrictions on Canadian escorts: "Difficulty is being found in maintaining necessary minimum number of escort oilers with convoy and risk of damaging equipment at outset of voyage is not acceptable. Request that oiling at sea by western local escorts be temporarily restricted to ON [westbound from the United Kingdom] convoys."[28] With no formalized training process and few opportunities to practice at sea, it was inevitable that the RCN's difficulties would continue to plague the escort groups and limit their endurance. Not all of the problems experienced by the RCN, however, related to poor seamanship skills and lack of experience. The nature of their ships' propulsion systems also helped to make refueling at sea difficult.

Part of the reason for Canadian problems in refueling astern was the reciprocating machinery in minor warships. The commanding officer of the Flower-class corvette HMCS *Sackville,* Acting Lt. Cdr. A. H. Ankin, RCNVR, reported that his ship took a long time to respond to engine orders, which often caused the corvette to put heavy strain on the steadying line.[29] Ankin advocated the use of a ten-inch manila hawser to prevent damage to the fueling hose. U.S. Navy ships and Coast Guard cutters, plus the Royal Navy's destroyers and most its sloops, were turbine powered, which gave them much more precise speed control.

Evans's article about refueling at sea concluded with an impassioned plea for other commanding officers, escort group commanders, and "higher authorities ashore" to consider adopting the alongside method of refueling as standard practice.[30] Evans recommended that one to three oilers be assigned to each convoy and that escort group commanders plan for fueling their escorts at sea "as frequently as conditions permit." He exhorted his fellow captains to try the alongside method and to be persistent: "We found the first ten times were the worst." Evans also hinted at the widespread resistance in the RCN to the idea: "Everyone from your No. 1 [i.e., first lieutenant] will tell you that it simply *can't be done.* Oh no? *It works!*" [emphasis original]. His article was a last-ditch effort to get his experiences out to a wider audience.

Evans had submitted an earlier formal report, dated 16 November 1942, through his chain of command.[31] He had completed five convoy operations since his first exposure to fueling at sea during convoy ON-125. In his report, Evans described the process in detail, and in a notably less ironic manner than his later article. He reported that the use of steadying ropes was a hindrance rather than a help and that it was possible to maintain position near a tanker at distances of twenty-five to seventy-five feet solely by the use of rudder and the engine. He asserted confidently that the operation was not difficult, "even in moderately rough weather. The worst condition is that of a following or a quartering sea."

There is no record of an official reply to Evans's report, but the document itself bears a marginal note from Capt. Horatio N. Lay, Director of Plans at Naval Staff Headquarters: "Never heard of this before—obsolete anyway on account of buoyant hose astern method." Lay's offhanded condemnation is particularly revealing as he was regarded as the only headquarters staff officer with recent seagoing experience.[32] He obviously did not recognize the superiority of the alongside method and was not prepared to consider the possibility that the American method could be used by Canadian warships, despite strong evidence to the contrary.

The first Canadian response to the knowledge that American escorts were experimenting with refueling alongside from convoy tankers was to ask the Admiralty for direction. A letter on refueling at sea from the secretary of the Naval Board was sent to the secretary of the Board of Admiralty on 26 August 1942. The Canadian letter indicated that it was understood that refueling at sea from a tanker in convoy could considerably increase the endurance of warships.[33] The letter admitted openly that the members of the Naval Board were "not completely aware of the latest methods developed for oiling small craft at sea." It suggested the provision of sets of refueling gear, specifically bronze-metallic hoses, to selected tankers in convoys.

On 9 September, a message from Rear Adm. Roland M. Brainard, Commander, Task Force 24, which was addressed to all American, British, and Canadian naval high command authorities, was the first important official warning on the issue of inadequate escort endurance. Brainard forecast escorts having to leave convoys due to fuel shortages and anticipated that the situation would worsen due to adverse weather. He took the unprecedented step of recommending a tanker be designated and appropriately equipped for refueling escorts.[34] Adm. Ernest J. King, the U.S. Chief of Naval Operations, added his support to Admiral Brainard's recommendation in a message sent on 11 September. He recognized the current endurance difficulties and endorsed the advantages of the proposal from Brainard. "As an immediate palliative," King suggested that the current western meeting point should be moved as far eastward as possible.[35] This was a not-too-subtle suggestion that the problem was largely British in origin. It was not until 7 October that Canadian Naval Staff Headquarters sent a message to the Admiralty with a direct request for guidance.[36] The Admiralty did not reply until 21 October and then said only, "Detailed reply is being forwarded by air."[37]

The Admiralty reply came in a letter dated 29 October. It assured the RCN that arrangements were being made for tankers to sail in convoys to and from New York for oiling escorts at sea "as far as may be found practicable." It went on to describe the trough, or alongside, method as "efficient in calm weather" and the stirrup (astern with bronze-metallic hose) and "derrick" (astern with floating rubber hose) methods as "designed for any weather when men can work on the forecastle of an escort vessel."[38] British reluctance to endorse the concept of refueling at sea is quite evident from the letter's characterization of the alongside method and obvious preference for the two astern methods. However, the stipulated limitation of ability to work on the forecastle of a small escort restricted refueling operations to fair conditions not often encountered in the North Atlantic.

An attachment to the Admiralty letter of 29 October was entitled "Guidance for Masters of Commercial Tankers Employed on Escort Fuelling Service in the Use of Buoyant Rubber Oil Hose by Boom Method."[39] In it, masters of escort oilers were particularly entreated to ensure that the greatest care was taken when using either rubber hoses or manila hawsers. It emphasized that the safety of the convoy and its escorts depended largely on the efficiency of the tanker selected for this important duty. The document equated the safety of the tanker, its equipment, and its personnel to that of the whole convoy. These important cautions soon proved prophetic.

On 6 November 1942, the Admiralty designated what must have been one of the first escort oilers—*British Valour,* which departed with convoy ONS-144 on 15 November. It was fitted with the floating-hose system and was loaded with approximately six hundred tons of fuel oil. *British Valour* was ordered to load a full cargo of fuel oil in New York and return with the first available homeward convoy. It would be available for fueling escorts at sea during both the outward and homeward voyages.[40]

By 21 November the Admiralty was able to signal that five tankers fitted with buoyant hose equipment for fueling over the stern were available for North Atlantic convoys. Four more were in the process of being converted, and other suitable candidates were being sought, with a view to providing sufficient tankers to cover all North Atlantic convoys. British escorts and tankers were to be supplied with Confidential Book 4080(42), *Oiling at Sea Instructions.*[41] The disagreement between American and British authorities over the most suitable method of fueling at sea now began to pick up energy.

An Admiralty message declared that canvas hose had been found to be "unsuitable repetition unsuitable," since it became porous after exposure to fuel oil and the rate of fueling by the 2.5-inch hose was too slow. The Admiralty claimed that American escorts had on several occasions been fueled by the British five-inch buoyant hose, and "no difficulties [had been] reported." The signal suggested that astern refueling become the standard method and that "the alongside trough method should be fitted in tankers as subsidiary."[42] A reply from the U.S. Navy was soon received.

Despite the Admiralty's assurances, American naval authorities were satisfied neither with the rate of arrival of British-provided escort oilers nor with adoption of the astern refueling method as standard practice. In an attempt to press their views with Royal Navy authorities, a meeting was organized for 21 December 1942 at Derby House, Londonderry, headquarters of Western Approaches Command. The subject was promulgated simply as "Oiling at Sea." Captain Heineman arrived on 17 December, after serving as escort commander for convoy SC-111. Heineman was well armed with information and experience, having used the convoy's passage to conduct operational experiments.

During the passage of SC-111, Task Unit 24.1.3 had refueled eleven times from two oilers: *British Progress* (seven times) and *Vacuum* (four times). Neither of these tankers had been designated officially as an escort oiler, nor had either been equipped with five-inch floating hoses. The regularly assigned escort oiler for SC-111 had put into Halifax for repairs and had not made the passage. The alongside method of fueling had been used, without towing lines. All fueling hoses, flanges, clamps, and slips had been provided by the American escorts and passed to the tankers while at sea. Standard 2.5-inch canvas deck-wash hose in fifty-foot lengths with screw couplings had been used; each tanker had been provided with 250 feet. A system of clips to support the hose from a derrick-supported carrying line had been improvised by *British Progress* and proved to be quite advantageous.[43] At the meeting, Captain Heineman tabled a letter from Capt. A. Kenney, master of *British Progress,* detailing which ships had received the 242 tons of fuel transferred: HMCS *Trillium,* eighty-three tons; USS *Badger,* sixty-two tons; HMCS *Rosthern,* forty-four tons; HMCS *Dauphine,* forty-two tons; and HMS *Wanderer,* eleven tons. The only other ship in Task Unit 24.1.3 was *Spencer,* Heineman's flagship, which had not required fuel, because of its superlative endurance. Captain Kenney's letter concluded that in his opinion the alongside method was the best for fueling small escorts at sea. It also recommended that the fuel oil be heated to one hundred degrees Fahrenheit, to ease the pumping process.[44]

A report of proceedings by HMS *Wanderer,* which had had the least success in fueling alongside, made its way to the Canadian Naval Board, by way of the Captain for Destroyers in Newfoundland, Capt. Harold T. Grant, RCN. *Wanderer* had made three attempts at alongside refueling. Its captain, Lt. Cdr. D. H. P. Gardiner, RN, classified two of these as "complete failures." The third attempt had resulted in receiving a small amount of oil before "the oiler's bow wave caused an outward sheer and the hose parted." Gardiner grudgingly acknowledged that the small amount of fuel transferred had allowed *Wanderer* to remain with the convoy until morning instead of departing in the middle of the night. Gardiner concluded, "Trough method could easily have been employed on the last two occasions if the gear had been available, but oiling a destroyer through a canvas [*sic*] hose without a tow of any sort is easier to imagine than to carry out."[45] As Evans had explained, the first attempts at alongside refueling were bound to be difficult. Gardiner was obviously not well practiced at this challenging maneuver.

Captain Grant forwarded the report from *Wanderer* to Naval Staff Headquarters in Ottawa. In his covering remarks, Grant commented that Lieutenant Commander Gardiner was "a competent seaman and ship handler." Grant used the report to discount the American alongside refueling method: "It is considered that the most practicable method of refueling at sea under all conditions is that finally adopted by the Admiralty as standard, i.e. astern by 5-inch rubber hose, adapter, and 3½-inch hose [led to the fuel tank tops] in each ship."[46] Grant neglected to mention in his memorandum that the Canadian corvettes *Trillium, Rosthern,* and *Dauphine,* as well as the American destroyer *Badger,* had all fueled successfully and that none of them had been required to detach from the convoy due to fuel shortage as *Wanderer* had. The credibility of a regular-navy British officer was for Grant enough to discount the quite evident and quantifiably superior seamanship skills of one U.S. Navy and three Canadian RCNVR commanders.

As a prelude to the meeting on 21 December at Derby House, Captain Heineman reported to Admiral Brainard that a "beautifully timed" signal had arrived at Western Approaches Command from his headquarters on the 18th. The signal was retransmitted by Admiral Horton to the base commander at Londonderry and to the captains commanding escort forces at Liverpool and Greenock on 19 December. It called for escorts to be "topped up with fuel from oilers on every possible occasion, even on the first or second day from the sailing port" and recognized that the permanent absence of an escort due to shortage of fuel was far more dangerous to the convoy than its temporary absence while refueling.[47]

Heineman would later assess that the issue of escort oilers had now risen to considerable prominence with the British. He recorded the presence at the meeting of a virtual who's who from Western Approaches Command, including Admiral Horton and twelve members of his senior staff: "The stage was all set." Heineman began by describing his experiences with refueling at sea by the various methods, and "a great discussion arose" regarding the merits of astern refueling versus the American alongside method. Heineman held nothing back, telling the Western Approaches staff that the British version of the alongside method using bronze hoses was "definitely impracticable in North Atlantic winter weather."[48] Although the point is not clearly elaborated on in his record of events, Heineman argued that only one practicable method of refueling at sea in winter weather existed, namely, the American alongside method.

Heineman's "ace in the hole" was his recent experience with *British Progress*. He explained that during a winter transit, all his short-legged escorts had been able to refuel, admittedly with differing success. The decisive factor was that *British Progress* had not been a designated escort oiler and that the entire affair had been accomplished with improvised equipment. At that point, Admiral Horton had heard enough. As Heineman described it, "When this was disclosed, the Admiral took charge." Horton announced that he considered the canvas-hose method the only one feasible at the present time for North Atlantic trade convoys. He made a number of decisions that he wanted carried out "at once." Three escort oilers were to be designated for each convoy and equipped with two thousand feet of canvas hose plus the necessary fittings and couplings. Even tankers already fitted with floating hose were to be equipped with canvas hose for use in an emergency, "so as to leave nothing to doubt." Captain Kenney was to be contacted and asked to explain the process to staff representatives, for relay to Western Approaches forces. Captain Heineman commented later, "To me, the whole affair was very satisfactorily handled by the Admiral, and I left the conference very well pleased."[49] This was as it should be, for he had won an important victory.

Unfortunately, Heineman's victory came too late for the RCN. Convoy ONS-154 departed Liverpool on 19 December 1942, two days prior to the conference at Derby House. The convoy's only escort oiler was *Scottish Heather,* which was equipped with buoyant rubber hose for refueling astern and Admiralty bronze-metallic hose for refueling alongside. The fragility of the metallic hoses and Admiralty resistance to alongside refueling meant it would refuel escorts only by the astern method. On 26 December, despite very rough weather, it managed to transfer one hundred tons of fuel to HMCS *St. Laurent,* the flagship of the senior officer of Escort Group C-1, Cdr. Guy S. Windeyer, RCN. Attacks by a U-boat wolf pack began on 27 December and continued almost without interruption until late on 28 December. The battle has been described as "a disaster of the first order."[50] The outcome led directly to the withdrawal of Canadian escort groups from North Atlantic service, just before the critical months of the Battle of the Atlantic, when the German U-boat force would reach its point of culmination.

Largely overlooked in accounts of the battle for convoy ONS-154 is the fact that *Scottish Heather* was heavily damaged on the afternoon of 27 December by a torpedo from *U-225,* commanded by Oberleutnant zur See Wolfgang Leimkühler. *Scottish Heather* was forced to leave the convoy and return to port for repairs. The related fact that the efficiency of Allied escorts in defense of ONS-154 declined quickly as they ran out of fuel due to the effects of heavy weather and sustained combat is also largely ignored. The British destroyers *Meteor* and *Milne,* as well as the Canadian corvettes *Battleford* and *Shediac,* were forced to detach from the convoy due to low fuel and make for the Azores on the afternoon of 30 December, even though it was known there were still five U-boats in pursuit. The fact that *Battleford* towed *Shediac* the last forty miles when the latter ran out of fuel and that *Milne* towed *Meteor* for the last five miles for the same reason merited only a footnote in the Canadian official history.[51] That *Scottish Heather* had dropped out of the convoy to refuel the Canadian corvette *Chilliwack,* in direct contravention of Commander in Chief, Western Approaches' signal of 19 December has yet to be properly recognized. The unnecessary risk to the convoy and its escorts caused by allowing *Scottish Heather* to leave the main formation is another charge of incompetence that has yet to be laid at the feet of the RCN in general, and of Commander Windeyer in particular. The damage done to the reputation of the RCN by the defeat of Escort Group C-1 has a large logistical component that has completely escaped the notice of naval historians.

Changes in the conduct of refueling at sea followed the disaster of ONS-154. On 9 March 1943, Admiral Horton sent a widely addressed message that declared, "Allied success in meeting the heavy U-boat threat depends largely on the ability to fuel expeditiously at sea." He was aware of the deficiencies in equipment and in the training of the oilers but could report that "all possible steps" were being taken to make improvements. Commanders of all escorts were urged to give refueling operations "their closest attention and to miss no opportunity to carry out this evolution at sea." Horton assured his command that the highest priority was being given to the manufacture of rubber hose and to the fitting out of oilers.[52] More support was soon lent to Western Approaches Command to solve the persistent problem of low escort endurance.

An Admiralty signal sent on 28 March 1943 made fundamental changes to British organization for escort of convoy operations: "It has been decided that tankers fitted with oiling at sea gear for service as escort oilers are to be recognised as forming an integral part of the convoy escort system in the proportion [of] 2 escort oilers to each escort group."[53] In order to implement this decision, the Admiralty assigned the highest priority, over all other work, to accomplishing four critical tasks: the fitting of fueling platforms or other type of oiling-at-sea gear; the maintenance, repair, or alteration of that gear; repairs to tankers that had been or were being fitted with gear; and the berthing and discharging of escort oilers. With such high-level support, escort oilers soon became available for service in all transatlantic convoys.

The Admiralty also signaled a major change in operating practices for the escort of convoys. Oilers were to be stationed well within the convoy, normally in the two columns adjacent to the convoy commodore's flagship, as would also be escort carriers when they were present. To facilitate refueling, the entire convoy would alter course if the planned track proved unsuitable due to conditions of sea and swell. Even the basic definition of an escort group was changed: "The composition of an Escort Group is thus, in effect, the vessels forming the Group *plus* two Escort Oilers."[54] Operational logistics had finally become an integrated concept within Royal Navy convoy doctrine.

An Escort Oiler Supervising Officer organization was established, with offices on both sides of the Atlantic. The staff assigned to the escort oiler offices were tasked to provide detailed information for every convoy at least six days before departure: the number of escort oilers ready to sail; the type of equipment fitted; what experience of oiling at sea the officers and crews possessed; and whether time would permit any of the tankers' proceeding to Moville, Ireland, to exchange practical instruction before sailing.[55] Records were kept on oiler and escort performance, and attempts were made to resolve difficulties. Observations from operations were soon being used as the basis for implementing improvements to procedures and equipment.

By mid-April 1943, escort-oiler numbers had increased substantially. Excluding Royal Fleet Auxiliaries, which were generally regarded as worthless for convoy service, eighty escort oilers were available for operations and another twelve were fitting out. Thirteen tankers had been inspected and judged suitable for fitting out when they became available, while another three had yet to be inspected.[56] Still, and despite the firm direction provided earlier by Admiral Horton, British-controlled tankers tended not to be fitted with the canvas-hose system. Moreover, the Royal Navy held firm to the belief that alongside refueling could not be conducted in rough weather. "Escort Tanker Listing Number Seven" carried the notice "Alongside or on the quarter (Not practicable for rough weather)."[57] The official guidance for escort oiler supervising officers said, "The means of oiling-at-sea to be fitted whenever possible is the buoyant rubber hose method with platform and rail. This is least at the mercy of the weather and consequently of best all-round efficiency."[58] There were some dissenting opinions.

In May 1943, the commanding officer of HMCS *Arvida,* Lt. D. G. King, RCNVR, one of Philip Evans's contemporaries in the A-3 group, sent a strongly worded report entitled "Fuelling at Sea" to the commanding officer of HMCS *Ottawa.* In it he advocated the alongside method and described the astern method as "clumsy in the extreme, difficult, and at times highly dangerous to personnel rigging the lines and hose."[59] By the time of this report, the A-3 escort group had been disbanded and *Arvida* was a member of Escort Group C-5. The commanding officer of *Ottawa* was Cdr. Hugh F. Pullen, RCN, Senior Officer Escorts for C-5.[60] Like his professional brothers, he did not attach any special significance to the unorthodox suggestions of *Arvida*'s reservist commander.

In the end, a wide variety of refueling arrangements were maintained. The majority were variations of the original British astern method. Incredibly, even the old and highly unreliable British bronze-metallic hoses were fitted into twenty-eight tankers for use in alongside refueling. The tendency of these hoses to fail under the most modest of pressure undoubtedly had much to do with the Royal Navy's reluctance to fuel alongside. The installation of these useless hoses also represented a challenge to the authority of Admiral Horton, who had clearly ordered the installation of American canvas hoses.

Failures by Canadian historians and naval authorities to examine the importance of operational logistics have led to some extraordinarily inaccurate conclusions about what actually took place in Royal Canadian Navy–U.S. Navy Atlantic relations. Admiral Murray's claim that it was he who had taught Admirals Bristol and Brainard the system for convoy organization and protection is a grotesque distortion of the facts. Moreover, Admiral King's offer to have Admiral Brainard take Murray as his deputy for a period to effect a transition in command and to have Brainard remain as a permanent adviser to Murray was almost certainly based on American concerns about Canadian logistical support and sustainment deficiencies and not due to reluctance on King's part to surrender control. Charges that King was "completely out of touch with the realities of the situation in the North West Atlantic and blatantly ignorant of the scope of the RCN's participation in escort work since September 1939" can now be rejected.[61] The volume and detail of information transmitted back and forth between the two commanders of Task Force 24, Bristol and Brainard, and King reveal that both the strategic and operational levels of command in the U.S. Navy were intimately aware of all events during the Battle of the Atlantic and of the Canadian part in them. Countercharges should be laid against both Canadian political and naval authorities that they were unaware of their force-generation and logistical-sustainment deficiencies. These shortcomings, which were clearly identified by U.S. Navy observers, had direct bearing on Canadian tactical effectiveness.

While Canadian commanding officers from Escort Group A-3 strongly advocated the wholesale adoption of the U.S. Navy refueling techniques, the cultural bias of the RCN prohibited the recognition of what practical experience clearly demonstrated—that high endurance, good sea-keeping characteristics, and practicable logistical support were essential to effective sustained naval operations. The inability of the Canadian naval staff to make its own judgments about the operational importance of refueling at sea without Admiralty guidance is another instructive insight into the intellectual immaturity of its members and their complete lack of understanding about the importance of operational logistics.

NOTES 1 Marc Milner, "RCN Participation in the Battle of the Atlantic," in *RCN in Retrospect, 1910–1968,* ed. James A. Boutilier (Vancouver: Univ. of British Columbia Press, 1982), p. 167.

2 Marc Milner, *North Atlantic Run: The Royal Canadian Navy and the Battle for the Convoys* (Toronto: Univ. of Toronto Press, 1985), app. 2, pp. 290–91.

3 Samuel E. Morison, *History of United States Naval Operations in World War II* (Boston: Little, Brown, 1947), vol. 1, p. 108.

4 Commander, Task Unit [hereafter CTU] 24.1.3 to Commander, Task Force [hereafter CTF] 24, "Fueling at Sea," 5 January 1943, Heineman Papers, box 9, folder 4, U.S. Naval Historical Center, Operational Archives, Washington, D.C. [hereafter NHC/OA].

5 Morison, *History of United States Naval Operations in World War II,* vol. 1, p. 337 note 42.

6 "Alumni Lookup, Classes, 1930," s.v. "Evans," *United States Naval Academy,* www.usna.com/.

7 Godfrey H. Hayes, *Days of Endeavour* (Victoria, B.C.: 1999), pp. 76, 81.

8 Evans received a "mention in dispatches" on 10 June 1944. The citation read, in part, "He has worked hard to develop new ideas and methods and has always conducted himself with courage and ability in numerous combats with enemy submarines." "WW 2, 'E,' Evans, Philip Cabell," *Awards to the Royal Canadian Navy,* www.rcnvr.com/.

9 "Fuelling a Corvette at Sea: A Little History," *RCN Monthly Review* (January 1943), pp. 31–38.

10 Samuel E. Morison, *The Two Ocean War: A Short History of the United States Navy in the Second World War* (Boston: Little, Brown, 1965), p. 135.

11 Thomas Wildenberg, *Gray Steel and Black Oil: Fast Tankers and Replenishment at Sea in the U.S. Navy, 1912–1995* (Annapolis, Md.: Naval Institute Press, 1996), pp. 30–45.

12 Royal Navy, *Manual of Seamanship,* BR 68 (London: His Majesty's Stationery Office, 1923), vol. 2, p. 80.

13 Ibid., p. 65.

14 Ibid., p. 85. The longer towing distance was used to reduce the strain on the hawser in heavy weather.

15 Royal Navy, *Manual of Seamanship,* BR 68 (London: His Majesty's Stationery Office, 1932), vol. 2, pp. 60–61.

16 Ibid., p. 19.

17 E. E. Sigwart, *Royal Fleet Auxiliary: Its Ancestry and Affiliations, 1600–1968* (London: Adlard Coles, 1969), p. 19. See also Jean-Yves Béquignon, "Ravitailler à la mer," *Chasse-marée,* no. 145 (August 2001), p. 5.

18 Royal Navy, *Manual of Seamanship* (1932), vol. 2, p. 64.

19 Jak Showell, *German Navy Handbook, 1939–1945* (Phoenix Mill, U.K.: Sutton, 1999), pp. 37–39.

20 For *Gonzenheim* and *Lothringen,* Stephen W. Roskill, *The War at Sea, 1939–1945* (London: Her Majesty's Stationery Office, 1956–61), vol. 1, pp. 542–46, table 24.

21 Sigwart, *Royal Fleet Auxiliary,* p. 20.

22 "Fuelling a Corvette at Sea," pp. 35–36.

23 "A Minor Operation in Mid-Atlantic," *Crowsnest* 1, no. 12 (October 1949), pp. 28–29.

24 "Report on Trip to U.K. in Connection with Escort Oilers," 6 March 1944, record group [hereafter RG] 24, series D-1-b, box 3960, file 1044-1-26, pt. 3, National Archive of Canada [hereafter NAC].

25 Capt. M. F. Wilson, Admiralty Trade Division, to Flag Officer Newfoundland, St. John's, "Oiling at Sea without Use of the Steadying Line," 17 December 1943, RG 24, series D-1-b, box 3960, file 1044-1-26, pt. 3, NAC.

26 Secretary of Naval Board to Flag Officer Newfoundland, "Fuelling at Sea," 6 June 1944, RG 24, series D-1-b, box 3960, file 1044-1-26, pt. 3, NAC.

27 Commander in Chief, Canadian Forces, North-Western Approaches [hereafter CinC CA NWA], to address indicating group [collective

address; hereafter AIG], and Naval Service Head-quarters [hereafter NSHQ], message 21 2020Z January 1944, RG 24, series D-1-b, box 3960, file 1044-1-26, pt. 3, NAC.

28 Admiralty to CinC CA NWA and NSHQ, message 23 1551A January 1944, RG 24, series D-1-b, box 3960, file 1044-1-26, pt. 3, NAC.

29 Commanding Officer, HMCS *Sackville* to Captain "D" St. John's, 4 February 1944, RG 24, series D-1-b, box 3960, file 1044-1-26, pt. 3, NAC.

30 "Fuelling a Corvette at Sea," p. 37.

31 Commanding Officer, HMCS *Trillium*, "Notes on Fuelling a Corvette at Sea," 16 November 1942, RG 24, series D-1-b, box 3960, file 1044-1-26, pt. 1, NAC.

32 David Zimmerman, *The Great Naval Battle of Ottawa* (Toronto: Univ. of Toronto Press, 1989), p. 82.

33 Secretary of Naval Board Ottawa to Secretary of Admiralty, "Oiling Escort Vessels at Sea from Tankers," 26 August 1942, RG 24, series D-1-b, box 3960, file 1044-1-26, pt. 1, NAC.

34 CTF 24 to Commander-in-chief, COAC [hereafter Cominch, COAC]; COAC, Western Approaches [hereafter CinC WA]; and COAC, U.S. Fleet [hereafter Cominch], message 09 1745Z September 1942, RG 24, series D-1-b, box 3960, file 1044-1-26, pt. 1, NAC.

35 Cominch to Admiralty, NSHQ; British Admiralty Delegation [hereafter BAD]; COAC; FONF; and CinC WA, message 11 2106Z September 1942, RG 24, series D-1-b, box 3960, file 1044-1-26, pt. 1, NAC.

36 NSHQ to Admiralty, message 07 1525A October 1942, RG 24, series D-1-b, box 3960, file 1044-1-26, pt. 1, NAC.

37 Admiralty to NSHQ, message 21 2301A October 1942, RG 24, series D-1-b, box 3960, file 1044-1-26, pt. 1, NAC.

38 Admiralty to Secretary Naval Board Ottawa, BAD, BATM Ottawa [hereafter BATM Ottawa], and HC [hereafter HC] for Canadian Deputy of Stores New York, 29 October 1942, RG 24, series D-1-b, box 3960, file 1044-1-26, pt. 1, NAC.

39 Admiralty to Secretary Naval Board Ottawa, BAD, BATM Ottawa, and HC for Canadian Deputy of Stores New York, "Guidance of Masters of Commercial Tankers Employed on Escort Fuelling Service in the Use of Buoyant Rubber Oil Hose by Boom Method," 29 October 1942, RG 24, series D-1-b, box 3960, file 1044-1-26, pt. 1, NAC.

40 Admiralty to CinC WA, NSHQ Ottawa, et al., message 06 1712A November 1942, RG 24, series D-1-b, box 3960, file 1044-1-26, pt. 1, NAC.

41 No copies of this manual have survived. None could be located in either British or Canadian public or military archives.

42 Admiralty to Commander, Naval Forces Europe, message 21 1319 November 1942, Heineman Papers, box 9, folder 4, NHC/OA.

43 CTU 24.1.3 (Heineman) to CinC WA, 20 December 1942, Heineman Papers, box 9, folder 4, NHC/OA.

44 A. Kenney, Master, SS *British Progress,* to CTU 24.1.3 (Heineman), "Report on Fuelling Escort Vessels," 14 December 1942, Heineman Papers, box 9, folder 3, NHC/OA.

45 Commanding Officer, HMS *Wanderer,* Lt. Cdr. D. H. P. Gardiner, RN, to Captain (D) Newfoundland, Report of Proceedings, 16 December 1942, RG 24, series D-1-b, box 3960, file 1044-1-26, pt. 1, NAC.

46 Captain for Destroyers [hereafter Captain D] Newfoundland, Capt. H. T. Grant, memorandum to Secretary of Naval Board, 20 December 1942, RG 24, series D-1-b, box 3960, file 1044-1-26, vol. 1, NAC.

47 CinC WA to Commander Liverpool, Captains D and all escorts, message 22 1235A December 1942, Heineman Papers, box 9, folder 3, NHC/OA.

48 CTU 24.1.3 to Chief of Staff, CTF 24, 16 January 1943, RG 80, Heineman Papers, box 9, folder 4, NHC/OA.

49 A transcript of Heineman's letter of 16 January 1943 is available from the author upon request.

50 Milner, *North Atlantic Run,* p. 210.

51 W. A. B. Douglas et al., *No Higher Purpose: The Official Operational History of the Royal Canadian Navy in the Second World War, 1939–1943* (St. Catharines, Ont.: Vanwell, 2002), vol. 2, pt. 1, p. 575 note 219.

52 CinC WA to AIG 32, message 09 1045A March 1943, RG 24, series D-1-b, box 3960, file 1044-1-26, pt. 1, NAC.

53 Admiralty to CinC CA NWA, message, 7 June 1943, RG 24, series D-1-b, box 3960, file 1044-1-26, pt. 1, NAC.

54 "Notes for Escort Oiler Supervising Officers, New York and Halifax: Duties and Responsibilities," memorandum, 22 May 1943, RG 24, series D-1-b, box 3960, file 1044-1-26, pt. 1, NAC [emphasis original].

55 Ibid.

56 Admiralty Naval Store Department, telegram to Admiralty, 12 April 1943, RG 24, series D-1-b, box 3960, file 1044-1-26, pt. 1, NAC.

57 "Escort Tanker Listing Number Seven," memorandum, 10 May 1943, RG 24, series D-1-b, box 3959, file NSS 1044-1-26, pt. 1, NAC.

58 "Notes for Escort Oiler Supervising Officers, New York and Halifax."

59 Commanding Officer, HMCS *Arvida* to Commanding Officer, HMCS *Ottawa,* "Fuelling at Sea," 16 May 1943, RG 24, series D-1-b, box 3960, file 1044-1-26, pt. 2, NAC.

60 Ken Macpherson and John Burgess, *The Ships of Canada's Naval Forces 1910–1993* (St. Catharines, Ont.: Vanwell, 1994), pp. 28, 231.

61 Wilfred G. D. Lund, "The Royal Canadian Navy's Quest for Autonomy in the North West Atlantic," in *RCN in Retrospect, 1910–1968,* ed. Boutilier, pp. 154–56.

X *See Fido Run*

A Tale of the First Anti-U-boat Acoustic Torpedo

KATHLEEN BROOME WILLIAMS

By March 1943 the Battle of the Atlantic had reached a crisis. That month, German U-boats sank 108 ships, coming close to forcing Britain out of World War II. In response to the escalating threat a new weapon was rushed into action. Fido—an American-created, air-launched, antisubmarine, acoustic-homing torpedo, and the first of its kind—was let loose against the U-boats. To preserve its secret Fido was officially called the "Mark 24 mine." Eventually it had several other code names, including the "six-hundred-pound depth charge" and "Proctor," while some of its users called it "Wandering Annie" or "Zombie."[1]

Although later deployed in the Pacific against Japanese submarines and in the Caribbean Sea and Indian Ocean, Fido is quintessentially an Atlantic story. No miracle weapon, technological device, intelligence breakthrough, industrial productivity, or even resolute warriors won the Atlantic campaign for the Allies. It took the combined weight of them all to defeat German admiral Karl Dönitz's skilled submariners, and Fido played an important part at a critical time.

How did this new weapon move—remarkably fast—from concept to effective operational use? The answer revolves around Allied cooperation, from top decision makers to ground technicians. While many accounts of the Battle of the Atlantic note Fido's use in action, none has examined the mechanics of day-to-day cooperation required to get it there.[2] The Fido saga demonstrates that cooperation depended on innovation, improvisation, flexibility, and compromise—across national borders and at micro as well as macro levels—among scientists, industry, civilian leaders, and the military, prefiguring the sorts of relationships so soon required by NATO operations.[3]

Creation

For fifteen years scientists at the Naval Torpedo Station at Newport, Rhode Island, had churned out reports claiming that an acoustic-homing torpedo was theoretically impossible, since torpedoes made too much noise themselves to be able to home on any external noise source.[4] Yet Capt. Louis McKeehan, a naval reserve officer whose peacetime job was director of the physics laboratories at Yale, was not constrained by the received wisdom of navy engineers. In November 1941 he asked scientists at HUSL, the Harvard Underwater Sound Lab, whether an acoustic torpedo was feasible.[5] In just over one year, physicist Harvey Brooks and his team at HUSL, working closely with engineers at the Bell Telephone Labs, proved that it was. They designed a small, slow-speed electric torpedo that was quiet enough to permit acoustic control. Its speed was too slow to use against enemy warships but sufficient to overtake the fastest submerged submarine. Small size also meant the torpedo could be launched from an aircraft instead of a destroyer or another submarine.[6]

The torpedo was endowed with canine attributes, the various parts referred to as Fido's "head," "body," and "tail." Fido was steered by connecting rudders in his tail to four hydrophones mounted near his nose, shielded to prevent him from chasing his own tail. The hydrophones were arranged for up/down and right/left directional control and, like a dog's ears, were very sensitive. Before launching, the rudders were tested by scratching Fido gently on the head near one of the hydrophones. When working properly the rudders responded by steering toward the scratching.[7] Unlike later, active (sonar pinging) torpedoes, Fido was passive. He listened, he chased, he bit, but he did not bark.[8] By May 1943, only seventeen months after the beginning of the project, Fido had entered service and made his first kill.[9]

As Brooks recalled years later, the team that created Fido included "musicians who had fiddled around with hi-fi in their spare time, bankers who were ham radio operators and ministers who had majored in physics in college."[10] Another HUSL member called the Fido group "electronicers, acousticians and screwballs."[11] Most were young, many of them graduate students. They worked twelve-hour days, six or seven days a week, thriving on innovation and experiment. To emphasize the urgency of their task, workers at HUSL were greeted each morning by a board bearing the tonnage of shipping lost to U-boats over the previous twenty-four hours.[12]

Warned by reports of deficiencies in conventional torpedoes that were filtering back from the Pacific, the "Fido Gang" planned a strenuous set of trials for its progeny. First, running tests and preliminary steering trials were conducted from rowboats. Later, the Naval Air Station at Squantum near Quincy, Massachusetts, provided aircraft, PBY Catalina patrol planes, for trials leading to the development of successful methods of dropping the torpedoes from the air.[13] There were many gaffes and bloopers, though, as Fido was put through his paces, due in part to lack of experience in conducting trials. For instance, the second torpedo body tested was lost when it struck the target boat during an acoustic attack. Later, one of the preproduction models being tested in an inland lake made a successful attack on a target but "in circling for a re-attack ran up a bank and nearly climbed a tree."[14] The torpedo suffered no damage, so it was run a second time, but just as it was launched in the vicinity of the artificial target a real target showed up in the form of a small motorboat. The torpedo chased the motorboat for almost a mile, running perfectly successfully until, fortunately, the lake became so shallow that the torpedo simply nosed into the mud.

When air tests of Fido began, one of the first trials of the torpedo's air stabilizers was a fiasco. Two of the stabilizer surfaces tore off as soon as the torpedo dropped from the PBY. As a result the body turned end over end, landed in the water tail first, broke up, and sank.[15] Another day the torpedo release mechanism in the aircraft failed to work. With the bomb bay open, two HUSL members struggled to free the stuck torpedo while the bomber pilot circled downtown Boston awaiting instructions. On yet another occasion an HUSL member was driving a truck carrying Fido to load him into the bomb bay when he rammed the tail structure of the aircraft, doing so much damage that testing had to be postponed for several days.[16]

The finished torpedo measured nineteen inches in diameter and was eighty-four inches long. It was propelled by an electric motor and could run at twelve knots for fifteen minutes. Fido weighed in at seven hundred pounds and carried ninety-two pounds of high-explosive Torpex.[17] HUSL's success in demonstrating an experimental device relatively simply made in its own workshop persuaded the navy to authorize immediate production.[18]

The tactical doctrine for using Fido was simple. When a surfaced U-boat dived, a torpedo bomber, slowing its airspeed to around 125 knots, dropped Fido slightly ahead of the U-boat's swirl from an altitude of some two hundred feet.[19] Once in the water, Fido circled at full speed under hydrostatic control (that is, operating at a depth controlled by water pressure) until he picked up propeller noises from a submarine. At that point, control switched from hydrostatic to acoustical homing, and Fido steered toward the target until he came into contact, at which point—as Harvey Brooks expressed it—Fido "was supposed to explode and fatally cripple the target." However, if Fido overshot on his first approach and lost the signal altogether, he searched in a circle until he picked it up again and renewed his approach. Under ideal conditions he could detect propeller noises at a maximum range of about 1.4 kilometers. In the absence of an acoustic signal, Fido circled until his battery ran down and he sank.[20]

Negotiation

By the time Fido came along the Allies had already set up channels of communication, established patterns of consultation, and begun an extensive exchange of scientific and technical information. In London, Prime Minister Winston Churchill chaired weekly meetings of the Anti-U-boat Warfare Committee, meetings that were attended by Averell Harriman, President Franklin Roosevelt's special representative for war aid, and Adm. Harold "Betty" Stark, commander of U.S. Naval Forces,

Europe.[21] Churchill also invited Maj. Gen. Ira Eaker to "give us the advantage of your knowledge of the work done by the squadrons of the 8th U.S. Air Force operating in the U-Boat war."[22] Cooperation among the major Allied forces was a critical factor in the defeat of the U-boats, but cooperation was never easy and Fido required sometimes problematic interservice, as well as international, cooperation.[23]

Word of Fido first reached the Admiralty in London in December 1942 from the British Admiralty Delegation (BAD) in Washington, D.C., the Admiralty's liaison with the U.S. Navy.[24] Soon, the Royal Air Force (RAF) was involved too.[25] By February 1943, Fido was in full production in the United States, with one thousand weapons expected to be ready by 1 May.[26] The British had still not received full details of Fido's dimensions and performance, but, having been at war for over three years, they prepared for its arrival with practiced speed.[27] Noting that Fido might "have a decisive effect on the course of the war," the Admiralty informed the RAF that a resolution of potential difficulties was of the "utmost importance."[28] The two agreed to create an interservice panel to deal with all aspects of Fido, including supply, maintenance, training, and operation.[29] Two days after its creation, the panel decided that Coastal Command would assign Fidos initially to Aldergrove RAF Station in Northern Ireland and to Reykjavík, Iceland. Eventually, Fidos would be deployed also from many airfields in England, and depots were established to supply them to naval forces afloat. Without having seen a single weapon, Air Marshal Sir John "Jack" Slessor, head of Coastal Command, believed he could be ready to operate with Fidos within one or two weeks of receiving them.[30] While the U.S. Navy Department controlled the supply and transportation of the torpedoes, it agreed that the Admiralty would determine the location of the stations in the United Kingdom to receive them and whether the torpedoes would be used for shore-based or shipborne operations.[31]

From February 1943, encrypted cable messages about Fido flowed almost daily between BAD in Washington and the Admiralty and Air Ministry in London, continuing unabated until the end of the war in Europe. Nevertheless, there were still differences to overcome. The British looked forward to using Fido against the Germans, while, predictably, the first inclination of the American Chief of Naval Operations, Adm. Ernest King, was to use Fido against the Japanese.[32]

Ultimately, the situation in the Atlantic proved decisive. By March, Admiral Dönitz had more U-boats at his disposal than ever before, and several convoys were severely mauled as they fought their way across the ocean.[33] Soon, BAD received word that the Mark 24 would be used first against the U-boats, the available weapons divided among Newfoundland, Iceland, and the United Kingdom.[34] Finally, on 6 May 1943, Fido was let loose.[35] After less than two weeks in action Jack Slessor wrote that "the Mark XXIV mine looks very promising."[36]

Close cooperation over Fido continued to the end of the war. There were regular meetings at Coastal Command headquarters in Liverpool between U.S. Navy representatives and those in Coastal Command responsible for Fido to iron out any problems that arose and to keep abreast of new developments and improvements in the weapon and its use.[37]

Tactical Employment

In the hands of the Allies, Fido proved his worth. His first success was on 12 May, when an Aldergrove Liberator (a B-24 heavy bomber) from RAF No. 86 Squadron sank *U-456*. An American, Iceland-based Catalina of Patrol Squadron (VP) 84 sank *U-640* two days later. Soon, too, British and American escort carriers were launching Fido attacks on U-boats.[38]

On 11 August an Avenger torpedo bomber from the escort carrier USS *Card* (CVE 111), on a routine submarine search north of the Azores, spotted a surfaced U-boat and executed a textbook Fido attack. An F4F-4 Wildcat—a fighter accompanying the bomber—went in for a strafing run, followed immediately by the Avenger, which dropped two depth charges, forcing the U-boat to crash-dive. Thirty seconds after the U-boat's disappearance, the Avenger released a Mark 24 mine. The pilot of the fighter "watched the mine hit the water about 20 feet to starboard and just ahead of the indistinct swirl left by the sub" and then saw the mine travel underwater and swing around toward the sub, striking it on the starboard side about halfway between the conning tower and the stern. Ten seconds later a large underwater explosion threw a geyser of water high into the air about 150 feet ahead of the spot where the U-boat had last been seen. Oil immediately came up in the center of the explosion area, eventually forming a crescent-shaped slick five to six hundred feet long.[39] The aircraft from *Card,* using Fido, had sunk *U-525*.[40]

Land-based aircraft accomplished similar feats. During the war more than four hundred airfields were built in the United Kingdom, and aircraft carrying Fido flew from a number of them. RAF Station Dunkeswell, in Devon on the south coast of England, became an important base for antisubmarine Fido-deploying squadrons tasked with patrolling the Bay of Biscay, gateway to the Atlantic operating areas for three of every four German and Italian submarines. Since most squadrons flying from Dunkeswell were American, the station represents a unique picture of Allied cooperation.[41] In June, some six weeks after Fido's first success, Group Captain E. C. Kidd, RAF, arrived at Dunkeswell to prepare the site as quickly as possible to operate several U.S. Army Air Forces (USAAF) squadrons. Initially, the station—still in a rudimentary state—was to function as a normal RAF Coastal Command station. Flying control, operational control, administration, and antiaircraft defense, as well as the special arrangements required for the accommodation of the Mark 24 mine, were to be provided from British sources.[42]

"Some US Liberators [of the 479th Antisubmarine Group] from Gander [in Newfoundland] have already arrived UK," Slessor wrote to the head of the U.S. Tenth Fleet, on 28 June. "They will need a little acclimatization and working up in Coastal Command procedure and none of their maintenance personnel will arrive for some time but hope they will soon be working in the Bay [of Biscay]." The 479th Group was under the U.S. Eighth Air Force for administrative purposes but came under the operational control of Coastal Command.[43] "Find the new patrol arrangements in the Bay working well," Slessor continued. He noted that he would be certain of success if Coastal Command could increase air strength in the bay and—in addition to other improvements suggested by the Admiralty—if the new group could use the Mark 24 mine.[44] "Whether the U-boats return to the North Atlantic . . . or go for independent shipping all over the Atlantic," Slessor concluded, "the Bay still remains the first place to get at them."

Over the next two months the station at Dunkeswell was hastily thrown together. Construction crews arrived to build necessary structures, including special reinforced storage areas for Fidos, and RAF personnel came from all over to fill them.[45] Living quarters—cold and perpetually clammy Nissen huts—were in a "rather damp valley" away from the airfield itself, adding to the general misery of the location.[46] On 29 July the ground echelons of the 479th's 4th and 19th Squadrons arrived, followed shortly by their aircrews. They had received training and some practice with the new Mark 24 mines, and on 7 August they began operational sorties from Dunkeswell.[47] The weather was "cloudy with drizzle," for which Dunkeswell became notorious.[48] Soon they were joined by two more U.S. Army squadrons, also flying Liberators on exhaustingly long patrols over the Bay of Biscay.[49]

Less than four weeks later Group Captain Kidd noted, with commendable understatement, that the smooth administration and efficiency of the squadrons had been "somewhat hampered" by the decision to move out the army units and substitute U.S. Navy units at the end of the month. "Loads of equipment" that had just been uncrated would have to be recrated, and although Kidd maintained that plans for the station were still proceeding on track, "inevitably," he confessed, "enthusiasm has been damped."[50] The change from army to navy was not just local. In July, Admiral King and army chief of staff George Marshall had agreed that the navy would take over all antisubmarine air activity. As the USAAF withdrew from the antisubmarine war it was replaced by U.S. Navy units.[51] Kidd had the impression that "the US Navy will differ considerably" from the army. "Therefore," he ended on a truly diplomatic note, "the Station Headquarters staff is now mainly concerned with dealing with the needs of the US Navy."[52]

In a June 2009 article, a professor of strategy at the Naval War College noted, "The side able to cope with—or, better yet, get ahead of—perpetual change holds the advantage over a less adaptive foe."[53] Dunkeswell tested everyone's adaptability.

Just one month after arriving, the USAAF 6th Squadron was transferred, and two days later advanced elements of the first U.S. Navy squadron, Bombing Squadron (VB) 103, took up residence. Together with VB-105 and VB-110, which had arrived in "dribs and drabs" at Dunkeswell by the end of October, the three squadrons were part of Fleet Air Wing 7 of the U.S. Twelfth Fleet, headquartered in nearby Plymouth. In an effort to ensure smooth relations with the squardons' British hosts, the air wing appointed a liaison officer to Coastal Command headquarters.[54]

In November, Kidd noted that the only thing worth recording was the final departure of the USAAF and the beginning of efforts to reorganize the station "to suit the needs of the US Navy." The operational role of the station continued without interruption amid the confusion. Liberators (the navy designated them PB4Y-1s) continued to rack up long patrol hours over the bay, interspersed with sporadic U-boat sightings and Fido attacks as well as air combat against German fighters and bombers.[55]

In March 1944, the U.S. Navy assumed command of Dunkeswell from the RAF, making it a U.S. Naval Air Facility, the only one in the European Theater of Operations.[56] By then there had already been exercises to "indoctrinate" U.S. Navy forces in the use of various RAF systems, and a civil engineer from Coastal Command visited to see what works were needed to meet American requirements.[57]

A year later, and after American planes had maintained a continuous, grueling schedule of air patrols from Dunkeswell, the enemy's situation on the continent had become critical, and Coastal Command called for extreme vigilance from its squadrons.[58] On 25 April 1945, *U-326* was destroyed off the Brest Peninsula by a Mark 24 mine from VPB-103 in the last Fido kill from Dunkeswell. The crew sighted smoke from a snorkel (*schnorkel*, which allowed U-boats to operate their diesels and recharge batteries submerged) and a wake at a distance of about two miles and on approaching could clearly see the snorkel, which looked like an enlarged periscope. The Liberator dropped two mines just ahead of the U-boat from a height of two hundred feet while making 132 knots. On entering the water both mines were seen to track straight to the target without "porpoising." The U-boat exploded, following which a large, green oil slick appeared. A man, apparently dead, was floating on his back in a prone position wearing a yellow Mae West.[59]

Overall, Fido's success in the Atlantic was impressive. By one count, based on Operations Evaluation Group study 289 in 1946, Fidos were dropped in 204 attacks against submarines. American aircraft made 142 of these attacks, sinking thirty-one submarines (22 percent of attacks) and damaged fifteen (11 percent). In the remaining sixty-two attacks other Allies, predominantly British, sank six submarines (10 percent) and damaged three (5 percent). Most of the submarines sunk were German U-boats in the Atlantic, although five Japanese subs were also sunk by Fidos, one in the Atlantic and four in the Pacific. The thirty-seven submarines sunk by Fidos represent about 15 percent of all submarines sunk by air escort or air antisubmarine warfare operations between May 1943 and the end of the war.[60] Between October 1943 and April 1945 Dunkeswell Liberators contributed to that record with thirty-four Fido attacks, resulting in seven U-boats sunk (21 percent of the attacks) and possible damage to another eleven (32 percent), a respectable record.[61]

A history of the Tenth Fleet noted that Fido, in conjunction with ahead-throwing weapons like Hedgehog and new depth charges, had "raised the probability of a 'kill,' once a U-boat had been located, to an amount which, although falling short of certainty, was an assurance of success."[62] Effective cooperation among the Royal Air Force, the U.S. Army Air Forces, and the U.S. Navy ensured that Dunkeswell played an important part in this success. After spring 1943 more than five thousand Americans served at the airfield, flying over 6,460 missions at a cost of some forty planes and 183 naval airmen killed in action. The Americans left Dunkeswell soon after VE Day, and the airfield reverted to the RAF.[63]

After the war, the scientists at Bell Labs who had worked on Fido returned to telephone work, Captain McKeehan returned to Yale, and Harvard took back its buildings and ended its classified work. The rapid and successful creation of Fido, however, had demonstrated the strengths enjoyed by civilian research labs and their unexpected potential for applying basic research to the development of naval technology. The navy recognized this. At its urging, in 1946 Congress created the Office of Naval Research to fund innovative research at universities across the country. The Cold War ensured that this federal funding would forever change the scientific landscape and solidify the new connection forged among science, industry, and the military. The lessons of wartime cooperation, exemplified in the creation and use of Fido, smoothed the way for the close and effective international defense partnership that would characterize NATO.[64]

NOTES   Not long before his untimely death, David Syrett, naval historian, teacher, mentor, and friend, suggested that Fido should be my next project. As ever, I owe David so much. My thanks are also due to Jock Gardner, Malcolm Llewellyn-Jones, Randy Papadopoulos, Michael Whitby, Joe Fitzharris, and Eugene Feit for comments, information, and advice on this project.

1 The Germans began working on an acoustic-homing torpedo in 1935, but it was a U-boat-launched antiescort weapon; early versions were ineffective until the T-5 Zaunkönig, which had its first confirmed hit in October 1943. When it was proposed to refer to the Mark 24, in some cases, as Proctor, one sensible correspondent—probably tired of Fido's many names—suggested "that we call the beast Proctor in *all* cases or not at all." Handwritten note, 4 August 1944, AIR 15/564, The National Archives, Kew, Surrey, United Kingdom [hereafter TNA]. The author's name is undecipherable.

2 See, for example, Peter Padfield, *War beneath the Sea* (New York: Wiley, 1995), p. 367; Clay Blair, *Hitler's U-boat War: The Hunted, 1942–1945* (New York: Random House, 1998), pp. 27, 251, 328, 395–97, 467, 557; Kenneth Poolman, *The Winning Edge: Technology in Action, 1939–1945* (Annapolis, Md.: Naval Institute Press, 1997), pp. 85, 88; Dan Van der Vat, *The Atlantic Campaign: World War II's Great Struggle at Sea* (New York: Harper and Row, 1988), pp. 350, 366; John Terraine, *The U-boat Wars, 1914–1945* (New York: G. P. Putnam, 1989), pp. 618–19; and Alfred Price, *Aircraft versus Submarine* (Annapolis, Md.: Naval Institute Press, 1973), pp. 107, 130–35, 141, 146, 159, 171, 178, 222, 224.

3 For an excellent overview of wartime cooperation see Mark A. Stoler, *Allies in War: Britain and America against the Axis Powers* (London: Hodder and Arnold, 2005).

4 "Final Report: Applied Acoustics in Subsurface Warfare," p. 11, 31 January 1946, file Final Report: Applied Acoustics in Subsurface Warfare, box 334, Record Group [hereafter RG] 181, National Archives and Records Administration [hereafter NARA] Northeast Region Waltham, Mass. [hereafter NARA-NE].

5 "Completion Report on No-94 (Fido) an Air-launched Acoustic Antisubmarine Mine," p. v, 1 January 1946, file Completion Report on No. 94 (Fido), box 334, RG 181, NARA-NE [hereafter "Completion Report on No-94 (Fido)"].

6 "Final Report," chap. 2, p. 4, file Historical Material, box 319, RG 181, NARA-NE. Torpedo expert Tom Pelick writes that Fido's small explosive power was sufficient to disable a submarine, forcing it to the surface, where it could be finished off by other air or surface forces. Fido, he maintained, "was designed as a mission kill torpedo versus a direct torpedo kill." See Tom Pelick, "Fido: The First U.S. Homing Torpedo," *Submarine Review* (January 1996), p. 68.

7 "Completion Report on No-94 (Fido)," p. 99.

8 *Fido Steering Report,* introduction, 27 February 1942, file H-55, box 330, RG 181, NARA-NE. The first *active* homing torpedo, the Mark 32, would come later.

9 For the roles of Bell Laboratories and Western Electric, see M. D. Fagen, ed., *A History of Engineering and Science in the Bell System: National Service in War and Peace (1925–1975)* (n.p.: Bell Telephone Laboratories, 1978), pp. 187–201.

10 Harvey Brooks, "Colleague's Viewpoint of F. V. Hunt," part 1, *Journal of the Acoustical Society of America* 57, no. 6 (June 1975), p. 1247.

11 "Harvard Underwater Sound Laboratory, 1941–1946," p. 37, unpublished reunion report, 9–10 October 1993, Cambridge, Mass., courtesy Harvey Brooks.

12 "Notes on Lectures Given by Dr. Boner for the Benefit of New Research Men and Technicians," p. 4, 2 September 1943, file Historical Material, box 319, RG 181, NARA-NE; Harvey Brooks, "Autonomous Science and Socially Responsive Science: A Search for Resolution," *Annual Reviews* 26 (2001), p. 31; "Harvard Underwater Sound Laboratory, 1941–1946," p. 34; Harvey Brooks, interview by author, Cambridge, Mass., January 2004; Brooks, "Colleague's Viewpoint of F. V. Hunt," pp. 1246–47.

13 F. V. Hunt to Fido Gang, 15 December 1942, file Historical Material, box 319, RG 181, NARA-NE.

14 "Completion Report on No-94 (Fido)," p. 7.

15 Ibid., p. 6.

16 "Harvard Underwater Sound Laboratory, 1941–1946," pp. 38–39.

17 "Glossary of Torpedoes," memorandum, 22 February 1944, p. 4, file Extra Copies of Index to HUSL External Reports, box 379, RG 181, NARA-NE;

Fagen, ed., *History of Engineering and Science in the Bell System,* p. 189. Conventional torpedoes carried payloads of about five hundred pounds.

18 "History of the Anti-submarine Measures Division of Tenth Fleet," p. 19, file History of A/S Measures Division, box 437, RG 38, NARA, College Park, Md. [hereafter NARA2]; "Completion Report on No-94 (Fido)," p. 7.

19 See, for example, "Report of Antisubmarine Action by Aircraft," 11 August 1943, file A/S Operations by US Escort Carriers (CVE), War History, case 8853, M.055386/43, 1943, ADM 199/1408, TNA.

20 "Data Sheet to Accompany 'Record of Invention' for Case 5," p. 2, file Invention Description No. 5, box 328A, RG 181, NARA-NE; Coastal Command Headquarters, "General Instructions for the Operation of the Mark 24 Mine," pp. 2–4, AIR 15/562, TNA; "Proposal for Fido Project," p. 12, file H-40, box 30, RG 181, NARA-NE; DTM [hereafter DTM] to Commander in Chief, Mediterranean, 21 March 1944, Part I Proctor: Policy Signals Covering Period February 1943–July 1945, War History "X," Director of Torpedo, Anti-Submarine, and Mine Warfare Division Domestic Records, 1943–45, case 163, p. 2, ADM 199/2404, TNA; for Harvey Brooks quote see Brooks, "Autonomous Science and Socially Responsive Science," p. 32.

21 On the Anti-U-boat Warfare Committee see W. J. R. Gardner, "An Allied Perspective," in *The Battle of the Atlantic 1939–1945: The 50th Anniversary International Naval Conference,* ed. Stephen Howarth and Derek Law (Annapolis, Md.: Naval Institute Press, 1994), pp. 516–37.

22 Portal to Prime Minister, 21 July 1943, AIR 20/848, Anti-U-Boat Warfare: Anglo-American Cooperation, TNA; Churchill to Eaker, 23 July 1943, AIR 20/848, Anti-U-Boat Warfare: Anglo-American Cooperation, TNA.

23 For an overview see Philip Lundeberg, "Allied Cooperation," in *Battle of the Atlantic,* ed. Howarth and Law, pp. 345–70. See also Kenneth P. Hansen, "King, Canada, and the Convoys: A Reappraisal of Admiral Ernest King's Role in Operation Drumbeat" (paper presented at the Naval History Symposium, Annapolis, Md., September 2007), for early difficulties in creating a cooperative working environment among the Allies in the Atlantic war. To be sure, Polish, Free French, Norwegian, Dutch, and other naval forces not considered in this chapter also played a part in the Allied coalition in the Atlantic.

24 RAF Delegation to Air Ministry, 11 December 1942, AIR 20/1101, Trials 12/42–9/43, TNA.

25 To Assistant Chief of Air Staff (Ops), n.d., AIR 20/1101, Trials 12/42–9/43, TNA.

26 BAD to Admiralty, 28 February 1943, Part I Proctor, case 163, ADM 199/2404, TNA; "Technical Procedure: Mark 24 Mine," 10 April 1943, file S-1943, box 3, RG 38, NARA2.

27 DTM to Assistant Controller (R&D), etc., reference sheet, 16 February 1943, AIR 20/1101, Trials 12/42–9/43, TNA; BAD to Admiralty, 28 February 1943, AIR 20/1101, Trials 12/42–9/43, TNA.

28 Admiralty to Under Secretary of State, Air Ministry, 8 March 1943, AIR 20/1101, Trials 12/42–9/43, TNA.

29 "Report No.1 Mark XXIV USA Mine," 15 March 1943, AIR 20/1101, Trials 12/42–9/43, TNA; "Minutes of Meeting Held at Admiralty, 16 March 1943, Subject: formation of an inter-service panel to deal with the introduction of the Mark XXIV mine into service," AIR 20/1101, Trials 12/42–9/43, TNA.

30 Notes of meeting held at Admiralty, 18 March 1943, AIR 20/1101, Trials 12/42–9/43, TNA; BAD to Admiralty, 21 March 1943, Part I Proctor, case 163, p. 16, ADM 199/2404, TNA; BAD to Admiralty, 26 March 1943, Part I Proctor, case 163, p. 24, ADM 199/2404, TNA; AOC RAF Iceland to Headquarters Coastal Command [hereafter HQCC], 16 August 1943, AIR 15/562, TNA.

31 Commander in Chief, U.S. Fleet [hereafter Cominch] to BAD, 25 April 1943, file S-1943, box 3, RG 38, NARA2.

32 BAD to Admiralty, 28 February 1943, Part I Proctor, case 163, p. 2, ADM 199/2404, TNA; D.A./S.W. to BAD, 6 March 1943, Part I Proctor, case 163, p. 6, ADM 199/2404, TNA.

33 Padfield, *War beneath the Sea,* p. 314.

34 Cominch to Vice Chief of Naval Operations, 13 May 1943, file S-1943, box 3, RG 38, NARA2; BAD to Admiralty, repeated Air Ministry, 17 March 1943, Part I Proctor, case 163, p. 10, ADM 199/2404, TNA.

35 BAD to Admiralty, 6 May 1943, Part I Proctor, case 163, p. 48, ADM 199/2404, TNA.

36 Slessor to Portal, 18 May 1943, AIR 20/848, Anti-U-Boat Warfare: Anglo-American Cooperation, TNA.

37 AOC RAF Iceland to HQCC, 16 August 1943, AIR 15/562, TNA; Notes on meeting held at HQCC, 13 August 1943, AIR 15/562, TNA; Commanding Officer, Fleet Air Wing 7 to Chief, Bureau of Ordnance, 2 January 1945, file S-76-1(1) 1945, box 37, RG 38, NARA2.

38 Price, *Aircraft versus Submarine,* p. 135; Terraine, *U-boat Wars,* has the dates right for the first two kills but wrongly identifies the U-boats: see J. Rohwer and G. Hummelchen, *Chronology of the War at Sea, 1939–1945,* rev. ed. (Annapolis, Md.: Naval Institute Press, 1992), pp. 211–12; DTM to Cominch, 13 May 1943, Part I Proctor, case 163, p. 14, ADM 199/2404, TNA; and Reykjavik, Iceland to HQCC, 15 May 1943, Part I Proctor, case 163, p. 17, ADM 199/2404, TNA. Part I Proctor, Case History 163, consists of 275 pages of operational signals recording Fido use. These reports came from Iceland and Aldergrove, from St. Eval, from Dunkeswell, and from the escort carriers HMS *Biter,* HMS *Striker,* and others. They give the facts as perceived at the time and illustrate how seldom analysts could be sure of results. They are testaments, however, to the extensive use of Fido from May 1943 onward. Some authors maintain the Catalina got the first kill; see Alan C. Carey, *US Navy PB4Y-1 (B24) Liberator Squadrons in Great Britain during World War*

II (Atglen, Pa.: Schiffer Military History, 2003), p. 20.

39 "Report of Antisubmarine Action by Aircraft," 11 August 1943, ADM 199/1408, TNA. I am indebted to Malcolm Llewellyn-Jones for finding this report for me.

40 Rohwer and Hummelchen, *Chronology of the War at Sea, 1939–1945*, p. 221.

41 Dunkeswell is active today, with air operations by Air Westward. It still has several of its World War II buildings, including the unusual control tower and a number of Nissen huts, the British equivalent of Quonset huts. A small museum on the site has a fine collection of memorabilia, much of it donated by former U.S. Navy personnel who served there. I am most grateful to Janet Shenfield for taking me to visit Dunkeswell in July 2008 on a cold, rainy, windy day that, I was assured, was quite typical.

42 "Summary of Events, 22–26 June 1943," RAF Station, Dunkeswell, RAF Operations Record Book, form 540, AIR 28/229, TNA.

43 Welsh to F. S. Low, 28 June 1943, file Air Marshall Welsh Misc., box 27, RG 38, NARA2; "Summary of Events, 26 June 1943," RAF Station, Dunkeswell, RAF Operations Record Book, form 540, AIR 28/229, TNA; Graham Smith, *Devon and Cornwall Airfields in the Second World War* (Newbury, U.K.: Countryside Books, 2002), pp. 98–99. I am grateful to Amyas Crump for bringing this book to my attention and getting a copy for me.

44 Welsh to F. S. Low, 28 June 1943, file Air Marshall Welsh Misc., box 27, RG 38, NARA2. For an excellent quantitative analysis of operations in the bay see Brian McCue, *U-boats in the Bay of Biscay* (Washington, D.C.: National Defense Univ. Press, 1990).

45 Group Captain Morris to RAF Stations Reykjavik, Ballykelly, St. Eval, and Dunkeswell, 26 August 1943, AIR 15/562, TNA; Group Captain Kidd to DTM, 13 September 1943, AIR 15/562, TNA.

46 "Administration, 3–19 September 1943," RAF Station, Dunkeswell, RAF Operations Record Book, form 540, AIR 28/229, TNA; Carey, *US Navy PB4Y-1 (B24) Liberator Squadrons in Great Britain during World War II*, pp. 40–41.

47 "Summary of Events, 26 June to 31 August 1943," RAF Station, Dunkeswell, RAF Operations Record Book, form 540, AIR 28/229, TNA.

48 A. F. Bennett and W. H. Scheer, "Recommendation Regarding Maintenance and Other Procedures: Mark 24 Mine," 5 August 1943, AIR 15/562, TNA; Group Captain Kidd to DTM, 13 September 1943, AIR 15/562, TNA.

49 "Summary of Events, 17 October 1943," RAF Station, Dunkeswell, RAF Operations Record Book, form 540, AIR 28/229, TNA.

50 "Station Commander's Resume, 24 August 1943," RAF Station, Dunkeswell, RAF Operations Record Book, form 540, AIR 28/229, TNA.

51 "History of the Anti-submarine Measures Division of Tenth Fleet," p. 42.

52 "Station Commander's Resume, 24 August 1943," RAF Station, Dunkeswell, RAF Operations Record Book, form 540, AIR 28/229, TNA.

53 James R. Holmes, "Where Have All the Mush Mortons Gone?," U.S. Naval Institute *Proceedings* (June 2009), p. 59.

54 "Administration, 21–30 September 1943," RAF Station, Dunkeswell, RAF Operations Record Book, form 540, AIR 28/229, TNA. A famous member of VB-110 was Lt. Joseph P. Kennedy, Jr., elder brother of a future president of the United States, John F. Kennedy.

55 Dunkeswell to HQCC, 6 November 1943, Part I Proctor, case 163, ADM 199/2404, TNA; "Station Commander's Resume, 30 November 1943," RAF Station, Dunkeswell, RAF Operations Record Book, form 540, AIR 28/229, TNA. The navy designated the B-24 as the PB4Y-1, and squadrons flying it were designated VB (Navy Bomber) until 1 October 1944, when the designation changed to VPB (Navy Patrol Bomber).

56 "Summary of Events, 31 March 1944," RAF Station, Dunkeswell, RAF Operations Record Book, form 540, AIR 28/229, TNA.

57 "Administration II," p. 2, 26 February 1944, RAF Station, Dunkeswell, RAF Operations Record Book, form 540, AIR 28/229, TNA.

58 Dunkeswell to HQCC, 11 March 1945, Part I Proctor, case 163, ADM 199/2404, TNA; to Director of Naval Intelligence to NID 0157, 13 March 1945, Part I Proctor, case 163, ADM 199/2404, TNA.

59 Dunkeswell to HQCC, 11 March 1945, Part I Proctor, case 163, ADM 199/2404, TNA; Smith, *Devon and Cornwall Airfields in the Second World War*, p. 110; Rohwer and Hummelchen, *Chronology of the War at Sea*, p. 345.

60 Frederick J. Milford, "US Navy Torpedoes: Part Four—WWII development of Homing Torpedoes 1940–1946," *Submarine Review* (April 1997). For another estimate see Pelick, "Fido," p. 69, citing E. W. Jolle, *A Brief History of US Navy Torpedo Development,* NUSCTD 5436 (n.p.: Naval Underwater Systems Center–Technical Director, 25 September 1978).

61 Carey, *US Navy PB4Y-1 (B24) Liberator Squadrons in Great Britain during World War II*, p. 147. Compare this with the record of the German homing torpedo Gnat: of 640 Gnats fired, only 3 percent hit; see Malcolm Llewellyn-Jones, *The Royal Navy and Anti-submarine Warfare 1917–1949* (New York: Routledge, 2006), p. 26.

62 "History of the Anti-submarine Measures Division of Tenth Fleet," p. 51.

63 Smith, *Devon and Cornwall Airfields in the Second World War*, p. 110; Carey, *US Navy PB4Y-1 (B24) Liberator Squadrons in Great Britain during World War II*, pp. 143–46, gives the total number of those who died in crashes, failed to return, or were shot down as 204.

64 Dr. Eric Walker, associate director of HUSL, went to Penn State after the war and set up the Ordnance Research Laboratory to continue acoustic torpedo research. See Pelick, "Fido," p. 70.

XI Hiding in Plain Sight
The U.S. Navy and Dispersed Operations under EMCON, 1956–1972

ROBERT G. ANGEVINE

The ability to operate freely, unthreatened by adversaries seeking to track and target them or interfere with their communications, that the U.S. Navy's aircraft carriers have enjoyed for the last two decades is unlikely to continue. China has been developing an antiaccess/area-denial capability, centered on antiship ballistic missiles, that may soon be able to locate and attack U.S. carriers at considerable distances.[1] The Chinese People's Liberation Army has also developed concepts for information warfare that integrate computer network operations, electronic warfare, and kinetic strikes to degrade an opponent's ability to collect, process, and disseminate information.[2] If combined effectively, antiship ballistic missiles and attacks on information networks could endanger the U.S. Navy's command of the sea.[3]

Although the specific problems presented by antiship ballistic missiles and information warfare are new, the broader operational challenges are not. During the Cold War, the threat posed by Soviet naval aviation and submarines prompted the U.S. Navy to stage a number of experiments examining the conduct of dispersed operations at sea. Spreading out across a wide area, it was believed, would make U.S. naval forces harder to detect, identify, and target. In order to lessen the chance of detection further, the U.S. forces in the experiments strictly limited their communications. Dispersed operations under emission control (EMCON) represented a significant departure from more active and overt methods of operation and posed new operational challenges. Navy experiments like the HAYSTACK and UPTIDE series therefore offer collectively an excellent opportunity to study organizational adaptation and change in response to new technologies and threats and to consider the conduct of distributed operations in the absence of a network.

The U.S. Navy in the 1950s

One of the primary challenges facing the U.S. Navy in the early years of the Cold War was how to employ its command of the sea to influence events ashore. The Soviet Union was essentially a land power; it did not possess a fleet capable of challenging American maritime supremacy. Instead, American and Western European policy makers expected a land attack against Western Europe and the Middle East to constitute the Soviets' principal offensive thrust in any future conflict.[4] As early as 1948, the U.S. Navy began envisaging an offensive strike force that would seek to slow the Soviet ground advance across Western Europe.[5] By 1956, the carriers of the Navy's Mediterranean-based Sixth Fleet were tasked with not only slowing any Soviet attack headed west and south but also striking key targets in the southern European part of the Soviet Union.[6]

In order for their aircraft to reach their targets, however, the Sixth Fleet's carriers had to move into the eastern Mediterranean, close to the Soviet Union, and survive there long enough to conduct launch operations. In the mid-1950s, the carriers' chances of doing so appeared slim. A series of air-defense exercises over the preceding years had demonstrated the fleet's inability to defend itself against even relatively small Soviet air raids.[7] In 1956, Admiral John H. Cassady, Commander in Chief, U.S. Naval Forces, Eastern Atlantic and Mediterranean, conceded in his annual report, "It is widely recognized that a carrier task force cannot provide for its air defense under conditions likely to exist in combat in the Mediterranean."[8]

The Haystack Concept

When Vice Admiral Harry Felt assumed command of Sixth Fleet in 1956, the fleet's ability to perform its primary mission was therefore questionable. Perhaps as a consequence, Sixth Fleet had the reputation of being a social rather than an operational fleet. Felt sought to change that reputation and improve the effectiveness of his new command by infusing the fleet's staff with new blood.[9]

One of the young officers Felt brought in was Lieutenant Jeremiah Denton.[10] Denton's background was in lighter-than-air aviation and electronic warfare. He had tested large airborne radars in blimps and served as the project officer for the WV-2, one of the Navy's first airborne-early-warning radar aircraft. Denton thus possessed a solid understanding of air defense operations, Soviet aerial attack capabilities, and airborne radar systems.[11]

Drawing on his extensive experience looking at radar scopes, Denton had developed an idea of how to extend the survival time of the Sixth Fleet's carriers during a general war.[12] He joined forces with Ralph Beatty, the Operations Evaluation Group analyst attached to Sixth Fleet, who had been working on mathematical techniques for calculating how a fleet of aircraft could find a carrier in a background of similar targets. Together, they began developing the new concept.[13]

Denton and Beatty argued that the Soviet bombers' greatest challenge was finding and identifying the Sixth Fleet's carriers. The fleet should therefore do everything in its power to "thwart and delay" recognition of the carriers. It should disperse widely and intermingle with commercial shipping in order to eliminate the unmistakable appearance on airborne radar scopes of the standard close, circular ("bull's-eye") formation. All nearby supporting units, including the destroyers serving as plane guards and screening the carriers against submarines, should disperse, and the carriers should operate independently. Strict control of all electronic emissions and the widespread use of deception would increase the effectiveness of the concept, which Denton dubbed "Haystack," because of its emphasis on making the carriers difficult to find.[14]

When Felt left Sixth Fleet after just six months to become Vice Chief of Naval Operations, he made a point of praising Denton, Beatty, and the Haystack concept in front of his successor, Vice Admiral Charles "Cat" Brown, and the entire Sixth Fleet staff.[15] Under Brown's command, Sixth Fleet began conducting experiments to test the Haystack concept. Small-scale tests began in October 1956.

The HAYSTACK Exercises

The first major exercise testing the Haystack concept, HAYSTACK CHARLIE, was conducted in January 1957 in the Mediterranean Sea about a hundred miles west of Sardinia. The primary objective of the two-day exercise was "to test the effectiveness of tactical deception as a method of striking force air defense." The exercise pitted two aircraft carriers, USS *Coral Sea* (CVA 43) and USS *Randolph* (CVA 15), their escorts, and their logistical support ships against a conventional submarine and land-based snooper and attack aircraft flying out of Naples and Malta. The carriers, which operated up to 250 miles apart, conducted simulated nuclear strikes against wartime targets and then retired, while the aggressor force tried to find and attack them as soon as possible.[16]

The exercise results suggested that tactical deception was effective. The carriers were able to avoid detection long enough to launch thirty to thirty-five simulated atomic strikes each day before being "attacked" by "aggressor" aircraft. Small groups of ships were employed effectively as decoys; they attracted attacks from several aircraft searching for the carriers. In particular, the guided-missile cruiser USS *Boston* (CAG 1) and two destroyers acted as an effective "missile trap" early in the exercise, shooting down several snooper aircraft trying to investigate the three closely packed radar blips.[17]

The results indicated, however, that the Haystack concept was still imperfect. Destroyers were frequently too close to the carriers. The three destroyers escorting *Coral Sea* were within ten miles of the carrier when the exercise began, enabling a snooper aircraft to detect the carrier in the first five minutes. The destroyers accompanying *Randolph* remained more distant, but they were still close enough to attract attention from snooper aircraft soon after the exercise started. Aircraft also tended to operate too close to the carriers. Aggressor aircraft attacked *Randolph* after intercepting the radar of an antisubmarine patrol plane circling the carrier. A snooper aircraft also detected the radar signal of an airborne-early-warning plane operating near a carrier.[18]

HAYSTACK DELTA, a seventeen-hour exercise, was held on 2 March 1957 in the Mediterranean Sea southeast of Malta and Sicily. The exercise emphasized passive air defense using traps and decoy groups. It matched two carriers, USS *Forrestal* (CVA 59) and USS *Lake Champlain* (CVA 39), against two conventional submarines and land-based attack, snooper, and electronic countermeasure (ECM) aircraft operating out of Naples and Malta.[19]

The exercise results again suggested that tactical deception was successful. The strike aircraft experienced significant problems identifying targets due to heavy cloud cover and squalls, careful emission control, and deceptive formations. Learning from past exercises, the destroyers in HAYSTACK DELTA remained farther away from the carriers and often paired with other ships to simulate carriers. The eight aggressor strikes detected thirteen possible military targets, but only one correctly identified a carrier *(Forrestal)* and its plane guard. Three strikes detected *Boston* and two accompanying destroyers, which were stationed in the expected direction of attack in order to draw strikes away from the carriers, and closed to investigate or attack. Two other strikes attacked oilers, which were paired with destroyers and being used as decoys for the first time.[20]

Emission control also proved effective. Only radar picket destroyers and sector air-defense ships, not carriers, used navigation aids. The aggressor ECM aircraft located the task force's operating area but could not locate or identify individual units, due to the suppression of electronic signals characteristic of particular ships.[21]

In order to experiment with the use of islands to hinder the identification of surface units by aggressor aircraft, the venue for HAYSTACK ECHO was moved to the Aegean Sea. The exercise, which was held from 9 to 11 April 1957, pitted *Forrestal*, *Lake Champlain*, and their escorts against two submarines and land-based snooper, ECM, and attack aircraft operating from Athens. The primary objective, again, was to practice tactical control and air defense in a dispersed disposition.[22]

Postexercise analysis was to indicate that it had not realistically tested the Haystack concept, because of the requirement for nighttime air operations and the consequent need for the carriers to employ plane guards and tactical air navigation systems (TACANs). An aggressor ECM aircraft had intercepted *Lake Champlain*'s TACAN emissions shortly after the exercise began and vectored in snooper aircraft to track the carrier and strike aircraft to attack it. The initial two attacks had been successful, as were two later strikes; snooper aircraft had tracked *Lake Champlain* almost continuously for the rest of the exercise. *Forrestal* had been detected visually at 7:14 AM on 10 April and had been tracked continuously thereafter, although it had not been attacked successfully until 3:01 PM. ECM aircraft had also detected and successfully attacked the carriers on several other occasions during the exercise. The analysis concluded, "Air control without the use of TACAN by carriers is essential."[23]

Other attempts at deception in HAYSTACK ECHO were only moderately success-ful. The heavy cruiser *Salem* (CA 139) and two destroyers decoyed snooper aircraft into shadowing them for several hours, until daybreak revealed that the group was not a carrier and its escorts. The many islands in the operating area, however, did not appear to hinder the aggressor force's ability to find the carriers. Instead, they complicated the task force's efforts to defend itself. Landlocking of radars (the ten-dency of radar return from landmasses to mask contacts around them) severely handicapped the ability of the task force to detect aggressor aircraft and control its own aircraft. Moreover, once the carriers and decoy groups were located, they were unable to relocate quickly. The aggressors could thus ignore the decoys and concen-trate their efforts on the carriers.[24]

The purpose of the Haystack concept was to develop tactics that would extend the survival time of U.S. carriers in the Mediterranean during the initial period of a nuclear exchange. After the conclusion of HAYSTACK ECHO, Brown declared the ex-ercises a success. In a letter to the Chief of Naval Operations (CNO) that also went to all the major commands in the Navy, Brown claimed, "Haystack tactics have been proved effective in increasing the critical survival time available for launching counter strikes against aggressor bases under today's war conditions in this area."[25] When the exercise series began, the expected survival time for carriers in the Medi-terranean had been less than two hours. During HAYSTACK CHARLIE, DELTA, and ECHO, the carriers, with one exception, survived for at least eight hours; half of the participating carriers survived for over fifteen hours.[26] Extending the survival time of the carriers by even a few hours gave them enough time to hit Soviet airfields and ports, thereby reducing the threat they faced thereafter. "As each hour without at-tack passes," Brown explained, "the chances of continued survival increases many fold."[27]

The U.S. Navy in the 1960s

The Sixth Fleet focused most of its attention on the threat posed by Soviet long-range aviation in part because there was no significant Soviet naval presence outside home waters at the time. In the mid-1950s Soviet surface combatants started to visit foreign ports occasionally, and they began conducting annual exercises in the North and Norwegian Seas in the late 1950s, but there were still relatively few Soviet submarines operating in the Mediterranean. The commander of the Sixth Fleet from 1958 to 1959, Vice Admiral Clarence E. Ekstrom, felt the submarine threat facing Sixth Fleet was "quite manageable."[28]

The developers of the Haystack concept expected that dispersing the destroyers screening the carrier would increase the carrier's vulnerability to submarine attack but considered the risk acceptable in areas where the submarine concentration was low or when the air threat exceeded the submarine threat.[29] By 1961 they were confident that the combination of dispersion, deception, and emission control would enable U.S. carriers to survive against enemy submarine attack long enough to conduct their retaliatory nuclear strikes, even in areas of relatively high concentrations of submarines, so long as those submarines were conventionally powered. Beatty estimated that a carrier could survive for an average of five days in a ten-thousand-square-mile area containing two conventional submarines.[30]

The introduction of the nuclear-powered submarine in the mid-1950s, however, revolutionized undersea warfare.[31] The first Soviet nuclear submarines began entering service in 1958 and soon threatened to render the Haystack tactics obsolete. By the early 1960s leading Navy officials were increasingly focused on how to counter the potential threat of nuclear submarines. A paper, "The Strategic Concept for Antisubmarine Warfare," circulated by the CNO, Admiral Arleigh Burke, identified hostile submarine activities as "foremost among the threats to our use of the seas."[32]

Compounding the challenge was the equipping of nuclear submarines with antiship cruise missiles. As early as 1960, Rear Admiral Jimmy Thach, one of the Navy's leading antisubmarine warfare (ASW) experts, predicted that submarine forces would increasingly rely on missiles as their primary weapons, even against shipping.[33] The Soviet Echo II class, a nuclear-powered submarine equipped with eight SS-N-3A (Shaddock) missiles, entered service in 1962. The SS-N-3A missile was, with the exception of certain aircraft, the longest-ranged antiship weapon in the world; it was capable of striking targets at sea from a distance of 250 nautical miles. Since the typical defensive perimeter of an American carrier battle group extended only a hundred nautical miles from the center, an Echo II could remain outside the perimeter and potentially launch an attack undetected. After an exercise to test performance against Soviet nuclear submarines firing "standoff" missiles, one U.S. Navy commander concluded, "It is evident that the force would have had essentially no capability against such an attack."[34]

Although the cruise missile–firing submarine presented dangers, it also had weaknesses. Its chief problem was detecting and identifying its targets while preserving its own stealth. As Beatty observed, "The ability of a submarine to identify carriers by sonar alone in large dispersed dispositions is poor. Visual identification is usually necessary."[35] He recommended testing the effectiveness of dispersed formations against nuclear submarines and placing an increased emphasis on the development of acoustic deception tactics and equipment, particularly expendable acoustic decoys.[36]

The UPTIDE Concept

By the late 1960s, the Navy increasingly emphasized improving its ability to defend against missile-firing nuclear submarines. In June 1968, the commander in chief of the Pacific Fleet, Admiral John J. Hyland, initiated Project UPTIDE (Unified Pacific Fleet Project for Tactical Improvement and Data Extraction). One of the primary objectives of UPTIDE was to devise and evaluate tactics Pacific Fleet antisubmarine warfare groups (typically an ASW carrier, its air wing, and a destroyer squadron) could use to frustrate and defend against missile and torpedo attacks by enemy submarines within moving or static areas of high tactical interest.[37]

The driving force behind the UPTIDE series was Vice Admiral E. P. "Pete" Aurand. An innovator and iconoclast, Aurand suggested shifting the focus of the ASW effort from killing submarines to reducing their effectiveness by preventing encounters.[38] Echoing Beatty, Aurand argued that although the nuclear submarine was very fast and could remain submerged indefinitely, it was still essentially blind. An unassisted submarine relied heavily on passive acoustic sensors to detect, classify, track, and localize carriers and other high-value targets. Degrading the information the submarine received could significantly reduce its effectiveness.

The UPTIDE experiments focused on reducing the probabilities that the submarine would detect, identify, and localize its target. The probability that the submarine would detect its target could be reduced by strict acoustic and electromagnetic emission control. Aurand may have drawn inspiration from his previous observation of Soviet naval operations in the Sea of Japan. Aurand had noticed that Soviet radar antennas neither rotated nor emitted. He speculated that the Soviet navy's policy was to leave its radars turned off unless there was no other way to obtain desired information. Although it denied the Soviets early warning, Aurand believed, "such a policy has merit, especially when compared to the predominant practice of most U.S. ships to emit constantly." He concluded, "Finesse in the handling of emitters, electronic, visual, and acoustic should be developed by our ships, especially in the vicinity of Soviet ships."[39]

The probability that the submarine would successfully identify a detected target could be decreased through acoustic deception. The probability that the submarine would localize it (i.e., close to within range of its weapons) could be diminished by forcing the submarine to move slowly, by deploying good passive acoustic systems in all antisubmarine vehicles, especially helicopters and destroyers.[40]

The UPTIDE Experiments

Project UPTIDE developed in three phases from January 1969 to November 1972. In each phase, an ASW group examined various dimensions of the challenge presented by nuclear submarines firing cruise missiles.[41] The purpose of Phase I was to lay the foundation for Phases II and III by exploring the broad outlines of the problem, refining the experimental design and methodology, and developing procedures for processing and analyzing data. It examined the situation from the perspective of the enemy submarine and derived data on the submarine's capabilities to detect, identify, and fire its missiles at high-value targets. Phase I also established a baseline for comparison of conventional antisubmarine warfare tactics with UPTIDE tactics.[42]

Phase I consisted of three continuous free-play experiments (each a Hunter-Killer Antisubmarine Warfare Exercise, or HUKASWEX), which took place from January to March 1969. In each exercise, USS *Kearsarge* (CVS 33), its aircraft, and Destroyer Squadron 23, constituting Antisubmarine Warfare Group 1, tried to defend *Kearsarge* against two opposing submarines with simulated cruise-missile capabilities. The submarines participating in Phase I were USS *Pomodon* (SS 486) and *Medregal* (SS 480) for HUKASWEX 1-69 and USS *Snook* (SSN 592) and *Scamp* (SSN 588) for HUKASWEX 2-69 and 3-69. The results of Phase I underscored the magnitude of the threat posed by the cruise-missile submarine and established the key metric that would be used in Phase II—the survival time of the carrier. In 144 exercise hours, the submarines conducted three torpedo attacks and nineteen launch events simulating the firing of seventy-eight missiles at the carrier. Eighty-seven percent of the missiles were judged to have met the bearing parameters for acquisition of their targets. The average survival time of the carrier was nine hours.[43]

Phase II was the major data-collection and tactical-evaluation phase of Project UPTIDE. It consisted of four major experiments from September 1969 to January 1971. The experiments were devoted to examining the effectiveness of dispersion, acoustic and electromagnetic emission control, simulation of the high-value target by surface escorts, and active acoustic deception against cruise missile–firing submarines in a scenario involving a carrier operating within a fixed area and simulating the launching of strike aircraft.[44]

The initial Phase II experiment, UPTIDE 2-B, took place in late September and early October 1969 and pitted Antisubmarine Warfare Group 3—consisting of USS *Hornet* (CVS 12), its aircraft, and Destroyer Squadron 31—against USS *Sculpin* (SSN 590) and *Razorback* (SS 394). By employing a dispersed formation, steaming below propeller cavitation speed (i.e., the speed at which the collapse of bubbles behind the blades becomes detectably loud), controlling emissions, and using escorts as "wolf trap" units to lure the submarines away, *Hornet* was able to avoid identification for the entire seven-day exercise. The submarines were deceived, lured, or confused for the majority of the exercise and spent nearly all the rest of the time in unproductive searches. Toward the end of the exercise, in frustration, *Sculpin* used strategic information to fire a spread of eight missiles at a range of two hundred miles. Significantly, two of them could have met the bearing parameters to acquire *Hornet*. Nevertheless, the commander of Antisubmarine Warfare Group 3 described the exercise as "an unprecedented success against the undersea adversary by an ASW group using a totally new concept in communications, formations, tactics, deception, and electronic/acoustic emission control."[45]

UPTIDE 2-C, held in January and February 1970, marked the introduction of a new tactical element—the acoustic deception device. The minesweeper USS *Leader* (MSO 490) was equipped with an active acoustic simulator called "Tergiversator," developed by the Naval Underwater Sound Center in New London, Connecticut. Tergiversator transmitted into the water carrier and escort propulsion noises and active sonar transmissions. Working together, *Leader* and the guided-missile cruiser USS *Chicago* (CG 11) were able to deceive the submarines USS *Plunger* (SSN 595) and *Snook*. After listening to the deception device's output for three hours, *Plunger* concluded that it was a heavy warship and fired two missiles at it. Meanwhile, *Hornet* was able to survive undetected for eighty-seven hours. Only when the carrier operated independently at high speed were the submarines successful in making a coordinated missile attack.[46]

The number and range of acoustic deception devices expanded significantly in UPTIDE 2-D, which was held in October 1970. Seven devices were employed, including an updated version of Tergiversator; two SADSAC (Small Acoustic Device Simulating a Carrier) buoys, developed by the Naval Underwater Research and Development Center; and four NYVOs (Nymph's Voices), developed by Magnavox. Once again the devices proved effective. They were able to mask the identity of USS *Ticonderoga* (CVS 14) for the first ninety-three hours of the exercise and induce *Sculpin* and *Snook* to dedicate two of their four launch events and nine of their sixteen missiles to them.[47]

The final exercise of Phase II, UPTIDE 2-E, underscored the dramatic impact that the experimental tactics could have on carrier survivability. Using UPTIDE tactics, *Ticonderoga* was able to avoid detection by *Plunger* and USS *Haddock* (SSN 621) for the entire 140 hours of the regularly scheduled exercise. On the last day, the carrier reverted to conventional tactics; it was targeted for simulated missile attacks within four and a half hours.

The principal finding from Phase II was that UPTIDE dispersion and deception tactics allowed carriers and their escorts to avoid consistently encounters with submarines. In nearly 650 exercise hours, there were just fourteen launch events, simulating the firing of fifty-six missiles. Moreover, less than one-third of the missiles met the bearing parameters for acquisition. On average, the submarines went a hundred hours between valid fire-control solutions on the carrier and were unable to conduct any torpedo attacks. In the four week-long exercise periods of UPTIDE Phase II, the "Blue" (i.e., U.S.) force achieved an average survival time of almost five and a half days for the high-value target between submarine-launched missile firings —an improvement by a factor of eighteen over Phase I results using conventional tactics.[48]

Phase III of UPTIDE, in two experiments from October 1971 to November 1972, examined transit scenarios and used a new measure of performance—miles safely traveled. The challenges the ASW group faced were increased to include integrated surface, subsurface, and air threats, but they were offset by corresponding increases in the group's capabilities. Among the new capabilities introduced were land-based patrol aircraft, towed passive sonar arrays, and helicopter-equipped destroyers. Acoustic deception devices were also used extensively, and with considerable success. Combining these new capabilities with UPTIDE tactics, the ASW group in UPTIDE 3-A was able to make good 86 percent of the nine hundred miles it attempted without a successful attack by a submarine. Only when three of the five acoustic deception devices being used broke down was the carrier detected and successfully targeted.[49]

The final exercise of the UPTIDE series, UPTIDE 3-B, occurred in October and November 1972. It added several new capabilities to the Blue forces, including two squadrons of land-based patrol aircraft and a helicopter-equipped destroyer. The Blue forces also successfully made tactical use of towed sonar arrays and Sound Surveillance System (SOSUS) information, although the slow towing speed of the towed arrays limited their utility in transit scenarios.[50]

Dispersed Operations under EMCON

The forces participating in the HAYSTACK exercises and those conducting the UPTIDE series struggled to command and control widely dispersed forces under EMCON. During the HAYSTACK exercises, Sixth Fleet sought to exploit "every available method of delivering message traffic that will permit the originating ship to maintain the highest practicable degree of electronic silence."[51] The fleet forbade the commanding officers of ships to use electronic means of communication unless absolutely necessary.[52] Instead, they were to employ visual signals, such as flag hoists or blinkers, to control flight operations and transmit messages.[53]

The fleet also urged the use of helicopters and airplanes to carry messages between ships. There was always the possibility of missing a message drop, but the helicopter or aircraft would typically carry extra copies of messages. The messages, enclosed in the equivalent of a buoy, would also float and could therefore be retrieved. Aircraft could also deliver messages to shore-based radio stations for relay to their ultimate destinations.[54]

In cases where electronic communication was necessary, the fleet relied on airborne relay of ultrahigh-frequency (UHF) transmissions, which are typically limited to horizon ranges and so are more difficult to detect than high-frequency transmissions. Although Soviet aircraft, submarines, and surface ships could intercept UHF transmissions, they had to be fairly close to the task force to do so. UHF was thus seen as a "relatively secure means of communication."[55]

Many of the methods UPTIDE forces employed were similar to those used during the HAYSTACK exercises. Among these were "bean-bag communications" (delivery of messages by helicopter) and airborne UHF relay. A central element of UPTIDE was the extensive use of an airborne-early-warning aircraft to relay UHF communications from the carrier to its escorts and other ships. During UPTIDE 3-A, antisubmarine aircraft and the carrier's combat information center used UHF so heavily that they nearly saturated the available circuits.[56]

The restriction to alternative methods and the near saturation of available circuits produced significant delays in communications. In HAYSTACK CHARLIE, inexperience with the alternative radio techniques used and the existence of too many units on the nets in each sector combined to produce long communications delays.[57] In UPTIDE 3-A, the delay times for messages with immediate operational relevance ranged from ten to 318 minutes. Even flash-precedence messages were delayed for up to sixty minutes.[58]

Diminished communications capabilities placed a premium on planning. To implement the Haystack concept, Sixth Fleet relied more heavily on doctrine and fixed plans.[59] According to the concept, "Movements of the fleet will be preplanned and promulgated as much in advance as possible, to allow maximum practicable electronic silence."[60] Before every port visit, Sixth Fleet would disseminate the "position and intended movement" (PIM), or route, that task forces would follow should there be a warning that nuclear war was imminent. To reduce the number of PIM-change messages, task force commanders were instructed to plan ahead and cover several days' movements with one message if possible.[61]

To minimize the volume of electronic emissions, Sixth Fleet also adopted a set of basic communications procedures. Preassigned alphanumeric groups indicated desired PIM changes or changes in ship stations. Simple aircraft codes were used to transmit classified information. Recipients of messages did not "Roger" or acknowledge receipt.[62]

UPTIDE similarly emphasized planning. Just prior to UPTIDE 3-A, the commander of Antisubmarine Warfare Group 3, Rear Admiral Carl J. Seiberlich, gave commanding officers of all his units the opportunity to work with his staff on the development of plans and options. The detailed and inclusive planning process produced significant benefits. As Seiberlich later explained to Aurand, he and his staff received valuable inputs, while "the commanding officers all feel that they have had a piece of the planning action, and understand our philosophy and objectives."[63] One of the focal points of the planning process was minimizing opportunities for detection of the carrier. UPTIDE tactics tried to reduce acoustic detectability through the use of noncavitating speeds where possible. Implementing the tactic required, according to the UPTIDE 3-A report, "judicious planning of the time and location when cavitating speeds were required.[64]

"There Might Be Some Useful Ideas There"

As Ralph Beatty once noted, interest in deceptive formations and dispersed operations under emission control seems to be cyclical. Every few years a version of the same basic idea emerges. Each iteration of the concept has been a response to a different specific threat—such as nuclear attack by land-based aviation in the HAYSTACK series, cruise-missile attack by submarines in the UPTIDE series—and has therefore approached the problem with little reference to past efforts. Yet the basic challenge has remained the same: How can naval forces conduct effective operations while dispersing widely and minimizing communications in order to avoid detection and attack? Since the U.S. Navy is likely to face similar challenges in the future, it might do well to heed Beatty's suggestion: "Pay attention to what's happened before. There might be some useful ideas there."[65]

One of the useful ideas highlighted by a review of the U.S. Navy's experiments with dispersed operations under EMCON during the Cold War is the utility of alternative methods of communication. During the HAYSTACK and UPTIDE exercises, the participating forces chose to limit their communications in order to minimize the adversary's ability to detect and identify them. They experimented with a wide variety of methods—both low-tech (flag hoists) and high-tech (airborne UHF relay). The ability to communicate and exchange information using a range of different methods and to relay communications from platform to platform proved invaluable.

As the participants in HAYSTACK and UPTIDE discovered, however, alternative communication methods typically have less capacity than more traditional ones. Consequently, it is important to develop detailed procedures for operating with diminished network capacity. Sixth Fleet included comprehensive appendices in its operations orders outlining the specific instructions for operating with diminished communications. The instructions spelled out which messages and which users should receive priority under various conditions and which procedures should be employed.[66]

It was also important to practice employing alternative means of communication. The forces participating in HAYSTACK CHARLIE experienced what analysts described as "excessive" delays, due in part to inexperience with the communications method employed. Similarly, air control in HAYSTACK DELTA was unsatisfactory due in part to controller inexperience.[67]

Even with the development of appropriate procedures and extensive practice, forces using alternative methods of communication experienced delays. According to the UPTIDE 3-A exercise report, the reduction in communications capabilities and use of alternative methods "extracted a price from the BLUE forces in terms of inadequate information exchange between the BLUE OTC [officer in tactical command] and his dispersed forces." "Information of value to the OTC from outlying units is often received late or not at all," the report explained, "and outlying units often lack the 'big picture' information held by the OTC."[68]

The delays and diminished flow of information inherent in the use of alternative communications methods underscored the importance of planning and decentralized decision making. The promulgation of plans as far in advance as possible enabled the commanders of the forces participating in the HAYSTACK and UPTIDE series to convey their intents before communications were diminished. The unit commanders, thus fully aware of their mission, were able to take the initiative, make decisions quickly, and implement them aggressively.

As U.S. naval forces increasingly operate under the threat of antiship-ballistic-missile attack while relying on rapid communication and information exchange, potential adversaries are likely to seek to detect, track, and target those forces and disrupt their communication and information networks. In future contests for control of information, as Beatty warned a decade ago, it will be important to understand what works and what does not work.[69] The principles and practices the U.S. Navy developed while experimenting with dispersed operations under EMCON appear to fall in the former category. As Rear Admiral George P. Steele told Aurand after receiving a briefing on UPTIDE, "I was able to make use of a great deal of it [the UPTIDE concept], and I am a believer; it works, and very well."[70]

NOTES   This chapter appeared, by permission of the author, as an article in the Spring 2011 issue of the *Naval War College Review*.

1 Andrew S. Erickson, "China's Evolving Anti-access Approach: 'Where's the Next (U.S.) Carrier?'" *China Brief* 10, no. 18 (10 September 2010), pp. 5–8; Andrew S. Erickson and David D. Yang, "Using the Land to Control the Sea? Chinese Analysts Consider the Antiship Ballistic Missile," *Naval War College Review* 62, no. 4 (Autumn 2009), pp. 53–86; Eric Hagt and Matthew Durnin, "China's Antiship Ballistic Missile: Developments and Missing Links," *Naval War College Review* 62, no. 4 (Autumn 2009), pp. 87–115.

2 Bryan Krekel, *Capability of the People's Republic of China to Conduct Cyber Warfare and Computer Network Exploitation,* prepared for the U.S.-China Economic and Security Review Commission (McLean, Va.: Northrop Grumman Corp., 2009); Timothy L. Thomas, "China's Electronic Long-Range Reconnaissance," *Military Review* (November–December 2008), pp. 47–54; Timothy L. Thomas, "Chinese and American Network Warfare," *Joint Force Quarterly,* no. 38 (3rd Quarter 2005), pp. 76–83.

3 Robert C. Rubel, "Talking about Sea Control," *Naval War College Review* 63, no. 4 (Autumn 2010), pp. 38–47.

4 Jakub J. Grygiel, "The Dilemmas of US Maritime Supremacy in the Early Cold War," *Journal of Strategic Studies* 28 (April 2005), pp. 191–206; Philip Alphonse Dur, "The Sixth Fleet: A Case Study of Institutionalized Naval Presence" (PhD diss., Harvard University, 1975), p. 72.

5 Dur, "Sixth Fleet," pp. 21, 33, 39.

6 Grygiel, "Dilemmas of US Maritime Supremacy in the Early Cold War," pp. 191–206; Dur, "Sixth Fleet," p. 72.

7 Adm. Jeremiah Denton, telephone interview, 26 and 27 May 2009.

8 Commander in Chief, U.S. Naval Forces, Eastern Atlantic and Mediterranean, to Chief of Naval Operations [hereafter CNO], ser. 00285, "Report of Operations and Conditions of Command, 1 July 1955–1 May 1956," 1 May 1956, quoted in Dur, "Sixth Fleet," pp. 76–77.

9 Adm. Harry Donald Felt, *Reminiscences of Admiral Harry Donald Felt,* Oral History (Annapolis, Md.: U.S. Naval Institute, 1974), p. 274.

10 Edward A. Smyth and Eugene P. Visco, "Military Operations Research Society Oral History Project Interview of Dr. Ralph Beatty, Jr.," *Military Operations Research* 9, no. 3 (2004) [hereafter "Interview of Dr. Ralph Beatty, Jr."], p. 66.

11 Denton, interview.

12 Smyth and Visco, "Interview of Dr. Ralph Beatty, Jr.," p. 66; "Men and Machines," *Naval Aviation News* (September 1974), p. 24.

13 Smyth and Visco, "Interview of Dr. Ralph Beatty, Jr.," pp. 66–67.

14 Operations Evaluation Group [hereafter OEG], *The Sixth Fleet Concept and Analysis of Haystack Operations,* OEG Report 77 (Washington, D.C.: Office of the CNO, 24 January 1958), pp. 3–4; "The Haystack Concept," Vice Adm. C. R. Brown, Commander U.S. Sixth Fleet [hereafter COMSIXTHFLT], to Adm. A. Burke, CNO, encl. 1, "Haystack Concept of Striking Forces; Report On," declassified, 2 November 1957, pp. 2–3, Sixth Fleet Files, 1957, Post-1946 Command File, Operational Archives, Naval History and Heritage Command, Washington, D.C. [hereafter OA, NHHC].

15 Felt, *Reminiscences of Admiral Harry Donald Felt,* pp. 282–83.

16 OEG, *Sixth Fleet Concept and Analysis of Haystack Operations,* p. 5; "Haystack Concept," in Brown to Burke, "Haystack Concept of Striking Forces," p. 3.

17 OEG, *Sixth Fleet Concept and Analysis of Haystack Operations,* pp. 13–14.

18 Ibid., pp. 14, 16, 19, 23.

19 Ibid., p. 25.

20 Ibid., pp. 27–31.

21 Ibid., pp. 25, 28.

22 Ibid., pp. 37, 42.

23 Ibid., pp. 42–46.

24 Ibid.

25 Brown to Burke, "Haystack Concept of Striking Forces," p. 3.

26 Ibid., p. 2.

27 Ibid., pp. 3, 6–7.

28 Vice Adm. C. E. Ekstrom to Philip Alphonse Dur, 3 January 1975, quoted in Dur, "Sixth Fleet," p. 75.

29 R. E. Beatty and L. S. Pocinski, *Submarine Opposition to Carriers in Large Dispersed Dispositions,* Operations Evaluation Group Study 642 (Washington, D.C.: OEG, Office of the CNO, 13 February 1961), p. 4.

30 Denton, interview; Beatty and Pocinski, *Submarine Opposition to Carriers in Large Dispersed Dispositions,* pp. 3, 10.

31 Owen Cote, *The Third Battle: Innovation in the U.S. Navy's Silent Cold War Struggle with Soviet Submarines,* Newport Paper 16 (Newport, R.I.: Naval War College Press, 2003), p. 52.

32 Adm. Arleigh Burke, CNO, "The Strategic Concept for Antisubmarine Warfare," declassified, 15 January 1960, file 3300, Anti-Submarine Operations, 1960, p. 1, Immediate Office Files of the CNO, OA, NHHC.

33 Rear Adm. J. S. Thach, "The Trend in ASW," declassified, 22 January 1960, file 3300, Anti-Submarine Operations, 1960, p. 3, Immediate Office Files of the CNO, OA, NHHC.

34 Jan Breemer, *Soviet Submarines: Design, Development, and Tactics* (Surrey, U.K.: Jane's Information Group, 1989), pp. 91, 103–106, 113, 117, 119; John Jordan, *Soviet Submarines, 1945 to the Present* (London: Arms and Armour, 1989), pp. 74–84, 103–108; Malcolm Muir, Jr., *Black Shoes and Blue Water: Surface Warfare in the United States Navy, 1945–1975* (Washington, D.C.: Naval Historical Center, 1996), pp. 74, 115–16, 135–36, 172; Norman Polmar and Jurrien Noot, *Submarines of the Russian and Soviet Navies, 1718–1990* (Annapolis, Md.: Naval Institute Press, 1991), pp. 155–56, 166, 177, 186–87, 333–34; Cote, *Third Battle,* pp. 60–61.

35 Beatty and Pocinski, *Submarine Opposition to Carriers in Large Dispersed Dispositions,* p. 3.

36 Ibid.

37 Vice Adm. Turner Caldwell, Director of ASW Programs, to CNO, "Comments on COMASWFORPAC's UPTIDE Proposals," declassified, 11 July 1969, Antisubmarine Warfare Folder, Immediate Office Files of the CNO, OA, NHHC; Capt. W. E. Sims to CNO, "Brief of Project UPTIDE Presentation to CAB," declassified, 23 November 1970, Antisubmarine Warfare Folder, Immediate Office Files of the CNO, OA, NHHC; R. F. Cross Associates,

Sea-Based Airborne Antisubmarine Warfare, 1940–1977, vol. 2, *1960–1977,* 2nd ed., declassified (Alexandria, Va.: 1978), p. 102. For more on UPTIDE, see Robert G. Angevine, "Innovation and Experimentation in the US Navy: The UPTIDE Antisubmarine Warfare Experiments, 1969–72," *Journal of Strategic Studies* 28 (February 2005), pp. 77–105.

38 Vice Adm. Eli T. Reich, *Reminiscences of Vice Admiral Eli T. Reich,* Oral History (Annapolis, Md.: U.S. Naval Institute, 1982), vol. 2, p. 617; Robert H. Smith, "Remembering Admiral Pete Aurand," U.S. Naval Institute *Proceedings* (December 1989), p. 108; Rear Adm. E. P. Aurand, "An Approach to Thinking about ASW Problems," declassified, [1966] file "An Approach to Thinking about ASW Problems," E. P. Aurand Papers, OA, NHHC.

39 Commander, Antisubmarine Warfare Group 1, "Report of Operations Northeast of Luzon to Conduct Overt Surveillance of Soviet Forces Which Had Exited the Sea of Japan," ser. 072, 26 February 1966, ASWGRU 1, 1966, p. 5, Post-1946 Command File, OA, NHHC.

40 Vice Adm. E. P. Aurand, "Speech to Destroyer Conference," declassified, 22 September 1971, COMASWFORPAC, 1969–1972, box 8, Aurand Office Files, OA, NHHC; Vice Adm. E. P. Aurand, "ASW in the Pacific," declassified, 20–21 May 1970, Tenth NSIA/Navy ASW Conference, Washington, D.C., COMASWFORPAC, 1969–1972, box 8, Aurand Office Files, OA, NHHC.

41 Vice Adm. E. P. Aurand, Commander, Antisubmarine Warfare Forces Pacific [hereafter COMASWFORPAC], to Dr. Joel S. Lawson, Jr., Director of Navy Laboratories, declassified, 17 April 1972, Personal Correspondence, 1970–1972, box 6, Aurand Papers, OA, NHHC. Management of Project UPTIDE actually began in October 1968, and Phase I commenced in December 1968, but the first exercise did not begin until January 1969; COMASWFORPAC Command History, 1968, pp. 5–6, box 839, Post-1946 Command File, OA, NHHC.

42 Sims to CNO; R. F. Cross Associates, *Sea-Based Airborne Antisubmarine Warfare, 1940–1977,* p. 150.

43 Sims to CNO.

44 Aurand to Lawson.

45 Sims to CNO; R. F. Cross Associates, *Sea-Based Airborne Antisubmarine Warfare, 1940–1977,* p. 150; Commander, Anti-submarine Warfare Group 3 [hereafter COMASWGRU 3], Command History, 1969, encl. 4, declassified, p. 2, Post-1946 Command File, OA, NHHC.

46 Sims to CNO; R. F. Cross Associates, *Sea-Based Airborne Antisubmarine Warfare, 1940–1977,* pp. 150–51.

47 Sims to CNO; Aurand, "Speech to Destroyer Conference."

48 Sims to CNO; Aurand, "Speech to Destroyer Conference."

49 Aurand to Lawson; Rear Adm. C. J. Seiberlich, COMASWGRU 3, to Vice Adm. E. P. Aurand, COMASWFORPAC, declassified, 28 December 1971, COMASWFORPAC Personal File, 1971, box 5, Aurand Papers, OA, NHHC.

50 R. F. Cross Associates, *Sea-Based Airborne Antisubmarine Warfare, 1940–1977,* p. 151.

51 Brown to Burke, "Haystack Concept of Striking Forces," p. 7.

52 COMSIXTHFLT, "Change 9 to Op Order 50-56," declassified, p. K-VI-3, Sixth Fleet Command File, 1957, Post-1946 Command File, OA, NHHC.

53 "Haystack Concept," in Brown to Burke, "Haystack Concept of Striking Forces," pp. 13, 16; Denton, interview.

54 Denton, interview.

55 "Haystack Concept," in Brown to Burke, "Haystack Concept of Striking Forces," p. 16.

56 Rear Adm. N. C. Gillette, Jr., COMASWGRU 3, to Vice Adm. E. P. Aurand, COMASWFORPAC, 12 January 1970, Personal File, 1970, COMASWFORPAC, 1969–72, box 5, Aurand Papers, OA, NHHC; Commander Third Fleet [hereafter COMTHIRDFLT], "UPTIDE Report 6: UPTIDE Exercise 3A [Transit Phase]," 4 September 1973, p. V-2.

57 OEG, *Sixth Fleet Concept and Analysis of Haystack Operations,* pp. 14, 16, 19, 23.

58 COMTHIRDFLT, "Uptide Report 6," pp. V-1, V-2.

59 OEG, *Sixth Fleet Concept and Analysis of Haystack Operations,* p. 4.

60 "Haystack Concept," in Brown to Burke, "Haystack Concept of Striking Forces," p. 15.

61 Ibid., p. 16.

62 COMSIXTHFLT, Op Order 50-56, app. I, p. E-I-10; "Haystack Concept," in Brown to Burke, "Haystack Concept of Striking Forces," p. 16.

63 Seiberlich to Aurand.

64 COMTHIRDFLT, "Uptide Report 6," p. II-3.

65 Smyth and Visco, "Interview of Dr. Ralph Beatty, Jr.," pp. 71–72. The challenge is not limited to naval forces. It is possible to envision a future security environment dominated by reconnaissance strike complexes that places a premium on detecting, tracking, and targeting stealthy forces and communicating in a degraded information environment. See Michael G. Vickers and Robert C. Martinage, *The Revolution in War* (Washington, D.C.: Center for Strategic and Budgetary Assessments, 2004).

66 COMSIXTHFLT, "Change 9 to Op Order 50-56," pp. K-VI-1 to K-VI-4.

67 OEG, *Sixth Fleet Concept and Analysis of Haystack Operations,* pp. 23, 35.

68 COMTHIRDFLT, "Uptide Report 6," p. VI-2.

69 Smyth and Visco, "Interview of Dr. Ralph Beatty, Jr.," p. 71.

70 Rear Adm. G. P. Steele to Vice Adm. E. P. Aurand, COMASWFORPAC, declassified, 30 January 1972, Personal Correspondence, 1970–1972, box 6, Aurand Papers, OA, NHHC.

XII *Turbulence and Terrorism*
The Story of Headquarters Support Activity Saigon, 1964–1966

JOHN DARRELL SHERWOOD

On Christmas Eve 1964, Lt. (j.g.) Anne Darby Reynolds, a U.S. Navy nurse assigned to Station Hospital Saigon, was in the living room of an apartment she shared with three other nurses in the Brink Bachelor Officers Quarters (BOQ)—a drab, seven-story hotel leased by the navy to provide housing for American officers in Saigon. As she gazed at the street through a French door, hoping to see Bob Hope, who had just arrived in town for his annual Christmas tour, a two-hundred-pound bomb in a panel truck went off in the building's garage. The French door blew into the room, and glass broke on top of Reynolds, cutting her leg. Since she was on call that evening, her first thought was, "Oh boy. Hospital OR [operating room] call. Here we go!" Dazed, Reynolds tried to go to her bedroom to retrieve her sneakers but was ordered to evacuate by another officer. She noticed fire and smoke as she made her way to the building's courtyard and then assisted the victims. When the ambulances arrived, she got into the first one and took some patients to the hospital, six miles away. Reynolds had no idea she was bleeding herself until a corpsman said, "You need to be sutured, so I am putting a suture set aside for you." Reynolds worked on patients until everyone was taken care of before requesting that her leg be examined.[1]

The Brink BOQ bombing destroyed three floors of the building, killing two U.S. servicemen and injuring sixty-three Americans, an Australian army officer, and forty-three Vietnamese civilians. Four navy nurses in the building, including Reynolds, were wounded in the attack; each one insisted on treating victims at the scene and helping with disaster response before tending to her own injuries.[2]

During the early 1960s, the navy ran nearly all of the major support functions in the capital city for the U.S. Military Assistance Advisory Group. Everything from medical facilities to food and billeting to headquarters security in Saigon was managed by the Headquarters Support Activity Saigon (HSAS). This role continued until May 1966, when HSAS was disestablished and many of its responsibilities were turned over to the army. Originally established as a housekeeping and logistics organization, HSAS ultimately found itself on the front lines of a wave of urban terrorism after the Viet Cong began attacking American facilities in Saigon in 1964.

The command also became mired in a controversy surrounding its second commanding officer, Capt. Archie C. Kuntze. Although he was later cleared of the charge, the press accused Kuntze of engaging in black-market activities in Saigon during a period when the black market represented a major supply source for the Viet Cong and was becoming a blight on South Vietnam's fragile economy.

The story of HSAS's struggles to feed, house, and supply America's intensive buildup in Vietnam, defend the capital city from terrorism, and handle an explosive controversy surrounding its second commanding officer is that of one of the navy's greatest and least understood achievements of the war.

Headquarters Support Activity Saigon

Headquarters Support Activity Saigon was commissioned on 1 July 1962 at a ceremony in Saigon's Kinh Do Theater. When Capt. Malcolm C. Friedman, the first HSAS commander, took over the activity, he knew that it would be a huge job for the navy, but the extent and rate of the activity's growth, especially in the year after he departed, surprised even him.[3] When the command was established, it was designed to support a maximum of nine thousand men; by June 1964, when Friedman left the job, it was directly sustaining over twenty-five thousand U.S. military and government personnel in 240 locations. HSAS grew from 445 active-duty personnel in 1962 to 1,600 in December 1965. By 1966, the command was providing housing, utilities, transportation, police protection, legal aid, medical care, food services, shopping, recreation, education, pay, and religious services for over fifteen thousand American and allied personnel in Saigon. It extended additional services to the over 180,000 U.S. soldiers, sailors, airmen, and Marines stationed throughout Vietnam. In just three years' time, HSAS had grown to become the largest and most important naval shore facility in the world.[4]

The navy traces its formal involvement in Vietnam to 1950, when the U.S. Military Assistance Advisory Group (MAAG) was established to take over from the French the role of training the South Vietnamese armed forces. As the advisory role expanded and MAAG became the U.S. Military Assistance Command Vietnam (MACV) in 1962, the U.S. armed forces recognized that they would need a dedicated logistics outfit to support the larger command. As "administrative agent" for all U.S. armed forces in the Pacific, the navy became responsible for providing logistics support for the MACV headquarters and other activities and units designated by the Chief of Naval Operations—a tall task for a service more accustomed to managing seaborne and port logistics than dry-land operations in an urban area.[5] The magnitude of the challenge was exacerbated further by the poor state of the Vietnamese infrastructure. When Captain Friedman arrived in Saigon in 1962, he found a city more than thirty years behind most American urban areas in terms of roads, electricity, water, and sewage systems. Only 203 miles of narrow roads existed for a city of two million people, 642,000 motor vehicles, a half-million bicycles and rickshaws *(cyclopousses),* and thousands of animal-powered carts. The smell of human and animal excrement permeated nearly every corner of the city.[6]

The poor sanitary conditions in Saigon made food service one of Friedman's top priorities. HSAS inherited six enlisted messes from the army, and one of its first challenges was supplying food for these facilities.[7] It had to acquire forty-two thousand cubic feet of additional refrigerated space in 1962 just to maintain its stocks of fresh and frozen food in a city where the average daytime high temperature was ninety degrees Fahrenheit.[8] A food-inspection service, complete with army veterinarians, had to be developed from scratch. By 1966 HSAS was feeding or providing basic foodstuffs for more than 180,000 troops in the country, serving over ten thousand meals a day, and racking up $500,000 worth of mess sales a month.[9]

In order to downplay the American presence in the city and placate South Vietnamese government officials sensitive about the issue, HSAS could not build a centralized American base complex in the heart of Saigon. Instead, it had to lease facilities throughout the urban area on an ad hoc basis. "There was always a problem in setting up a lease that was acceptable to the Vietnamese and also to our military requirements," explained Friedman, but "the Vietnamese did build things for us on a handshake and lease them to us."[10] By December 1965, HSAS was managing 318 construction contracts at a cost of four million dollars and had signed real-estate leases worth nearly nine million.[11]

The facility that perhaps best illustrated the real estate, maintenance, and construction challenges confronted by HSAS was Station Hospital Saigon. South Vietnamese government restrictions on building new facilities compelled HSAS to acquire a building on the open market and then convert it to a functional hundred-bed hospital.[12] The HSAS real-estate department eventually found a dilapidated five-story apartment house on Tran Hung Dao, one of downtown Saigon's busiest thoroughfares.[13]

Since the hospital initially had no kitchen, food had to be transported to patients from nearby enlisted quarters. The "cast room" was an open-air space near some sheds.[14] Ambulatory patients had to walk cross the busy Tran Hung Dao to reach the X-ray department, located in the Metropole Hotel; nonambulatory patients had to be transported there by one of the hospital's four ambulances or by stretcher and gurney.[15]

The hospital was surrounded by a concrete wall topped with wire grenade screens and guarded by military police and Vietnamese soldiers. Ten medical officers, two medical service officers, sixteen nurses, and ninety hospital corpsmen worked in the hospital.[16] The navy obtained permission from the Vietnamese government to construct several new facilities near the hospital, including a modern kitchen, a dining room, and a surgical suite. During the construction of the 1,500-square-foot surgical suite, local construction workers routinely defecated on the floors of unfinished bathrooms, compelling HSAS to disinfect those spaces completely on a daily basis.[17] "I learned a great lesson there," Captain Friedman later recounted. "You cannot convert these people into indoor plumbing overnight. They are just not ready for it."[18]

Such were the challenges of building and operating a modern hospital in Saigon in the early 1960s, but it should be stressed that HSAS stood up the hospital in just six weeks.[19] During its first year of operation, it treated three hundred inpatients and 1,800 outpatients, and by 1965 these numbers had grown to 2,500 and 53,000, respectively.[20] In the end, the professionalism and expertise of the navy medical staff compensated for the physical deficiencies of the hospital.

Upon commissioning, HSAS assumed responsibility for nine BOQs and seven bachelor enlisted men's quarters (BEQs), with the capacity to hold two thousand men; by 1965 it was running fifty-four such facilities plus four transient hotels, housing more than 6,400 military personnel. Most of these facilities were converted hotels and apartment buildings, spread out in the downtown area of Saigon. HSAS generally provided quarters with air-conditioning, maid service, and potable hot and cold running water.[21]

During the Vietnam War, the navy operated fifty-three commissaries in the continental United States and thirty-six overseas. These stores did over $224 million in business. On 18 August 1965, HSAS opened a brand-new commissary in Saigon. The new store stocked over 1,400 items, such as 130 varieties of chilled and frozen food and fifty kinds of produce. It supported the entire allied military community in Saigon and 260 military clubs in the field. During 1965, the store registered over $300,000 worth of sales per month and managed an inventory approaching three million dollars. Using a local contractor, HSAS built the flagship store in just three months.[22]

HSAS also operated the largest Navy Exchange system in the world, with a central store in Saigon and a hundred satellite operations in the field.[23] The system offered servicemen a wide variety of retail goods plus such specialized services as watch repair, engraving, photograph development, tailoring, dry cleaning, and hot food served in a cafeteria. The exchange in Saigon stocked basic items like toiletries, candy, tobacco, stationery, and uniforms, as well as appliances, cameras, and electronics. By December 1965 it employed eight hundred people and required 160,000 feet of storage space. Exchanges received little appropriated-fund support from the government. They mainly supported themselves through their operations, but they still managed to keep prices lower than equivalent commercial stores.[24]

The profits earned by the Vietnam operation went to support the Special Services Division, which provided recreation for all U.S. forces in Vietnam. The division operated bowling alleys, craft shops, movie theaters, swimming pools, libraries, and even a waterskiing concession. It also ran rest-and-recreation (R&R)

flights to Hong Kong, Bangkok, Taiwan, the Philippines, and Japan. The Pershing Field athletic complex offered softball, tennis, handball, volleyball, basketball, and archery. The hobby shop sold ten thousand dollars' worth of merchandise per month to over 1,700 patrons. By the end of 1965, a library system with nine branches maintained a collection of twenty-four thousand volumes. It also mailed out over sixty thousand newspapers and magazines a month to more than 750 field units.[25]

To manage its burgeoning workforce of Vietnamese civilians, HSAS established an Industrial Relations Department, which among other things created an employee classification system, pay schedules, career development plans, and management practices. As Friedman later put it, "We ended up with a small civil service commission" to administer a civilian workforce that by 1966 had grown to seven thousand people.[26] This large, well organized civilian workforce enabled HSAS's compact military staff to provide logistics support for the American buildup in South Vietnam at very low cost.[27]

The scale of HSAS's mission can perhaps best be defined by the amount of money it handled. By 1966, it accounted for over two hundred million dollars in appropriated funds. Ninety percent of this money went to support other military commands, including 237 cash accounts held by units in the field. In Saigon alone, the HSAS disbursing officer spent over thirteen million dollars per month and completed over 91.2 million piastres ($1.2 million) in foreign-currency transactions.[28]

HSAS not only pumped millions of dollars into the Vietnamese economy and employed thousands of locals but also sought to help bolster MACV's popular support through a variety of civilian assistance or "civic action" programs designed to help "win hearts and minds." Project HANDCLASP, administered by the HSAS chaplain's office, distributed over two hundred tons of supplies to remote villages and hamlets in South Vietnam in 1965. Established in 1959, HANDCLASP was designed to enhance perceptions of the United States and the U.S. Navy through the distribution of humanitarian, educational, and goodwill material to disadvantaged people in foreign countries throughout the world. Through direct person-to-person contact in the conduct of community-relations endeavors, the operation simultaneously allowed U.S. Navy personnel to gain insight into other nations and cultures. HANDCLASP received donated goods from U.S. companies and nonprofit organizations and transported them to Vietnam and other locations worldwide on navy ships, utilizing chaplains and navy volunteers to distribute the items. Goods included toys, clothes, educational materials, food and household items, medical supplies, tools, and construction materials.[29]

A cornerstone of navy civic action in Vietnam, medical civic-action programs (MEDCAPs) provided free medical care, vaccinations, and medicines to Vietnamese civilians in Saigon as well as in the countryside. When twenty thousand Saigon-area civilians were struck with cholera in 1964, fifteen navy medical personnel from Naval Medical Research Unit 2 helped establish a 160-bed treatment facility at Saigon's Cho Quan Infectious Disease Hospital, where, along with 425 Vietnamese medical staff, they treated 1,877 cholera victims and largely brought the disease under control in just one month's time.[30] Working on weekends, dental teams from the HSAS dental department often treated two hundred Vietnamese patients in a single ten-hour village MEDCAP.[31] In 1965, Station Hospital Saigon performed surgeries on fifty civilian patients suffering from harelips and cleft palates, in an operation called CLEFT LIP.

HSAS was the navy's most complex, multifaceted command of its size in the early 1960s. It performed a tremendous variety of roles, ranging from those of a traditional navy supply organization to others more appropriate to a municipal government. That the HSAS staff rose to the occasion and ran most of the command's diverse and far-ranging activities in a professional and efficient manner speaks volumes about the talent of its naval personnel. Whether it involved building a new commissary in Saigon or dealing with a cholera epidemic, HSAS personnel proved willing to take on nearly any task assigned, no matter how large or small. Despite the difficult living and working conditions of Saigon, most HSAS sailors performed their jobs with good cheer and optimism, but few activities in Saigon proved simple, even running basic medical facilities. This was especially true during the wave of terror that struck the city beginning in early 1964.

A New Kind of War: Terrorism in Saigon, 1964–1966

The first major terrorist attack against an HSAS facility occurred on 9 February 1964 at the Pershing Field recreational complex in Saigon. A bomb fabricated from a mortar shell exploded under the bleachers of a baseball park during a game, killing two Americans and wounding twenty-four others. Witnesses noted that the Vietnamese children who usually played around the field had left before the blast. Investigators later found a wire leading from the crater to a toilet area used by a Vietnamese national employed by the facility. HSAS reluctantly closed this popular R&R facility after the attack.[32]

The Viet Cong struck again on the 16th at the Capital Kinh Do Theater, where HSAS had been commissioned. A group of Viet Cong terrorists gunned down Pvt. 1st Class Peter M. Feierabend, an army military policeman guarding the facility.[33] They then rolled an explosive device in a coffee can down the center aisle of the theater during a Sunday showing of *The Diary of Anne Frank* (1959). An alert Marine, Capt. Donald E. Koelper, noticed the device and leaped to the stage to warn everyone to take cover. The bomb killed Koelper and wounded thirty-six other Americans, including three dependent children.

When the navy established HSAS, it viewed its major mission as logistics support, not force protection or counterterrorism. In fact, from 1962 to 1964, HSAS

Saigon's entire security element consisted of a 181-man U.S. Army Military Police (MP) company.[34] This unit, augmented by Vietnamese National Police and Vietnamese Military Police, was responsible for guarding all major American military installations in Saigon. After the Brink Hotel bombing in December 1964, MACV decided to reinforce the 560th MP Company with the 575-man 716th MP battalion, but USAID officials initially refused to sign off on the plan, arguing that security should be left to the Vietnamese.[35] Instead, HSAS had to beef up its security force by activating a sixty-five-man navy landing force to provide additional guards for facilities.[36] Not until after attacks on American bases at Bien Hoa and Pleiku did MACV prevail in this debate, but even with an expanded MP force HSAS never had enough security resources to defend properly all of its facilities from Viet Cong terrorists. In 1965, MACV estimated that HSAS needed a minimum of 1,500 additional American troops to grapple with the problem.[37] America was slow to recognize that terrorism, far from being an occasional annoyance, was a core strategy of the Viet Cong and that Saigon was its central front.[38]

The decentralized nature of HSAS facilities made them particularly vulnerable to terrorist attacks. Friedman noted, "It was a major problem. . . . [W]e had to lease facilities where they were."[39] HSAS was responsible for the security of 190 manned structures and hotels in Saigon, as well as the streets surrounding those buildings.[40] Even buses for American servicemen and dependents traveling between facilities had to be guarded.[41]

The port of Saigon posed a particularly daunting security challenge. It was far and away Vietnam's busiest port, ranking for much of the war as one of the world's top twenty ports in terms of cargo handled. In 1964, HSAS's Port Terminal Division handled thirty ships and over thirty thousand tons of cargo a month. Port personnel worked twelve-hour, seven-day-a-week shifts to keep up with the mountain of supplies arriving in Saigon. One of the navy's biggest concerns was that the Viet Cong might severely disrupt this flow by sinking a vessel in Saigon harbor or the forty-six-mile shipping channel that ran from Vung Tau to Saigon.[42] That fear almost came true on 2 May 1964, when Viet Cong saboteurs blew a three-by-twelve-foot hole in the hull of USNS *Card* (T-AKV 40), a former escort carrier converted into an aircraft ferry. The explosion occurred amidships, just above the waterline, and twenty-four minutes after the blast *Card* settled to the bottom of the forty-eight-foot-deep channel. In a matter of minutes, Viet Cong sappers had done what no German U-boat had accomplished in World War II—sink *Card*, which had won a Presidential Unit Citation and three battle stars in that conflict. It was the first major U.S. vessel to be sunk in action in the Vietnam War.[43]

Although no one died in the attack and the ship was refloated and towed away two days later, the *Card* incident proved a public-relations disaster, especially since it occurred right under the eyes of the entire Saigon-based foreign press corps. "The incident gave further evidence of growing Viet Cong boldness and the frequent in-efficiency of South Vietnamese security procedures," a *Time* magazine correspon-dent wrote.[44] An editorial in the *Boston Globe* noted that "American prestige in Southeast Asia has been severely damaged. Even more disturbing are indications of laxity that could make such a serious disaster possible."[45] Army of the Republic of Vietnam (ARVN) troops had been responsible for guarding the channel, and a company of airborne troops had been in the area during the attack, but these secu-rity forces had failed to prevent the attack. According to Friedman, "the Vietnamese had been sort of lackadaisical" about security.[46]

One year after the *Card* attack, military port operations in Saigon reached a new high: in October 1965, HSAS supervised the unloading of 330,000 measurement tons of military cargo from ninety-six ships and shipped forty thousand measure-ment tons to other ports in Vietnam via Military Sea Transportation Service ships. To ensure that the shipping lanes in Saigon would be quickly reopened in the event of a future mining attack, the navy assigned Harbor Clearance Team (HCT) 1 to Phu An, just outside of Saigon, in December 1965. The team, which comprised var-ious pieces of salvage, dewatering, and lift equipment and sixteen navy divers, stood ready to clear the Saigon waterways of wrecks quickly. Three additional harbor-clearance teams based out of Subic Bay, in the Philippines, could be quickly airlifted to Saigon should personnel or equipment be needed to augment HCT-1.[47]

Viet Cong terrorism in the Saigon area tapered off during the summer of 1964 and then resumed 1 November, with an attack on the Bien Hoa air base, twenty-five kilometers northeast of Saigon.[48] Following the Bien Hoa attack, Gen. William C. Westmoreland, the MACV commander, airlifted U.S. Army and Marine troops to augment the defenses of Da Nang, Bien Hoa, and other airfields, but he rejected the idea of utilizing American ground troops in a static-defense role over the long term. He strongly believed that the proper role for U.S. ground forces was offensive oper-ations against enemy units in the field. Base defense, he reasoned, was the responsi-bility of tenant forces, security police, and the ARVN.

The Viet Cong attacks on the Brink Hotel on 24 December and on Camp Hollo-way in Pleiku province on 7 February 1965 again highlighted the inadequacy of the base security countrywide. At Pleiku, the Viet Cong fired 81-mm mortar, 57-mm recoilless rifle, and rifle grenade rounds into the U.S. adviser compound and the 52nd Aviation Battalion area for fifteen minutes, killing eight American servicemen and wounding another 108.[49] Pleiku helped convince President Lyndon B. Johnson to evacuate U.S. government and military dependents from Vietnam.

No building symbolized the American involvement in Vietnam more than the American embassy in Saigon. A former French commercial house, the chancery was located near the Caravelle Hotel and the Central Market. Wooden road barricades surrounded the building to prevent cars from parking near it, and six Vietnamese

National Police stood guard at all times. Nonetheless, at 10:46 AM on 30 March 1965, a Viet Cong terrorist detonated a 250-pound bomb hidden in a sedan in front of the embassy while a second terrorist opened fire on the guards from a scooter. The bomb blast, which could be heard as far as Tan Son Nhut airfield, blew out every window in the five-story chancery and turned the first floor into knee-deep rubble. It also destroyed the Vietnamese restaurant across the street and numerous vehicles parked across the street. Casualties included seventeen killed and twenty-seven wounded.[50]

A favorite hangout for Americans in Saigon was the My Canh Café, a floating restaurant on the Saigon River renowned for its good Vietnamese food and riverside views. On 26 June 1965, a grenade exploded in the establishment at the height of the dinner hour. Then, as dazed and wounded customers tried to flee to shore by way of a gangplank, a mine planted in the riverbank exploded, causing mass casualties among them. In all, thirty-two people were killed, and another forty-two were wounded.[51] According to Construction Electrician (Wiring) Third Class William Gary Hadley, a twenty-year-old Seabee who assisted in recovering bodies after the attack, "There were pools of blood and shattered glass everywhere. This is the first time I had ever seen so many dead and wounded people. I remember carrying a decapitated body out of the restaurant. After I got back to my billet, I was covered in blood and had to throw out all my clothes. Blood had even gotten inside my boots."[52]

The next big attack occurred approximately six months later. Just before dawn on 4 December 1965, a grey panel truck packed with 250 pounds of plastique blew up in front of the Metropole Hotel, a large enlisted billet housing 160 American servicemen. The blast sheared off several stories of the converted hotel's facade, killing eight and wounding another ninety-five.[53]

One of the last major bombings before HSAS was disestablished occurred at the Victoria Hotel BOQ on 1 April 1966. At 5:15 in the morning, a group of terrorists approached the billet, which housed two hundred junior officers from all services, and began firing automatic weapons at the American and Vietnamese guards at the building's entrance. A grey panel truck containing two hundred pounds of explosives then drove up and detonated in front of the building, destroying the first two floors and damaging the third. The blast killed three Americans and wounded another 113.[54]

As these examples reveal, the terrorist bombings that occurred in Saigon between February 1964 and April 1966 represented a completely new type of war for American forces—one the military assistance command had not anticipated. HSAS developed American facilities in Saigon according to the wishes of South Vietnamese officials. Where possible, as noted above, these politicians wanted the Americans to lease preexisting facilities in Saigon rather than build a centralized base complex. The policy was designed to downplay the American presence and also pump money into the hands of local property owners and businessmen. However, it also made these facilities perfect targets for urban terrorists. The buildings were not only hard to defend but also poorly constructed. "They did not use enough rebar [reinforcing bars] in the concrete," explained Maj. I. Thomas Sheppard, a former army intelligence officer attached to MACV, "so when bombs went off near them, the devastation was horrible." The Vietnamese affection for floor-to-ceiling glass windows and sliding glass doors exacerbated the problem. The back of the Metropole, for example, was mostly glass, and no one had been instructed to tape windows before the blast. According to Hadley, "There was so much glass in some of the bodies that they couldn't be safely picked up."[55]

After the bombings commenced, HSAS tried to improve the physical security of its structures by adding more guards and placing vehicle barriers near major buildings, but in the end HSAS never had the manpower to defend Saigon adequately from terrorism.[56] By 1966, it still had only one battalion of MPs, augmented by Vietnamese police, to provide security for nearly two hundred installations. Furthermore, even heavily guarded buildings proved vulnerable to bombing, given their locations on busy city streets. After the Victoria attack, HSAS actually had to block many boulevards with concrete cylinders filled with sand or concrete. By 1966 MPs had also fortified all of their posts with sand-filled fifty-gallon drums and sandbags.[57] Such measures made Saigon look like an armed American camp, greatly inconvenienced the local citizenry, and yet failed to prevent the capital city from once again becoming an urban war zone during the 1968 Tet Offensive. A base complex outside the city within a fortified and well defended perimeter would not only have been much easier to secure but also have mitigated the U.S. presence and appeased the local populace.

The Mayor of Saigon

The man at the center of the U.S. battle against terrorism during the 1964–66 period was Capt. Archie Kuntze, who replaced Malcolm Friedman as the commander of HSAS in June 1964. Informally known as the "mayor of Saigon," Kuntze visited nearly every bombing scene during his tenure, occasionally assuming the role of on-scene commander for first responders.[58] The twin demands of the rapid U.S. military buildup and the increasing incidents or terror attacks made his job one of the most demanding in the navy. To feed, house, and guard Saigon's burgeoning American population, Kuntze occasionally had to cut corners.

Sometimes this meant writing sole-source contracts with local contractors rather than taking the time to open contracts for competitive bidding. In other cases, it meant buying American goods or changing money for Vietnamese officials at the army Post Exchange (PX) for the sake of relationship-building. As Kuntze put it in a 1966 memorandum to the secretary of the navy,

> The assignment in Saigon was a difficult one. The rapid escalation of the conflict placed tremendous demands upon me and my staff. There was no precedent in navy manuals for this type of command in the situation existing in Vietnam. Problems that did not have answers in the rule books were constantly placed before me requiring immediate solutions that might otherwise have been considered irregular. I cannot overemphasize the fact that I was a road builder without signs to point the way.[59]

Kuntze's superior, Vice Adm. Edwin B. Hooper, the commander of Service Force, U.S. Pacific Fleet, wrote that Kuntze was "never inhibited by red tape, never bashful, but always energetic, imaginative, aggressive, and ambitious."[60]

The very skills that made Kuntze the perfect man to run HSAS also made him vulnerable to charges of impropriety. On 14 November 1966, a general court-martial found him guilty on three specifications of a charge of conduct "unbecoming of an officer." The navy had not court-martialed a navy captain for personal conduct since 1951, and the Kuntze trial emerged as one of the most famous navy courts-martial of the twentieth century.[61] The fall of Kuntze and the legacy of his command proved to be a public-relations fiasco for the navy in Vietnam. The story demonstrates how appearances of impropriety in a military context often cause more damage than the improprieties themselves, especially in a command under the microscope of the press and subject to petty jealousies of the other services. Given the challenges of working in a corrupt third-world country, Kuntze might have survived the controversy had he bent rules only for the good of the navy, but he also broke a few for his girlfriend, and it was those violations that ultimately led to his conviction.[62]

A native of Sheboygan, Wisconsin, Kuntze graduated from the Naval Academy in 1943 and saw extensive combat in the Pacific during World War II as a destroyer officer. In Korea he commanded USS *Begor* (APD 127), a high-speed transport that inserted partisans onto the coast of North Korea in 1951. After the war, he commanded Mine Squadron 7 and held various staff assignments with Seventh Fleet and the Bureau of Personnel. Kuntze took over HSAS on 6 June 1964 and immediately began raising some eyebrows with his lifestyle. He established his quarters in an elegant former French villa, elaborately decorated the mansion's many rooms in various styles, and placed two stuffed Asian tigers at the base of its grand stairway. Recently separated, he lived in his palatial digs with a beautiful twenty-six-year-old Taiwanese girlfriend, Jannie Suen, and soon gained a reputation in Saigon for holding "lavish" parties and rubbing shoulders with many of the town's elite.[63]

Kuntze's lifestyle may have led to some grumbling, but it was not unusual. The Vietnamese had been accustomed since the French colonial period to foreign military officers living in glamorous villas. What initially sparked an investigation of Kuntze was allegations of corruption and black marketeering. In 1965, several beer distributors accused Kuntze, who controlled all liquor procurement for the U.S. military, of giving contracts to one or two vendors and excluding the rest. Since Jannie Suen worked for one of the liquor distributors under contract with HSAS, its competitors assumed that Kuntze was steering business toward her company. That same year, the press learned that the Saigon HSAS had ordered 150,000 cans of women's hair spray for an American female population of just 750. Apparently GIs wanted the spray for their Vietnamese girlfriends, and Kuntze's policy was to sell goods that servicemen demanded. Unfortunately for Kuntze, these so-called girlfriends later resold many of the hair-spray bottles to street vendors. Given Saigon's problems with the black market, any hint that Kuntze's actions might be fueling such activity caused a storm of controversy.[64]

As the U.S. presence had grown in South Vietnam, so too had the black market for foreign goods in Saigon. Black markets and currency manipulations had become major causes of inflation and were to be parasites on the Vietnamese economy for the entire war. By the mid-1960s, one could buy anything from American lipstick to NATO-caliber ammunition and M-16 rifles in Saigon street stalls. Essentially, any item sold through the exchanges or brought into Vietnam to supply the U.S. armed forces could end up in the black market and be resold. Because Vietnamese did not have exchange privileges, they were willing to pay a premium for these goods. The black market was also an important supply source for the Viet Cong. Some historians estimate that 80 percent of the Viet Cong supplies during this period came from the Saigon open and black markets. Some of the goods originated from GIs, who purchased merchandise in the exchange and resold it for a profit to the vendors, but much of the black-market merchandise was stolen. During 1965 alone, exchange losses from pilfering amounted to $2.25 million out of $50 million in total sales—a loss rate of 4.5 percent. Goods disappeared literally by the truckload from poorly guarded warehouses. By 1966, some items even had to be rationed to curb black marketeering, and the Vietnamese National Police began making raids on stalls suspected of selling black-market goods.[65]

The catalyst that finally prompted MACV to initiate an investigation of Kuntze, however, was not the hair-spray controversy but the arrest of Jannie Suen by the Vietnamese Military Security Service (MSS) on 7 January 1966. A shipment of cloth from Thailand to her apartment with no proof of duties paid prompted the arrest. Since Suen's father ran a dress shop in Taipei, MSS officials suspected that she might be involved in the illegal importation of cloth. Although Suen was released a few days later without any charges filed, the incident prompted MACV to go ahead with an investigation of Kuntze.[66]

Commander, Naval Forces Vietnam launched two separate investigations: a board of inquiry, consisting of four navy captains, and a Naval Investigative Service (NIS) investigation. Both investigations examined Kuntze's purchases of merchandise abroad "for the accommodation of Miss Jannie Suen" and the possible misuse of government aircraft for such junkets. They also looked at his financial records, to see whether there was any evidence of illegal currency exchanges or other types of fraud. Finally, they explored his relationship with Suen, to determine whether Kuntze had engaged in conduct unbecoming of an officer with her. Kuntze was in the process of divorcing his first wife during his tour in Vietnam, so the board chose not to investigate him for adultery, but they did investigate the lesser offense of cohabitation outside of marriage.[67]

The investigations into Kuntze's financial transactions revealed interesting details about Kuntze and HSAS but not enough hard evidence of wrongdoing to convict the captain of money laundering. From August 1965 to March 1966 Kuntze had executed sixteen "ex-cash" transactions totaling $14,372. These transactions had involved the exchange of piastres for U.S. Treasury checks denominated in dollars. Kuntze had then mailed these checks to his account at Chase Manhattan Bank in New York. The acceptance of military payment certificates as a repayment of debt from a foreign national would have been against regulations, but neither the board nor the court-martial uncovered enough evidence to convict him of this charge.[68]

Some of Kuntze's transactions needed to be kept confidential for political reasons. When asked by the board of inquiry to produce a full accounting of the transactions, Kuntze refused, arguing that such "explanation would certainly, in many instances, be most embarrassing to officials high in the government of both the United States and Vietnam. . . . [S]ome [are] matters which cannot be explained without possible political repercussions, particularly on the local scene."[69] In his court-martial he provided more details, claiming that some of the transactions had been repayments from Vietnamese for "radios and fans and other items for Vietnamese officials." Kuntze believed that doing small favors for Vietnamese officials "was in the best interest of the United States."[70] Others were for CIA agents, who had requested that he change money for them.[71]

The net effect of individuals or companies converting piastres to dollars and then shipping those dollars overseas was runaway inflation and continued loss of confidence in the South Vietnamese economy. As historian William Thomas Allison puts it, "The South Vietnamese government, U.S. aid programs, and the U.S. military PX, club, and mess systems . . . fertilized an already well-tilled black market with cash, from which the weedy seeds of corruption took even greater root."[72] Many of the enterprises controlled by HSAS indirectly (in some cases directly) fueled black-market activity. As a consequence, allegations that Captain Kuntze may have been fanning the flames of corruption even further by changing money or buying exchange merchandise for Vietnamese officials created a furor in the press.

In its final report, the board of inquiry chastised Kuntze for buying goods for Vietnamese: "The board considers that by the purchase of merchandise from the Navy Exchange and the importation of liquors for sale to Vietnamese nationals, without reference to their entitlement to such materials under either MACV

Directives or Vietnamese law, Captain Kuntze showed utter disregard for both U.S. regulations and Vietnamese law and thereby acted in a manner reflecting adversely upon the position of Commanding Officer, HSAS."[73] In the end, however, no charges were filed for these actions. Ultimately, the court-martial found enough hard evidence of wrongdoing to convict him only of permitting a foreign female to "reside openly and notoriously" in his official quarters, allowing her to use an official vehicle, and unlawfully importing 250 yards of cloth from Thailand. As punishment, he was given a reprimand and "bumped" a hundred numbers on the lineal list, effectively ending his chances of promotion. He retired soon after the trial ended. "Had I adhered strictly to 'The Book' heavens knows where we would be today," Kuntze later wrote in a letter to Rear Adm. Isaac C. Kidd, Jr. "To do the job was the most important thing and the job was done. What must be remembered is that the orient is another world compared to the staffs and business methods; dealings and politics are very different."[74]

Despite an increasing terrorist threat, a chaotic business environment, and a mushrooming influx of American troops, HSAS met nearly all of its fundamental logistic goals, and Kuntze deserves much of the credit for this success. However, his "damn the torpedoes" attitude also caused problems. Cutting corners by securing sole-source contracts with proven vendors may have saved HSAS valuable time, but it also created enemies. Kuntze's flamboyant lifestyle caused even more difficulties for the command. As Lt. Cdr. Bill Manthorpe, the officer in charge of the NIS investigation of Kuntze, put it, "What was most irritating to the increasing number of army generals in town was seeing a mere navy captain driving around town in an air-conditioned car with white-walled tires and other alleged aspects of high living."[75] Clearly, these officers believed that a man in charge of millions of dollars should have behaved more modestly, especially given the media climate in Saigon.

The international media presence in Saigon guaranteed that anything happening in Vietnam would be immediately broadcast across the international news wires. From hair-spray deliveries to barracks bombings, the media covered it all, and not always in a manner favorable to HSAS. Press interest in the American buildup and in the "mayor of Saigon" also guaranteed that the navy's reputation would be sullied by the trial. It revealed a world where twenty-three million dollars was kept in an icebox, black marketeering and currency manipulations were the norm, and American officers lived like James Bond, complete with villas and exotic young women. Despite all the sacrifices made by HSAS sailors and officers during the 1964–66 battle of Saigon and all the good work they did in supporting the American buildup and providing humanitarian aid to the Vietnamese, HSAS would be forever remembered for its flamboyant commander, Archie Kuntze, and his various misdeeds.

Some popular histories and journalistic accounts of the episode contend that the U.S. Army initiated the Kuntze investigations to help convince MACV to transfer the Saigon logistics function immediately to the army.[76] In truth, planning for the transfer had begun several years before the controversy erupted. In November 1964, the Joint Chiefs of Staff directed Adm. Ulysses S. Grant Sharp, Commander in Chief, Pacific, to develop a logistics operation to support the American buildup. Sharp's staff studied the issue, concluded that existing arrangements were inadequate to meet "the present intensity of operations," and recommended that HSAS be replaced with an army logistics command. The final MACV plan, which Admiral Sharp signed in December 1964, envisioned a new army logistics command of 2,100 men to support a buildup of forty thousand men. HSAS would not be disestablished immediately, but planning would begin for an eventual turnover of most of its responsibilities to the army.[77]

Port operations were transferred in the fall of 1965, followed by exchange services in December. By February 1966, purchasing, contracting, and civilian administration had been turned over, and by April medical, maintenance, supply and engineering, clubs and messes, special services, billeting, and provost operations as well. On 17 May 1966, HSAS was awarded a Navy Unit Commendation and disestablished. It would be the end of an era. Not until the first Gulf War would the navy again run such a large logistics operation.[78]

NOTES 1 Capt. Darby Reynolds, USN (Ret.), interview by Dr. Jan K. Herman and Capt. Patricia Collins, USNR, 27 April 1998, Navy Bureau of Medicine History Office, Washington, D.C., pp. 1–7; Lt. Cdr. Ann Darby Reynolds, Officer Bio File, 13 April 1970, Operational Archives [hereafter AR], Naval History and Heritage Command [hereafter NHHC]; U.S. Pacific Fleet, "Annual Report," 26 June 1964–30 March 1965, p. 98, Post-1946 Command Files, AR, NHHC; Peer de Silva, *Sub Rosa: The CIA and the Uses of Intelligence* (New York: Times Books, 1978), p. 254; Naval History Division [hereafter NHD], Office of the Chief of Naval Operations, "History of U.S. Naval Operations in Southeast Asia," vol. 3, pt. 3, February 1971, p. 843, Vietnam Command Files [hereafter VCF], AR, NHHC.

2 Commander in Chief, U.S. Pacific Fleet [hereafter CINCPACFLT] message 250002Z December 1964, CINCPACFLT Message Collection, AR, NHHC; Edward J. Marolda and Oscar P. Fitzgerald, *The United States Navy and the Vietnam Conflict: From Military Assistance to Conflict, 1959–1965* (Washington, D.C.: Naval Historical Center, 1986), pp. 482–83; F. O. McClendon, Jr., "Doctors and Dentists, Nurses and Corpsmen in Vietnam," *U.S. Naval Institute Proceedings,* Naval Review Issue (May 1970), p. 279; National Military Command Center [hereafter NMCC] Operational Summary [hereafter Opsum], 26 December 1964, p. 2, box 94, NMCC Opsums, Post-1946 Command Files, AR, NHHC.

3 NHD, "History of U.S. Naval Operations Vietnam," vol. 2, "1964," p. 135; Marolda and Fitzgerald, *United States Navy and the Vietnam Conflict,* p. 357; Lt. Cdr. Bobbi Hovis, USN (Ret.), *Station Hospital Saigon: A Navy Nurse in Vietnam, 1963–1964* (Annapolis, Md.: Naval Institute Press, 1991), pp. 113–16.

4 "Four Years in Vietnam: HEDSUPPACT—Big Job," *All Hands* (June 1966), p. 16; NHD, "History of U.S. Naval Operations in Southeast Asia," vol. 3, pt. 3, p.

835; HSAS Command Fact Sheet, 15 December 1965, item 15210104001, Vietnam Archive, Texas Tech University, Lubbock, pp. 1–2; Marolda and Fitzgerald, *United States Navy and the Vietnam Conflict,* pp. 255, 361.

5 Edwin Bickford Hooper, *Mobility, Support, Endurance: A Story of Naval Operational Logistics in the Vietnam War, 1965–1968* (Washington, D.C.: U.S. Navy Dept., NHD, 1972), p. 14.

6 Hovis, *Station Hospital Saigon,* pp. 46, 50.

7 HSAS, Draft History, Commander, Naval Forces Vietnam [hereafter COMNAVFORV] Records, AR, NHHC.

8 Malcolm C. Friedman, "Comments Concerning the Establishment and Problems of HEDSUPPACT Saigon," Edward J. Marolda Papers, AR, NHHC. Temperature data derived from "Average Weather Conditions in Ho Chi Minh City," *BBC,* www.bbc .co.uk/.

9 "Four Years in Vietnam," p. 16; NHD, "History of U.S. Naval Operations in Southeast Asia," vol. 3, pt. 3, pp. 837–39.

10 Friedman, "Comments Concerning the Establishment and Problems of HEDSUPPACT Saigon"; Capt. Malcolm C Friedman, USN, interview with Oscar P. Fitzgerald, p. 9, Oral History Collection, AR, NHHC [hereafter Friedman, interview].

11 Hooper, *Mobility, Support, Endurance,* pp. 63–64; "Four Years in Vietnam," p. 17.

12 Friedman, "Comments Concerning the Establishment and Problems of HEDSUPPACT Saigon," p. 3; Commander, U.S. Military Assistance Command Vietnam [hereafter COMUSMACV] message 1600Z September 1963, Hospital Saigon, Marolda Papers, AR, NHHC; Head, Medical Department to Commanding Officer, HSAS, memorandum, "HSAS Medical Department, Saigon," 17 November 1965, Marolda Papers, AR, NHHC.

13 Hovis, *Station Hospital Saigon,* p. 39.

14 Ibid., pp. 36–37, 42–43.

15 Lt. Cdr. Alvina Harrison, "Military Nursing in Viet Nam, January 1965 to 17 February 1966," p. 2, NAVSUPPACT Saigon Hospital, Nurse Corps Files, box 36, AR, NHHC.

16 Jan Herman, "Navy Medicine in Vietnam," draft manuscript, 2 January 2007, p. 29; McClendon, "Doctors and Dentists, Nurses and Corpsmen in Vietnam," p. 279.

17 Hovis, *Station Hospital Saigon,* pp. 25, 41.

18 Friedman, interview, p. 5.

19 Friedman, "Comments Concerning the Establishment and Problems of HEDSUPPACT Saigon," p. 3.

20 Head, Medical Department to Commanding Officer, HSAS, 17 November 1965, p. 4.

21 Marolda and Fitzgerald, *United States Navy and the Vietnam Conflict,* pp. 255–57; HSAS, Command History, 1965, p. 5, Post-1946 Command Files, AR, NHHC; "Four Years in Vietnam," p. 18.

22 HSAS, Press Release 060-65, 18 August 1965, Sheboygan County Historical Research Center, Sheboygan Falls, Wis.; "The Big Four," *Navy Supply Corps Newsletter* (April 1966), p. 16; "Four Years in Vietnam," p. 21.

23 NHD, "History of U.S. Naval Operations Vietnam," vol. 2, "1964," p. 135.

24 Cdr. J. Scott Kirkwood, "The Renaissance Man," *Navy Supply Corps Newsletter* (April 1966), pp. 24–31; NHD, "History of U.S. Naval Operations in Southeast Asia," vol. 3, pt. 3, pp. 842–43; "The Big Four," pp. 14–15.

25 HEDSUPPACT Chronology, box 182, VCF, AR, NHHC; NHD, "History of U.S. Naval Operations in Southeast Asia," vol. 3, pt. 3, p. 843; Hooper, *Mobility, Support, Endurance,* p. 62.

26 Friedman, interview, p. 22.

27 HSAS's substitution of Vietnamese and contract workers for American military personnel greatly impressed Glen Gibson, the Deputy Secretary of Defense for Installations and Logistics, who toured HSAS's facilities in January 1965. See Marolda and Fitzgerald, *United States Navy and the Vietnam Conflict,* p. 364, and "Four Years in Vietnam," p. 21.

28 "Four Years in Vietnam," p. 19; NHD, "History of U.S. Naval Operations Vietnam," vol. 2, "1964," p. 142.

29 Withers M. Moore, "Navy Chaplains in Vietnam, 1954–1964," draft manuscript, p. 116, LY NHHC; "Four Years in Vietnam," p. 21; HSAS Command Fact Sheet, 15 December 1965, p. 21.

30 Chief, Bureau of Medicine to Op-09B92, ser. 38, 11 February 1966, in Marolda Papers, AR, NHHC.

31 "Four Years in Vietnam," p. 22.

32 Marolda and Fitzgerald, *United States Navy and the Vietnam Conflict,* p. 358; Hovis, *Station Hospital Saigon,* p. 62; Silva, *Sub Rosa,* p. 250.

33 He served with the Army's 560th Military Police Company, which was attached to HSAS. See

34 HSAS, Command History, 1 July 1962, p. 10, box 182, VCF, AR, NHHC.

35 Graham A. Cosmas, *The United States Army in Vietnam: MACV, the Joint Command in the Years of Escalation, 1962–1967* (Washington, D.C.: Center of Military History, 2006), p. 172.

36 "U.S. Bomb Squads Search Military Barracks," *Saigon Daily News,* 26 December 1964, p. 6.

37 COMUSMACV to CINCPAC, message 3004087 March 1965, "Request for Additional Security Personnel," March 1965 folder, box 219, Vietnam Flag Plot, AR, NHHC.

38 Silva, *Sub Rosa,* pp. 220, 247, 250.

39 Friedman, interview.

40 Hooper, *Mobility, Support, Endurance,* p. 65.

41 HSAS, Command History, 1965.

42 Marolda and Fitzgerald, *United States Navy and the Vietnam Conflict,* pp. 357–59; Capt. William H. Hardcastle, interview with Oscar P. Fitzgerald, 22 April 1975, p. 81, Oral History Collection, AR, NHHC.

43 CINCPAC to Joint Chiefs of Staff [hereafter JCS], message 040201Z May 1964, "Sinking of USNS *Card,*" *Card* folder, box 205, CNO Flag Plot, AR, NHHC; Associated Press, "U.S. Ship Is Sunk by Vietnamese Reds; Crewmen Escape," *New York Times,* 2 May 1964, p. 1.

44 "Remember the *Card!,*" *Time,* 8 May 1964, p. 31.

45 Editorial, *Boston Globe,* 4 May 1964, cited in Commander, First Naval District to Chief of Naval Information, message 041720Z May 1964, "CNO Press Briefing Item," *Card* folder, box 205, CNO Flag Plot, AR, NHHC.

46 HEDSUPPACT Saigon to Naval Support Activity Philadelphia, message 070715Z May 1964, "USNS *Card,*" *Card* folder, box 205, CNO Flag Plot, AR, NHHC; Friedman, interview, p. 30.

47 Marolda and Fitzgerald, *United States Navy and the Vietnam Conflict,* p. 356; Commander, Seventh Fleet to Seventh Fleet, message 120718Z May 1964, "Antiswimmer and Antisaboteur Measures during RVN Visit," Seventh Fleet Message Traffic, AR, NHHC; Hooper, *Mobility, Support, Endurance,* p. 62; "COMNAVFORV Monthly Summary," April 1966, pp. 7–8, VCF, AR, NHHC.

48 The most significant attack in Saigon during the summer of 1964 occurred at the Caravelle Hotel, where many foreign journalists stayed during the war, and also the site of the Australian and New Zealand embassies. At 11:30 AM on 25 August, a bomb exploded in Room 514 of the Caravelle, damaging nine rooms and sending glass flying into the street. Several people were injured, but no one died in the attack, because most of the journalists were out on assignments that day. For more on the incident see Silva, *Sub Rosa,* pp. 252–53, and "Memoirs of the Caravelle," www.caravellehotel.com/images/newsletter/pressroom/caravellememoirs.pdf.

49 COMUSMACV to JCS, message 0710001 February 1965, roll 18, CINCPACFLT Message Traffic, AR, NHHC; NMCC Opsum, 8 February 1965, February 1965 folder, box 94, NMCC Opsums, Post-1946 Command Files, AR, NHHC.

50 Among the wounded were Lt. Cdr. Donald G. Scully, a naval adviser visiting the embassy that day; Silva, the CIA station chief; and Deputy Ambassador Ural Alexis Johnson. For more, see "Outrages like This," *Time,* 9 April 1965; NMCC Opsum, 30 March 1965, box 95, NMCC Opsums, Post-1946 Command Files, AR, NHHC; COMUSMACV to NMCC, message 300918Z March 1965, Marolda Papers, AR, NHHC; American Embassy Saigon to USINFO WASHDC, message 300920Z March 1965, box 219, Vietnam Flag Plot, AR, NHHC; Donald G. Scully, Bronze Star Citation, Awards and Special Projects Branch files, AR, NHHC; "Bomb Blast in City Kills 16, 150 Hurt; U.S. Embassy Damaged," *Saigon Daily News,* 31 March 1965, pp. 1, 6.

51 The dead included thirteen Americans, and the wounded, seventeen.

52 CEW1 William Gary Hadley, telephone interview with John Darrell Sherwood, 11 March 2008 [hereafter Hadley, interview].

53 The casualties included one American serviceman killed and another seventy-two wounded. See "250 Lbs. of Plastique," *Time,* 10 December 1965, available at www.time.com/; NMCC Opsum, 4 December 1965, p. 1, box 101, NMCC Opsums, AR, NHHC.

54 NMCC Opsum, 1 April 1966, p. 6, box 103, NMCC Opsums, AR, NHHC.

55 I. Thomas Sheppard, telephone interview with John Darrell Sherwood, 19 March 2008 [hereafter Sheppard, interview]; Hadley, interview, 28 March 2008.

56 Ironically, the relative lull in terrorism between the Metropole and the Victoria attacks convinced HSAS to remove some of the barriers, including ones near the Victoria, to show that it did not fear the Viet Cong. Barriers went back up after the 1 April 1966 attack. See "BOQ Blasted in V.C. Attack," *Saigon Daily News,* 2 April 1966, p. 1.

57 R. W. Dietrich, "Saigon MPs Guard 'City within a City,'" COMSERVPAC [Commander Service Force, Pacific] Information Bulletin, May 1966, pp. 17–19, item 15210107001, Vietnam Archive, Texas Tech University.

58 Charles Mohr of the *New York Times* interviewed Kuntze at the Victoria bombing, and UT1 T. E. Tomlin remembered seeing Kuntze at the Metropole attack. Charles Mohr, "Saigon G.I. Billet Bombed in Vietcong Terror Attack," *New York Times,* 4 December 1965, pp. 1, 3; Hadley, interview, 28 March 2008.

59 Capt. Archie C. Kuntze to Secretary of the Navy, memorandum, "Request for Voluntary Retirement under Provisions of Title 10 USCA 6823," 8 September 1966, 00 Files, AR, NHHC.

60 Hooper, *Mobility, Support, Endurance,* p. 60.

61 "Navy Captain Convicted of Unofficerlike Conduct," *New York Times,* 15 November 1966, p. 7.

62 Ibid.

63 Rick Johnson, "South Vietnam, the American Waterloo: Saigon's Navy Mayor in Trouble," unpublished article, courtesy of Paul A. Johnson, available at walterzoomiesworld.blogspot.com/; "The 'Mayor,'" *Time,* 12 August 1966, available at www.time.com/; Sheppard, interview; Hadley, interview, 28 March 2008.

64 "Captain's Paradise," *Newsweek,* 15 August 1966; Sheppard, interview; Johnson, "South Vietnam, the American Waterloo."

65 In 1967, the U.S. embassy and the MACV staff judge advocate general established an Irregular Practices Committee in 1967 in an attempt to curb black marketeering. This committee monitored exchange purchases and currency exchanges in an effort to catch servicemen involved in the black market. Nevertheless, black marketeering continued in Saigon throughout the war. See Maj. Gen. George S. Prugh, *Law at War: Vietnam 1964–1973* (Washington, D.C.: U.S. Army Dept., 1975), pp. 103–105; William Thomas Allison, *Military Justice in Vietnam: The Rule of Law in an American War* (Lawrence: Univ. Press of Kansas, 2007), p. 40; and 2nd Lt. Courtney Frobenius, USA, telephone interview with John Darrell Sherwood, 15 June 2009.

66 Sheppard, interview; Capt. Archie C. Kuntze, Board of Inquiry, 12 June 1966, Findings of Fact, para. 50a, 00 Records, 1966, AR, NHHC.

67 "State Summary of War Casualties from World War II for Navy, Marine Corps, and Coast Guard Personnel," Records of the Bureau of Naval Personnel, Record Group 24, National Archives II, College Park, Maryland, via wwwa.nko.navy.mil/; Archie C. Kuntze to Rear Adm. I. C. Kidd, 12 May 1966.

68 Kuntze, Board of Inquiry, Opinions, para. 32a.

69 Capt. Archie C. Kuntze to Convening Authority, 2 May 1966, as cited in Kuntze, Board of Inquiry, Findings of Fact, para. 100a.

70 Kuntze, as cited in Joseph Di Mona and Birch Bayh, *Great Court-Martial Cases* (New York: Grosset and Dunlop, 1972), p. 208.

71 Ibid.

72 Allison, *Military Justice in Vietnam,* p. 141.

73 Kuntze, Board of Inquiry, Opinions, para. 45a.

74 Capt. Archie C. Kuntze to Rear Adm. Isaac C. Kidd, Jr., 2 May 1966, 00 Records, 1966, AR, NHHC; Isaac C. Kidd, Jr., Bio File, AR, NHHC.

75 Lt. Cdr. William Manthorpe, as cited in Douglas H. Hubbard, Jr., *Special Agent, Vietnam: A Naval Intelligence Memoir* (Washington, D.C.: Potomac Books, 2006), p. 26.

76 For an example, see Hubbard, *Special Agent, Vietnam,* p. 26.

77 Marolda and Fitzgerald, *United States Navy and the Vietnam Conflict,* pp. 360–65; CINCPAC, Command History, 1964, pp. 329–33.

78 Hooper, *Mobility, Support, Endurance,* pp. 61–65.

ABOUT THE AUTHORS

Dr. Robert G. Angevine is the author of *The Railroad and the State: War, Politics, and Technology in 19th-Century America* (2004) and articles on military approaches to technology, naval experimentation, and American military and naval intelligence. He received his PhD in military history from Duke University in 1999 and currently works as a defense analyst in the Washington area. He has taught at Duke, American, and George Mason Universities and now serves as Adjunct Assistant Professor of History at George Washington University.

Dr. Michael Barrett is a professor of history at The Citadel, teaching courses on World War I, modern Germany, and geography, among others. A graduate of The Citadel, he did his PhD at the University of Massachusetts, where he was a Fulbright Scholar (Germany). He is the author of *Operation Albion: The German Conquest of the Baltic Islands* (Indiana University Press), and *Clausewitz Revisited* (Praeger–ABC CLIO), coauthored with H. P. Willmott. He is a retired brigadier general in the U.S. Army Reserve.

Laurence M. Burke II is a PhD candidate in history and public policy at Carnegie Mellon University. His research interests lie in the history of technology and military history. He was awarded the Ramsey Fellowship in Naval Aviation History (National Air and Space Museum) and the General Lemuel C. Shepherd, Jr., Memorial Dissertation Fellowship (United States Marine Corps) in 2008, both of which have greatly assisted his research. This paper is drawn from his dissertation, whose working title is "What to Do with the Airplane? Determining the Role of the Airplane in the US Army, Navy, and Marine Corps, 1908–1930."

Capt. Craig C. Felker graduated from the United States Naval Academy in 1981. A naval aviator and helicopter pilot, he served in a variety of operational and staff assignments, the most notable of which included Operations DESERT SHIELD and

DESERT STORM in 1991, and as the director of the President's Emergency Operations Center in the White House from 1995 to 1997. While serving as an instructor in history at the Naval Academy, Commander Felker was selected for the Naval Academy's Permanent Military Professorship Program. He received his PhD from Duke in May 2004, and returned to the Academy the following June. In February 2007 Texas A&M University Press published his book *Testing American Sea Power: The U.S. Navy Fleet Problems, 1923–1940,* which examined the ways in which warfare simulation tested the Navy's Mahanian vision, and provided a means of adapting the vision to include new technologies. Captain Felker was the director of the 2009 Naval History Symposium.

Dr. Kenneth P. Hansen, Commander, Canadian Navy (Ret.), is the Visiting Defence Fellow in the Centre for Foreign Policy Studies at Dalhousie University, Halifax, where he is the Director of the Maritime Security in the 21st Century Project and Deputy Director for the center's Maritime Studies Programme. His research interests include concept development, operations planning, and logistical sustainment. His thirty-two-year naval career included a variety of positions in several ships of the Canadian Atlantic Fleet, a number of senior operations and staff appointments, and the Military Co-Chair of the Maritime Studies Programme at the Canadian Forces College, Toronto.

Dr. Marcus O. Jones is associate professor of German economic and military history at the U.S. Naval Academy. He is the author of a study of German industry and occupation policy in the Second World War, as well as of articles on Bismarckian strategic policy and the U-boat campaigns of both world wars. Dr. Jones earned his PhD at Yale University in 2005.

Dr. John T. Kuehn is a former naval aviator (EP-3/ES-3) who has completed cruises aboard four different aircraft carriers. He flew EP-3 missions during the last decade of the Cold War, the first Gulf War (DESERT STORM) and the Balkans (DELIBERATE FORCE, over Bosnia). CDR Kuehn has served on the faculty of the U.S. Army Command and General Staff College since July 2000, retiring from the naval service in 2004. He earned a PhD in history from Kansas State University in 2007. He is the author of *Agents of Innovation* and *Eyewitness Pacific Theater* with Dennis Giangreco.

Dr. Christopher P. Magra is Assistant Professor of Early American History and Director of the Atlantic History Center at the California State University at Northridge. He has published articles related to maritime history in the *International Journal of Maritime History,* the *New England Quarterly,* and the *Northern Mariner.* The Canadian Nautical Research Society honored him with the Keith Matthews Award for his scholarship. Cambridge University Press published his first book, *The Fisherman's Cause: Atlantic Commerce and Maritime Dimensions of the American Revolution,* in 2009. He has already begun research on his second book, a comparative analysis of British naval impressment in the Atlantic world.

Dr. Heather Pace Marshall received a PhD from Duke University. The daughter and wife of Marines, she has always been fascinated with understanding the origins of and developments in the Marine Corps's institutional culture. Her dissertation explores changes in the Corps's image and identity from the Civil War to World War I.

Dr. John Darrell Sherwood is a historian with the Naval History & Heritage Command, and the author of five books in military and naval history, including *Nixon's Trident: Naval Power in Southeast Asia, 1968–1972* (2009), *Black Sailor, White Navy: Racial Unrest in the Fleet during the Vietnam War Era* (2007), and *Afterburner: Naval Aviators and the Vietnam War* (2004). Sherwood holds a PhD in military history from The George Washington University, and is currently working on a history of U.S. Navy coastal and riverine operations during the Vietnam War.

Dr. Andrew Stewart studied for his doctorate in the Department of War Studies, King's College London, and was awarded his PhD in December 2001. The following year he joined the Defence Studies Department, King's College London, based at the Joint Services Command and Staff College. His research examines various issues connected to the British Empire and the Second World War. His book *Empire Lost: Britain, the Dominions and the Second World War* was published in September 2008 by Continuum and his next project is centered on the British Commonwealth military effort in East Africa during the Second World War.

Dr. Bruce Taylor was born in Chile in 1967 and educated at the University of Manchester and at Oxford, where he received a DPhil in modern history in 1996. He is author of *The Battlecruiser HMS* Hood: *An Illustrated Biography, 1916–1941* (2005) and together with Daniel Morgan is completing *Annals of the Wolves: U-boat Sinkings of Allied Warships as Recorded in German Logs.* He lives in Southern California.

Dr. Kathleen Broome Williams is the Director of General Education and professor of history at Cogswell Polytechnical College in Sunnyvale, California. Her published work includes *Secret Weapon: U.S. High-Frequency Direction Finding in the Battle of the Atlantic* (Naval Institute Press, 1996), *Improbable Warriors: Women Scientists and the U.S. Navy in World War II* (Naval Institute Press, 2001), and *Grace Hopper: Admiral of the Cyber Sea* (Naval Institute Press, 2004), as well as articles and book chapters on naval science and technology. She serves on the board of trustees of the Society for Military History and the advisory board of H-Maritime.

Dr. Carlos Alfaro Zaforteza was born in Spain in 1957. After a career in the building industry he graduated in war studies from King's College London. He is presently finishing his PhD and teaching naval history at that institution. His main interests are Spanish naval policy, international naval history, and the role of medium/small navies in the nineteenth century. He has published in British, American, and Spanish journals, including *War in History, Warship International,* and *Revista de Historia Naval.*

NAVAL WAR COLLEGE HISTORICAL MONOGRAPH SERIES

1. *The Writings of Stephen B. Luce,* edited by John D. Hayes and John B. Hattendorf (1975).

3. *Professors of War: The Naval War College and the Development of the Naval Profession,* Ronald Spector (1977).

4. *The Blue Sword: The Naval War College and the American Mission, 1919–1941,* Michael Vlahos (1980).

5. *On His Majesty's Service: Observations of the British Home Fleet from the Diary, Reports, and Letters of Joseph H. Wellings, Assistant U.S. Naval Attaché, London, 1940–1941,* edited by John B. Hattendorf (1983).

7. *A Bibliography of the Works of Alfred Thayer Mahan,* compiled by John B. Hattendorf and Lynn C. Hattendorf (1986).

8. *The Fraternity of the Blue Uniform: Admiral Richard G. Colbert, U.S. Navy and Allied Naval Cooperation,* Joel J. Sokolsky (1991).

9. *The Influence of History on Mahan: The Proceedings of a Conference Marking the Centenary of Alfred Thayer Mahan's The Influence of Sea Power upon History, 1660–1783,* edited by John B. Hattendorf (1991).

10. *Mahan Is Not Enough: The Proceedings of a Conference on the Works of Sir Julian Corbett and Admiral Sir Herbert Richmond,* edited by James Goldrick and John B. Hattendorf (1993).

11. *Ubi Sumus? The State of Naval and Maritime History,* edited by John B. Hattendorf (1994).

12. *The Queenstown Patrol, 1917: The Diary of Commander Joseph Knefler Taussig, U.S. Navy,* edited by William N. Still, Jr. (1996).

13. *Doing Naval History: Essays toward Improvement,* edited by John B. Hattendorf (1995).

14. *An Admiral's Yarn,* edited by Mark R. Shulman (1999).

15. *The Memoirs of Admiral H. Kent Hewitt,* edited by Evelyn M. Cherpak (2004).

16. *Three Splendid Little Wars: The Diary of Joseph K. Taussig, 1898–1901,* edited by Evelyn M. Cherpak (2009).

17. *Digesting History: The U.S. Naval War College, the Lessons of World War Two, and Future Naval Warfare, 1945–1947,* Hal. M. Friedman (2010).

18. *To Train the Fleet for War: The U.S. Navy Fleet Problems, 1923–1940,* Albert A. Nofi (2010).

19. *Talking about Naval History: A Collection of Essays,* John B. Hattendorf (2011).